Atticus Finch

Also by Joseph Crespino:

Strom Thurmond's America

The Myth of Southern Exceptionalism
(co-editor)

*In Search of Another Country: Mississippi and
the Conservative Counterrevolution*

JOSEPH CRESPINO

Atticus Finch
The Biography

HARPER LEE, HER FATHER,
AND THE MAKING OF AN AMERICAN ICON

BASIC BOOKS
New York

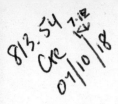
Basic Books
Hachette Book Group
1290 Avenue of the Americas, New York, NY 10104
www.basicbooks.com

Printed in the United States of America

First Edition: May 2018

Published by Basic Books, an imprint of Perseus Books, LLC, a subsidiary of Hachette Book Group, Inc. The Basic Books name and logo is a trademark of the Hachette Book Group.

The Hachette Speakers Bureau provides a wide range of authors for speaking events. To find out more, go to www.hachettespeakersbureau.com or call (866) 376-6591.

The publisher is not responsible for websites (or their content) that are not owned by the publisher.

Print book interior design by Amy Quinn.

Library of Congress Cataloging-in-Publication Data
Names: Crespino, Joseph, author.
Title: Atticus Finch: the biography : Harper Lee, her father, and the making
of an American icon / Joseph Crespino.
Description: New York : Basic Books, 2018. | Includes bibliographical
references and index.
Identifiers: LCCN 2017056457 (print) | LCCN 2017056513 (ebook) | ISBN
9781541644953 (ebook) | ISBN 9781541644946 (hardback)
Subjects: LCSH: Lee, Harper. | Finch, Atticus (Fictitious character) | Lee,
Harper--Family. | Lee, Harper. To kill a mockingbird. | Lee, Harper. Go
set a watchman. | Lee, Harper--Criticism and interpretation. | Authors,
American--20th century--Biography. | BISAC: BIOGRAPHY & AUTOBIOGRAPHY /
Literary. | HISTORY / United States / State & Local / South (AL, AR, FL,
GA, KY, LA, MS, NC, SC, TN, VA, WV). | LITERARY CRITICISM / American /
General.
Classification: LCC PS3562.E353 (ebook) | LCC PS3562.E353 Z58 2018 (print) |
DDC 813/.54 [B] --dc23
LC record available at https://lccn.loc.gov/2017056457

ISBNs: 978-1-5416-4494-6 (hardcover), 978-1-5416-4495-3 (ebook)

LSC-C

10 9 8 7 6 5 4 3 2 1

For Carrie and Sam

Blameless people are always the most exasperating.

—George Eliot, *Middlemarch*

Contents

Prologue

Like the Christ child himself, Atticus Finch was born on Christmas. It was 1956, and Nelle Harper Lee would not be heading home to Alabama for the holidays. She couldn't get time off from her job as an airline reservationist, so she spent Christmas with her closest friends in New York, Michael and Joy Brown and their two boys. Nelle had shared with the Browns the short stories that she wrote in the little free time that she had—humorous, heartwarming tales of small town southern life that reminded Michael of his own childhood growing up in east Texas. He liked them so much that he recommended Nelle to his agents, Maurice Crain and Annie Laurie Williams, a husband-and-wife team who ran one of the most successful agencies in New York. Crain read Nelle's stories and saw real promise in them. But he thought that she should write a novel, which would be easier to sell. It was good advice, but no simple thing to do, not with her airline job, which she needed to make ends meet. Around this same time, Michael experienced a windfall from a musical comedy special that he had sold. That's when he and Joy had an idea. On Christmas morning, they put an envelope on the tree marked "Nelle." Inside was a note: "You have one year off from your job to write whatever you please. Merry Christmas."

Stunned, Nelle responded with a litany of objections. Were they crazy? It was too much money. What if the children got sick? As the Browns batted down each one, it dawned on her that this wasn't an act of gener-osity, it was an act of love. Emboldened by their "fearless optimism," Lee was determined to honor the faith that her friends had shown in her.

She got to work immediately. In January, she started dropping by Crain and Williams's office each week to hand over new pages. By the end of the month, she had written 150. In another month, she had a full manu-script with the title "Go Set a Watchman."

It was the story of a struggling young writer in New York who returned to her small Alabama hometown to find that the town and her family had been transformed by racial crisis. The central conflict was between the young woman and her beloved father, a man she knew to be decent and principled but who had inexplicably fallen in with the racist reactionaries. The last name of the father she took from her own family, her mother's maiden name, Finch. The first name she drew from Roman history, Titus Pomponius Atticus, the friend of Cicero, a "wise, learned and humane man," she would later explain to a reporter.

On February 28, 1957, Crain sent the manuscript to Lois Cole, an edi-tor at G. P. Putnam's Sons who was best known for having discovered Mar-garet Mitchell, author of *Gone with the Wind*. Lee had "very real promise," Cole thought, but the novel was thin. "[T]here is not very much story, or plot, or suspense," she wrote, "and the last hundred pages do resolve into a series of debates, which are certainly sound and well-expressed, but still debates. It seems, to us, that people can be, and should be, instructed, but that they will take it better if it is all accomplished by a real story." She asked Crain to send her Lee's second novel if he failed to place this first one. She included with her letter an application for the New Campus Writ-ing Fellowship, in case Lee wanted help with her next book.

Five days later, Crain sent "Watchman" to Evan Thomas at Harper & Brothers, pitching it as "an eye-opener for many northerners as to southern attitudes, and the reasons for them, in the segregation battle." Thomas, a Princeton graduate and the son of the six-time Socialist Party presidential candidate Norman Thomas, had recently published *Profiles in Courage* by the young Massachusetts senator John F. Kennedy, which would win the Pulitzer Prize the following month. Lee was "a good writer . . . damned good," Thomas told Crain over the phone, but the novel didn't have enough story. He wished that Lee "wouldn't put her heroine in trousers. Somehow having her wear pants just rubs me the wrong way." Neither did he like how the character cursed her father. But Lee had "potential indeed," and, like Cole, Thomas asked Crain to send him Lee's next book if this one didn't sell.

Crain kept after it, sending the book to Lynn Carrick at J. B. Lippincott on May 13. Meanwhile, since finishing the draft of "Watchman," Nelle, intent on making the most of her year of artistic freedom, had started a new novel. It grew out of the childhood stories that she had initially shown Crain. The best of those, in Crain's opinion, had been "Snow on the Mountain," about a boy who takes out his frustration with the elderly neighborhood shrew by destroying her flowers. Another, "The Cat's Meow," Lee had revised in January and given back to Crain when she had passed along the first fifty pages of "Watchman." By mid-May, Nelle had decided to incorporate these two stories into her new novel. Two weeks later Nelle gave Crain the first 111 pages of a manuscript that she had titled "The Long Goodbye."

She kept writing, and in roughly another two weeks, on June 13, Crain sent Carrick a complete version of this new, second novel. "[T]his childhood stuff is wonderfully appealing," Crain wrote. "Possibly this longer and more substantial book would make a better starter than the one you have. She says this could go on and on." Crain advised Lee to keep writing and eventually she could drop out the duller stuff, holding the book to around 350 or 400 pages. Lee planned to break the novel off after the brother character entered high school, "leaving the four-year-younger sister to a lonely childhood."

It seems that this second novel, which grew out of Lee's short stories, is the one that would eventually become *To Kill a Mockingbird*. The book focused on the childhood and earlier lives of the characters that she had written about in "Watchman." In July 1957, Nelle described to Joy and Michael Brown how frustrated she had become trying to merge the two books. It was Crain who explained to her that this was a fool's errand, and that she should go ahead and finish the childhood novel. Then later she could write a bridge novel that would flow into "Watchman." He showed her sections of a novel in progress by Bonner McMillion, another writer with whom he worked whose fiction was set in the small town South, and who, like Lee, had the ability to "create living characters" and to "recall childhood scenes and moods with complete clarity," with "the same gentle underlying humor which adds charm to the telling." Lee loved the passages from McMillion's work. It hadn't seemed feasible to her at first to divide the material into separate books and let the childhood novel stand on its own, but then she found herself doing exactly as Crain had said.

By the middle of June, the editors at Lippincott had both of Lee's manuscripts. The one that Crain had first sent to Carrick under the title "Go Set a Watchman" would be listed in Lippincott's records as "Atticus." But the novel that Lippincott eventually signed to a contract on October 17, 1957, was untitled, and Carrick wasn't the book's editor. That task fell to Tay Hohoff, the firm's only female vice president. It seems that the editors changed because the manuscript that Lippincott was interested in changed. Instead of Carrick editing "Watchman," a political novel set in the midst of the segregation crisis, Hohoff was given the childhood novel that Lee continued to supplement with new pages throughout the summer. Amid the card files that Annie Laurie Williams kept is one with a header labeled "Go Set A Watchman." It is neatly struck through in pencil, and above it is typed "To Kill A Mocking Bird."

Two different manuscripts with two different fates. One found its way to a safety deposit box in Monroeville, Alabama, where it sat all but forgotten for over half a century before being discovered by Lee's lawyer and published in 2015. The other, revised and reworked for another two years and published in 1960, became one of the most successful books in American publishing history. In some ways, it's a familiar story. Many if not most successful novelists have a drawer in which an earlier, apprentice manuscript is tucked away. Yet Harper Lee's novels are different. Conceived back-to-back in the first six months of 1957 but published fifty-five years apart, both became a kind of Rorschach test for the politics of race in the period that they were published. They are unusual, too, in their paradoxical treatment of one of the most beloved characters in all of

American literature, the orienting figure of both novels, that touchstone of decency and goodness himself, Atticus Finch.

THIS BOOK TELLS Atticus's story, from his origins in the life and example of Harper Lee's father, Amasa Coleman Lee, to his creation and evolution in her two novels, his adaptation in the film version of *To Kill a Mockingbird,* and his public reception during the critical years of the southern civil rights struggle. Harper Lee famously described *To Kill a Mockingbird* as "a love story pure and simple." But with the discovery of *Go Set a Watchman,* we know that how she came to write that story, and to construct the character of Atticus, the source and the object of that love, was anything but simple. Thanks to *Watchman,* we know, too, that Harper Lee set out to write a novel not just about love, but about politics. To understand Atticus Finch, it is necessary to recover the political struggles that preoccupied her father, a lawyer, state legislator, and newspaper editor in Monroeville, Alabama, which were the same struggles that preoccupied Harper Lee herself.

A variety of new or previously unexamined sources make this possible. They include exclusive letters and other documents from the files of Harper Lee's publisher; privately held letters, previously unavailable to scholars, written by Lee from Monroeville in the mid- and late 1950s, that shed light on her relationship with her father and developments in her hometown that influenced her fiction; and interviews with Harper Lee's two oldest living nephews and oldest living niece, who offer fresh insights into the life of their grandfather and famous aunt alike. Most important perhaps are the hundreds of editorials written by A. C. Lee during his years as editor of the *Monroe Journal,* from 1929 to 1947, in which he commented on a remarkable range of state, national, and even international issues.

Previous biographers and journalists have almost completely ignored these editorials, which are crucial for a proper assessment of Harper Lee's fiction. Indeed, while we have long understood that A. C., as he was called, was the inspiration for Atticus, what has been lost is that he was a man deeply engaged with the momentous events of his times. His precocious daughter absorbed his sense of civic responsibility and belief that the nation's problems, not to mention the world's, were also Monroeville's. In his life and in his writings, A. C. Lee demonstrated a principled, conservative opposition to demagoguery and fascism, at home and abroad. A lifelong Democrat and loyal admirer of Franklin Roosevelt, he turned against the New Deal in the late 1930s and early 1940s as labor and civil rights politics moved to the fore of national Democratic Party politics. One consequence was a political rift between Lee and his spirited, nonconformist, politically unorthodox daughter. In the years immediately following World War II, when Harper Lee was an undergraduate, progressive candidates briefly found success in southern politics. Nelle produced her first published writings in this period: some short stories, but much of it political satire, including some aimed squarely at people like her father.

By the time Nelle sat down to write her novels in 1957, however, those days were long past. The Supreme Court's 1954 decision in *Brown v. Board of Education* set loose extremist forces across the Deep South. White southerners established new organizations to defend segregated schools, and they revived old ones, such as the Ku Klux Klan, which in Alabama enjoyed direct access to the state's most powerful politicians, including the governor himself. Alabama's leaders turned a blind eye to Klan violence against black protest, as well as to the intimidation and harassment of whites who didn't toe the line of strict racial orthodoxy. Conservative white southerners such as A. C. Lee, who in an earlier era might have objected to the demagoguery and fear-mongering, fell silent.

Watchman was Harper Lee's effort to make sense of her father's conservatism amid the madness of massive resistance. Yet that first novel didn't succeed, either as a work of fiction or as a defense of her father's politics, and potential publishers recognized as much. It would be *Mockingbird,* with its more careful, selective, and allusive evocation of a principled, decent white southerner, that coincided with and provided cultural reinforcement for a quiet oppositional politics in the white community, one that defied the essential, foundational myth of the militant segregationists:

the idea that the white South, united by blood, soil, and the tragic history of the Lost Cause, would resist racial integration to the bitter end. The puncturing of this myth marked the beginning of the end of the Jim Crow South.

That collapse owed most importantly and most fundamentally to the protest of black southerners themselves, and it would have happened regardless of whether Harper Lee ever published her novel. It was a fitting irony that Gregory Peck's portrayal of Atticus Finch in the film adaptation of *Mockingbird* won the Academy Award the same month, April 1963, that Martin Luther King Jr. wrote "Letter from Birmingham Jail," the quintessential statement of how well-meaning whites can often get in the way of genuine racial progress. Yet King himself would later recognize the "moral force" in Harper Lee's novel, and in Atticus in particular.

During the heyday of massive resistance, when Harper Lee was struggling to write her first novel, she could not have dreamed how the character that she invented would become an essential symbol of empathy and tolerance in American public life. Fifty-seven years after the publication of *To Kill a Mockingbird,* Barack Obama, reflecting in his Farewell Address on the lingering divisions of race, reminded Americans of the advice that Atticus gave to Scout: "You never really understand a person until you consider things from his point of view, until you climb into his skin and walk around in it."

It would have been impossible, too, for Harper Lee to have imagined in the late 1950s the changes that would come to her native South. That was when the militant segregationists were still in the driver's seat, and the common bit of cynicism among even progressive white southerners was that the law can't change people's hearts. But stories can. And Harper Lee's story did, in a way that's hard to measure—aside from the astronomical book sales—but hard to deny.

Her North Star in those chaotic, confusing days was her father. However much she might have disagreed with him on the particulars, she knew her father to be a man of character and substance, someone who deserved a serious hearing. That was the idea with which she started her first novel, after the Browns gave her that extraordinary gift. In her imagination, she returned to her childhood, to when she had grown up at the foot of a fair and decent man in a tucked-away, forgotten corner of the country. That is where the story of Atticus Finch began for Harper Lee, and it is where it begins for us as well.

PART I

ORIGINS

Chapter 1

The View from the Square

Do all the good you can. By all the means you can. In
all the ways you can. In all the places you can. At all the
times you can. To all the people you can. As long as ever
you can.

—John Wesley

The best way to understand A. C. Lee is to read what he wrote. There
is plenty to choose from—more, in fact, than his famous daughter
ever published. In the hundreds of editorials that he produced over nearly
eighteen years as editor of the *Monroe Journal*, all the quaint fare one
would expect from a rural weekly is on display: reports on prize hogs or
gargantuan turnips, pictures of beauty queens, respectful obituaries, and
long columns of short paragraphs noting who came or went visiting which
relative or friend at Christmas or Easter. Yet so, too, is coverage and original commentary on an extraordinary range of issues and concerns. Under Lee's leadership, the *Journal* didn't merely report local happenings;

it interpreted the world for its readers, only a small minority of whom had even a high school education.

A. C. Lee himself didn't have that. Eighth grade was the highest he completed. His formal education, such as it was in a rural schoolhouse five miles outside the tiny panhandle town of Chipley, Florida, ended at age sixteen, when he passed an exam that qualified him to teach at another meager schoolhouse elsewhere in the county. Yet Lee was Lincolnesque in his reading habits and devotion to self-education. He was a thoroughgoing Anglophile, a trait that he would pass down to his daughters. A grandson would recall hearing the names of Addison and Steele, Macaulay, and Gladstone in family conversation long before he had any idea who they were. A. C. read mostly legal and political history and biography. Southern history was a particular favorite. He consumed every book ever written by Douglas Southall Freeman, the editor of the *Richmond News Leader* and two-time Pulitzer Prize winner for his multivolume biographies of Robert E. Lee and George Washington. A. C.'s copy of W. C. Oates's *History of the 15th Alabama* was so worn that his daughter Alice would be on constant lookout for reprints. A. C.'s father, Cader A. Lee, had fought with the regiment for four years, battling Chamberlain's men on the fateful second day at Gettysburg, taking the bloody road south, stacking arms at Appomattox with what remained of the army of northern Virginia.

Albert James Pickett's *History of Alabama* was a cult classic in the Lee family. From it A. C. learned the history of the aboriginal tribes with their ancient burial mounds and fortifications, and of de Soto's explorations. Pickett wrote about the colonial rule of the Spanish and the French, and the arrival of English settlers, who came to the area that would become Monroe County either by traveling north up the Alabama River from Mobile, or coming down the Federal Road, which the United States had established as a postal route through Creek territory. A. C. would have read of the brutal fighting between whites and Indians in 1813 and 1814 that culminated in the Treaty of Fort Jackson. Pickett wrote a dramatic account of the Battle of Burnt Corn, considered the first real battle of the Creek War, which took place just south of Monroe County. At the beginning of the war, in Pickett's telling, "[e]verything foreboded the extermination of the Americans in Alabama, who were the most isolated and defenceless people imaginable." In addition to reading about local history, A. C. enjoyed taking his grandchildren and out-of-town visitors to the historical markers in and around Monroe.

In the official accounts written by white settlers and their descendants, the Creek War made Alabama safe from "Indian uprisings." Over the ensuing decades ambitious white men from the eastern states flocked to the southwestern frontier with their families and their slaves to take part in the cotton boom. The farms in Monroe were never as large or as prosperous as those just to the north in the Black Belt counties, named for the rich, black soil. Throughout much of the nineteenth century, there were some four hundred small farms spread throughout the county. As rail spurs penetrated deeper into the Alabama backwoods later in the 1800s, a market for timber developed and sawmills sprang up in the area.

A. C. Lee's first real job was as a clerk at a sawmill. He learned how to keep books and made himself indispensable to a series of small businesses in rough-hewn hamlets across north Florida, south Alabama, and southwest Mississippi. It was easy to like A. C. Lee, or Coley as he was sometimes called. He had a pleasant, earnest face, a gentle disposition, and an even temper. It was at one of his bookkeeping jobs, in the village of Finchburg in Monroe County, Alabama, that he met the woman whom he would marry, Frances Finch, the daughter of the local postmaster and prominent farmer and landowner. They married in 1910 and their first child, Alice Finch Lee, was born the following year. They would add three more to their brood: Frances Louise Lee, born in 1916, Edwin Coleman Lee, born in 1920, and their youngest daughter, Nelle Harper Lee, six years the junior of her closest sibling.

A. C. settled his family in Monroeville in 1913, when he took a job managing a small branch railroad line recently built by two lawyers by the name of Barnett and Bugg. After a year in their office, A. C. read for the Alabama bar under the two men's tutelage, which, in that day, for a person of Lee's background and means, was a common way to receive a legal education. He was admitted to the bar in 1915, and shortly thereafter Barnett and Bugg became Barnett, Bugg, and Lee. The firm did well enough that

A. C. Lee as a young man.

in 1922 Lee decided to remodel and enlarge the home that he had bought on Alabama Avenue.

If he was not at home or at work, chances are A. C. was at the Methodist church, where for decades he served as the lay representative to the annual Methodist conference, a position that his oldest daughter Alice would eventually take over. Among A. C.'s earliest memories was his mother, Theodosia Windham Lee, gathering up the children for the weekly three-and-a-half-mile trip to the community church. For seven of her eight children Theodosia chose conventional names—Fannie, Jessie, Mary, Stephen, Henry, George, James—but her second youngest child she named Amasa, the son of Abigail, the nephew of King David, derived from the Hebrew word meaning "burden bearer." Throughout his life Amasa bore many burdens of family, church, and community. Perhaps it was one reason that, as an adult, it became A. C.'s habit each Sunday to sit by himself during church, apart from his family at the front of the sanctuary, his attention given over fully to the service.

He was a pillar of his community as well. A member of the board of directors for the county bank, he was elected to the Monroeville town council in the early 1920s, where he helped bring electrification to the town. A. C. Lee and Monroeville practically grew up together. When he settled his family there, the population was only around five hundred. The new courthouse, built in the Romanesque style with a Georgian influence, was less than a decade old, which was the case as well with the First National Bank. Before the construction of those two buildings, Monroeville had been little more than an outpost at the crossroads of the county's only thoroughfares, which is why it had been made the county seat back in 1832. Monroeville was neither a river town—the Alabama River runs roughly eighteen miles to the west—nor a rail town—the main line of which would be laid eighteen miles to the southeast in Repton—which meant that while it was prominent locally, as the center of county business, the town would always be isolated from the wider world.

To counter that isolation was one reason A. C. Lee got into the newspaper business. Lee learned the trade from years of reading local papers along with the metropolitan dailies that circulated in south Alabama out of Montgomery, Mobile, and Birmingham. His journalistic interests were a matter of public service, but also political calculation. He won a seat in the state legislature in 1926. For an enterprising politician looking to have a voice in local and state affairs, gaining a stake in a newspaper was a savvy move. It was a good way to cultivate a constituency, promote pet bills or projects, or weigh in on party and state politics.

A. C. made a name for himself throughout Alabama, both as a politician and as an editor. In Montgomery, he was well-known as one of the legislature's most prominent fiscal conservatives. In 1932, he took the lead in opposing Governor B. M. Miller's proposed constitutional amendment allowing for a state income tax. When it became clear that the governor had the votes he needed to pass the measure, Lee maneuvered to limit the size of the tax. His signature achievement came three years later with the passage of a bill that required counties to pay off existing debts and operate solely on a cash basis. The *Anniston Star* called it "one of the most attractive measures" of that year's legislative session. There was some talk even of A. C. Lee running for governor, although it never came to pass.

As a newspaper editor, Lee was a member of a tight fraternity. Editors in Alabama read each other's columns and commonly debated public issues. A. C. wasn't shy about handing out plaudits or calling out colleagues when he disagreed with them, and he could be prickly. A measure of his ambition and standing was the frequency with which he quarreled with prominent editors of Alabama's major dailies, particularly Grover C. Hall, the Pulitzer Prize–winning editor of the *Montgomery Advertiser*. Hall and Lee kept a running argument in their respective newspapers in 1933 and 1934, debating Governor Miller's income tax proposal and other matters. Hall thought Lee had not been sufficiently forthcoming about the size of the state debt that had prompted Governor Miller to pursue an income tax. Lee chastised Hall for addressing the debt only by increasing revenues rather than reducing expenses. Things got heated. Speculating on why Hall so frequently sided with the governor against the legislature, Lee wrote, "Oh yes, it was the Governor and not the Legislature who appointed the Advertiser editor to a lucrative position recently." During another wrangle, Hall described Lee as "a smirking opportunist" who "regards all political journalism of a 'low order' which is not practiced in behalf of his side." Lee could only shake his head at Hall's "resort to the puerile practice of calling us names."

Prominent though he was, if Lee had personal ambitions for wider office or acclaim, he kept them well hidden. The overarching theme of both his politics and his editorship was of an unstinting propriety bordering at times on the sanctimonious. He took seriously his role as servant of the public good, both as a representative in the legislature and as agent and operator of a free press. On display year after year on the *Journal's* editorial page, in Lee's earnest, labored prose, are many of the attributes commonly associated with the Atticus Finch of *Mockingbird:* integrity, idealism, and seriousness of purpose, along with a bedrock commitment to the political and legal structures of government by the people, and a determination to ensure that the individuals who administered those structures lived up to the high ideals necessary to ensure their success.

Lee loved a good political sermon. And he was not afraid to repeat himself, nor to test his readers' patience with lengthy editorials on arcane matters, a significant number of which had to do with the intricacies of local and state finances. Harper Lee's portrait of Atticus Finch as a state legislator—consider Jem's explanation to Scout that Atticus "spends his time doin' things that wouldn't get done if nobody did 'em"—seems as true to life as anything in her book.

A. C. Lee also loved the Democratic Party, and, more even than the party itself, its incomparable standard-bearer, Franklin Roosevelt. Lee was ambivalent about the New Deal, yet his admiration and respect for Roosevelt himself were unwavering. No matter how much he may have disagreed with certain policies or proposals, Lee would never believe that Franklin Roosevelt had anything less than the best interests of the nation at heart.

That might not have been the case had Lee been concerned solely with domestic matters. Yet from his newspaper office on an unpaved street in his tiny south Alabama town, A. C. Lee looked out on all the world. It was the march of fascism in Europe, its ominous parallels in American politics—to A. C., none more ominous than Huey Long—and the portent of another world war that preoccupied him by the late 1930s, and reaffirmed his faith and hope in Roosevelt's leadership. Lee knew Roosevelt to be the heir to the Wilsonian ideals of international justice and peace. He deplored the Republican isolationists who stood in the way of what he saw as the inevitable mobilization necessary to assist Great Britain and defend freedom and democracy around the globe.

His editorials were ambitious and high-minded, and sometimes he produced four for a single issue. Showing up for work every day in a three-piece suit and a felt hat, a personal uniform that he adhered to years after most men in Monroeville abandoned jackets and ties (his entire life, Lee's only concession to informality would be when he took off his suit jacket for golf or to play with his grandchildren), he wrote for the cotton farmers

and sawmill workers, bank employees and traveling salesmen, shopkeep-
ers and schoolteachers, widows and churchwomen who made up the rolls
of *Journal* subscribers. Who could say how much of it any of them read?
Yet these were the constitutionally empowered citizens of the state of Alabama and the United States of America. With their vote and through
their elected officials they made real the promise of free government. The
proper fulfillment of their duties required a free flow of information and an
informed opinion on vital matters of the day. If they didn't get it from the
Monroe Journal, then where else were they going to get it? Given the tireless attention and care of Lee's editorials over his many years at the paper,
it's not hard to imagine that this thought, or something similar to it, passed
through his mind pretty much every single day of his working life.

ATTICUS FINCH IS a hero because he vigorously defended a black man
wrongly accused of raping a white woman. He did it because it was the
right thing to do, pure and simple. The pages of the *Monroe Journal,* however, show that for A. C. Lee himself, the moral calculus of Jim Crow law
and politics was considerably more complicated.

Consider a scandalous interracial sex crime that occurred in Monroe
County in the summer of 1930, roughly a year into Lee's editorship of
the *Journal.* Local judge F. W. Hare impaneled a special grand jury to
deal with an incident that had outraged the local citizenry. A man named
Archie Sheffield, a twenty-three-year-old common laborer, was indicted
for "carnal knowledge" of a girl under twelve years of age. The judge immediately convened a special petit jury and placed Sheffield on trial. The
Monroe County solicitor L. S. Biggs waged a "vigorous and unsparing"
prosecution of Sheffield. The jury returned a guilty verdict that same day.
No notice of appeal was given. Sentencing was imposed, again on that
same day, and Sheffield was sent to the penitentiary.

The episode looks like a commonplace example of precipitous, rail-
roaded "justice" in a southern courtroom, and perhaps it was. Yet there
was an unexpected wrinkle: Archie Sheffield was a white man, and his
young victim was black.

The conviction was front-page news in the *Journal*. Failing to respect the usual distinction between reportage and editorializing, the *Journal* reporter was quick to make clear the meaning of the event. It was proof "to the public" that "our courts do function promptly when an unusual situation demands it." A letter to the editor signed by two local white ministers elaborated. "[T]he jury that faced the facts and the law without prejudice," the men said, "wrote a new page—a bright page—in the history of human progress in our section—declaring the sacredness of human personality without distinction of racial heritage or of 'the pigmentation of the epidermis.' Under the administration of men of such courageous attitude and sincerity of purpose as these we bear with added pride the name Alabamians."

The historical record leaves little trace of who Archie Sheffield was and where he might have stood in the pecking order of Monroe County's white community, although it's unlikely that his position was very favorable. Yet even as a presumably poor white man with few influential friends, Sheffield's sentence was only fifteen years. It is impossible to imagine a black man receiving such a sentence for the same crime against a white woman.

Nonetheless, Archie Sheffield's conviction showed that Monroe County courts functioned properly, or at least that was A. C. Lee's understanding of it. Lee gave the Sheffield conviction front-page coverage in part because he himself had had personal experience with the improper functioning of county courts. In 1919, only a few years after he passed the bar, Lee was appointed by a local judge to defend two black men, Frank and Brown Ezell, a father and son accused of having robbed and murdered a white storeowner. Passions ran high throughout the county; a lynch mob gathered outside the Monroe County jail where the men were being held, leading the sheriff to move them to another county for safekeeping. The trial they received was a farce, a fact that Lee highlighted in his defense of the men. Lee objected to the fact that among the members of the jury was one of the victim's own sons. Lee lost the objection and the case. The Ezells were hanged in the Monroe County jail. It was the first and last criminal case that A. C. Lee ever took.

In *Mockingbird,* the adult Jean Louise notes that the hanging of Atticus Finch's first two clients "was probably the beginning of my father's profound distaste for the practice of criminal law." If the same was true for A. C. Lee and the Ezell hangings, it was because Lee knew that the case had been, in effect, a legal lynching. A. C. Lee detested lynching, and the sentiment went to the core of his religious beliefs. As a devout Methodist layman, Lee would have taken his cue in such matters from prominent leaders of southern Methodism. He held none in higher regard than Warren A. Candler, the Methodist bishop and longtime president of Emory University in Atlanta. As an editorialist, Lee recommended to his readers various sermons and moral teachings of Candler's, and when Candler died in 1941, Lee memorialized him in an editorial titled "A Truly Great Man Passes." The bishop's views on lynching provide a good proxy for Lee's.

Candler was a deeply conservative racial paternalist, and certainly no crusader. As lynchings across the South increased in number in the 1890s, he was slow compared to other white religious leaders in speaking out against them. Yet by 1903, in a public letter reprinted in newspapers as far away as New York and St. Louis, Candler roundly rejected lynching as "an outburst of anarchy" and denounced the politicians and newspaper columnists who agitated on its behalf. Over the years in letters and sermons published in the *Atlanta Journal* and reprinted in newspapers throughout the South, Candler denounced lynching as "an inexcusable outrage." Anyone who promoted it was "in the sight of God an accessory to murder, if not an outright and downright murderer" whom "God will not hold . . . guiltless when the Lord 'maketh inquisition for blood.'" Included in this admonition were courts that "ought not to try with indecent haste prisoners . . . nor sentence men to death to appease the passions of the mobs."

In his newspaper, Lee valorized southern politicians and lawmen who stood up to the lynch mob. A front-page story from June 1930 told of South Carolina governor John G. Richards's scathing denunciation of a sheriff who had failed to notify the governor's office in time to protect the life of a black man alleged to have attacked two young white women. The governor called the sheriff's actions "utterly reprehensible," and implied that he had been complicit with the mob, a common occurrence and one that anti-lynching groups had been drawing attention to for years. Perhaps Lee had this problem in mind when he ran another front-page story the following month about the sheriff in Jefferson County, Texas. This "robust and stout hearted" man was reported to have singlehandedly dispersed a mob that had come for a black prisoner accused of attacking a white woman.

The danger of the lynch mob and the threat it posed to civilized society was no abstraction for A. C. Lee. One of the most gruesome mob lynchings in the entire history of the practice hit close to home for Lee, literally. It took place in 1934 outside Marianna, Florida, the county where A. C. Lee was raised, where his mother and father were buried, and where all of his brothers and sisters still lived. In a scene similar to the one that Harper Lee would imagine in *Mockingbird,* a group of men traveling in four or five cars abducted a black prisoner from the jail in Brewton, Alabama, just forty miles south of Monroeville near the Florida state line. The black man, Claude Neal, was accused of having raped and murdered a white woman, Lola Cannidy, in a rural area in Jackson County, Florida. Neal, along with his mother and aunt, was initially taken to the jail in the nearby town of Chipley, A. C. Lee's hometown. Neal confessed to the crime, although investigators would later suspect that he had been coerced. In a detail that was similar to how in *Mockingbird* Tom Robinson testified that he had encountered Mayella Ewell on the day of the alleged rape, Claude Neal told how he had been walking along the fenced border of the Cannidy farm when Lola Cannidy saw him and asked if he would come across the fence and clean out a hog trough that she had been struggling with (Mayella Ewell asks Tom Robinson if he would bust up a chiffarobe for her).

The men who took Claude Neal from the jail in Brewton carried him back to the Cannidy family farm outside Marianna. A crowd estimated at several thousand people had gathered there, stoked by radio announcements and newspaper headlines earlier in the day. The horde became so large and unruly that Neal's abductors worried that they couldn't control it. So they took Neal to an alternative location and murdered him, but not before subjecting him to two hours of sadistic torture, including castration, forced autocannibalism, stabbing, burning with hot irons, and dismember-ment of toes and fingers. They tied Neal's body to the back of a car and dragged it to the Cannidy family home, where the remnants of the mob performed their own barbaric acts. Eventually Neal's mutilated corpse was hung from a tree on the northeast corner of the courthouse square in Marianna.

The *Monroe Journal* ran a story about the grand jury investigation into Neal's abduction from the Brewton jail, though it included none of the sickening details of the lynching. That was the first news about the lynching to appear in the *Journal*, yet it was unlikely to have been the first time that A. C. Lee had heard of the incident. The *Monroe Journal* office received wire reports from the major news agencies. On October 21, the Associated Press sent a dispatch from Lee's hometown of Chipley that reported that hundreds of men swarmed the streets all night threat-ening to destroy the jail if the sheriff didn't hand over Neal and the other prisoners.

Or perhaps Lee learned directly from his brothers or sisters about the mayhem in Marianna the day after the lynching. Neal's body was cut down from the tree on the courthouse lawn early on a Saturday morning. The rest of that day, a busy Saturday when rural whites and blacks customarily came into town to shop and do business, was, according to one local white man, "a day of terror and madness, never to be forgotten by anyone." Mobs of whites began attacking blacks around the town square who were there buying or selling goods, or who worked for white store owners. Marianna's mayor searched for policemen but couldn't find any; apparently members of the mob had already found them and threatened them with reprisals if they came to the square. The mayor attempted to deputize special officers, but could find no volunteers. One black man who was assaulted on a side-walk raced across the street into the courthouse where a group of friendly white men, armed with a machine gun, offered protection for him and an-other black man. The mob attacked a black porter helping a customer. The porter had to slash his way through the crowd with a knife to make it back to his employer's store, where the owner locked the door and held the mob at bay with a shotgun. A white woman only narrowly managed to protect the black maid that she had brought to town to help with her shopping. After emptying the streets downtown, the mob turned to the nearby white neighborhood with the oldest, grandest homes in town, looking for other black maids to attack. Some white women had already sent their maids home; others hid them in closets. Order was not restored in Marianna until late Saturday afternoon when a detachment of National Guardsmen, called up by the governor, arrived from Apalachicola.

This was utter chaos, the kind of thing loathed by mayors, town councilmen, bankers, members of the bar, newspaper editors, storeowners—in short, people of A. C. Lee's class. Blacks were the targets of the mob's violence in Marianna, but the mob's message was not to blacks alone. It was a warning also to whites who ran the town council and the businesses on the square, who employed blacks in their stores or in their fancy homes nearby, that if they couldn't protect white women in Jackson County, then the mob would. This was an example of the common confrontation within the southern white community between town folks and rural whites. The Claude Neal lynching showed the violence and the evil of which the mob was capable. It also showed the fragility of law, order, and civility in a small southern town. A man like A. C. Lee would not have taken any of these for granted.

William Faulkner had a metaphor that captured well the challenge for town folk. In *Intruder in the Dust* (1948), a large crowd comes in from the country to see if Lucas Beauchamp, a black man imprisoned in the county jail, will be lynched. A sullen group of men gather in the street in front of the jail, blocking traffic. The sheriff instructs a marshal to move them back onto the sidewalk. "Come on, boys," the marshal says, weakly. "There's other folks besides you wants to get up where they can watch them bricks." Faulkner continued,

They moved then but still without haste, the marshal herding them back across the street like a woman driving a flock of hens across a pen, she to control merely the direction not the speed and not too much of that,

the fowls moving ahead of her flapping apron not recalcitrant, just un-
predictable, fearless of her and not yet even alarmed.

The unpredictability of country folks was an everyday reality for a
town leader like Lee. His daughter would invoke this tension in *Mockingbird* in the calculations of men like Sheriff Heck Tate and Link Deas, Tom
Robinson's employer, who pay a visit to Atticus after dinner one evening
to share their concerns about the suspected activities of the rural white
families who lived out at Old Sarum.

By the 1930s, it wasn't just law and order that was at stake, but
home rule itself. In his thinking on this issue, A. C. Lee diverged starkly
from the Atticus of *Mockingbird*. The Claude Neal lynching is again revealing. The National Association for the Advancement of Colored People (NAACP) sent a young white minister to Marianna to investigate the
lynching and write a report, which the organization published in pamphlet
form and sent to thousands of ministers around the country. The horrific
details of mob violence, combined with the fact that the abduction that
had resulted in a lynching had taken place across state lines, led to a re-
newed effort in the US Congress for a federal anti-lynching law. The first
such proposal had been introduced back in 1922 and was blocked by a
filibuster by southern senators. The southerners would do the same to the
bill introduced in 1935 following the Neal lynching, and again in 1938.
A. C. Lee lauded the opposition to the 1938 bill in his newspaper. He was
convinced that its backers did not have law or morality on their minds, just
raw politics. "They seem to think such efforts will win the negro votes in
the northern states," he wrote in an editorial.

Lee knew that powerful interests outside of Alabama were looking
closely at how southern courts operated. This was why he had been eager
to publicize Archie Sheffield's conviction in 1930, and it would have factored into his 1934 decision to lead citizens of Monroe County to petition
Governor B. M. Miller to commute the sentences of two black men in the
county from death to life in prison, a request with which Miller complied
in both cases. It was why Lee castigated the white citizens of Tuscaloosa

County who had participated in a lynching in 1933. There was "no shadow of excuse," he wrote. The victim had been charged with a crime and apprehended; every indication was that "punishment commensurate with the offense would probably have been meted out to him in due course and in the orderly way."

But the outside attention also irritated Lee and made him defensive, a nearly universal feeling among white southerners of his generation, and one that survived into his daughter's generation as well. They were extremely sensitive to any mockery, condescension, or suspicion from a northern audience. For A. C. Lee, the political forces that threatened state and local control of Alabama's courts were of a piece with the cultural forces that looked down upon white southerners as denizens of a hopelessly backward, impoverished, and uncouth region—the "Sahara of the Bozart" in the famous phrase of H. L. Mencken.

A. C. Lee's resentment appeared, albeit in a characteristically subdued way, in his editorials on the most controversial case to come out of Alabama courts in the 1930s. In the town of Scottsboro in northeast Alabama, authorities arrested nine black youths in 1931 and charged them with having raped two white women. The accused had only barely escaped a lynch mob, and, hoping to avoid such an outcome, local officials organized a hasty trial in which eight of the nine accused were convicted and sentenced to death. News of the case made it into the *Monroe Journal* only after the International Labor Defense took up the boys' appeal, but even then the details were sketchy. A. C. Lee editorialized about some unnamed organization "principally from outside of Alabama" that would only irritate competent, well-meaning state and court officials and make it all the more unlikely that the defendants would get a fair hearing. He scoffed at a February 1936 article in *Time* magazine that, according to Lee, gave the impression that, for Negroes, Alabama courts were "simply perfunctory farces, and never utilized as an instrumentality for the disposition of justice." Interestingly, he wrote nothing about the June 1933 decision by Judge James E. Horton Jr., the white, native Alabaman who set aside the verdict against the defendants in the second court case and ordered a new trial. Horton's decision has often been cited as a real-life example of the kind of bravery that Atticus Finch showed in defending Tom Robinson. If Horton's decision was any inspiration to Harper Lee in crafting *Mockingbird*, it was not because her father took much note of it in print.

A. C. Lee's most heated commentary came in reaction to a widely publicized quote by New York attorney Samuel Leibowitz, the lawyer hired to defend the boys after their original conviction was vacated by the US Supreme Court. Leibowitz called the conviction in the second trial "an act of bigots spitting upon the tomb of the immortal Abraham Lincoln." Lee wrote in response,

> This brazen insult was hurled at a jury of twelve representative citizens of Morgan County, Alabama, who listened patiently to the testimony submitted at the trial and returned their verdict under oath.

> At least indirectly it was aimed at the people of Alabama, and the most charitable comment that can be fairly made is that the perpetrator has forfeited any claim he may have had to the respect of thoughtful citizens of this state.

> It is greatly to be hoped that the interests of the other defendants under the same charge will be in the hands of attorneys with some conception of the proprieties.

Reading the *Monroe Journal* today, it is easy to forget that the paper served a community in which some 40 percent of the population was African American. Occasionally, and always buried in the middle of the paper, there would be a "Negro News" column listing births or deaths in the black community. Every so often the principal at the black school would write a letter to the editor asking white citizens for donations to the school, or expressing thanks for white support for various ventures. The most frequent appearance of African Americans in the *Journal* was on the front page in reports of auto accidents or black-on-black assaults or murders.

On the sporadic occasion of black violence against whites, the coverage was extensive, as was white interest in the trial that followed.

The casual racism of Jim Crow Alabama pervaded the *Journal*'s pages. Included among them were advertisements and announcements for blackface minstrel shows, performed at school auditoriums throughout the county by high school or church groups. In February 1935, for example, the Young Women's Circle of the Methodist Missionary Society promised "plenty of laughs and fun" at the performance of a "Coon Town Wedding," which included tap dancing and a "Negro quartette." The sample ballot of the Democratic Party that the *Journal* printed included an emblem of a rooster below the banner "White Supremacy." Also evident in the *Journal*'s pages was the racial paternalism common to southern whites of Lee's social status. A July 1930 reprint of an article from a Virginia newspaper, for example, reported the death at age ninety of Evelina, a "much-loved colored mammy." Born in slavery, she had refused emancipation, so profound was her love of "her white people."

A. C. LEE would be an inspiration for his daughter's fiction not because he was ahead of his time, as the character of Atticus Finch of *Mockingbird* might imply, but rather because he was *of* his time and *of* his place, and yet still aspired to worthy ideals and noble values. Possessing no more than a middle school education, and with few resources for travel or other enlightening experiences, he was nevertheless a person of broad mind and high principle. There is plenty of evidence of those qualities in his editorials, particularly those he devoted to good government.

It was his favorite subject, and likely the thing that motivated him to get into the newspaper business in the first place. On his editorial page he delivered treatises denouncing government officials who took private salaries along with their public ones, which Lee argued led to "a lowering of the standards of official fealty and integrity." He criticized legislators who mingled too closely with lobbyists, and held forth on the proper relationship between corporations and government. The most consistent subtheme in this line of discourse was his condemnation of the political boss: Any politician who interpreted his duty as one of wringing spoils from government to be doled out to his constituents was on the road to bossism, Lee believed. Spoils delivered created debts to be repaid. It was through the collection of debts that politicians amassed personal power. Power invested in persons, rather than in the offices of government, weakened democracy as a whole. The slope was slippery. At the bottom was dictatorship.

Lee was not alone in these fears in the 1930s. Anxiety about government spoils being used for political advantage was common on editorial pages throughout the nation at the time. The proliferation of New Deal agencies that combated the Great Depression by providing direct relief to suffering Americans created unprecedented opportunities for political abuse. The 1930s was also the era of the strongman. Dictatorships were on the rise around the globe, and, as we will see, Lee connected the problem directly to that of the political boss. Yet to a remarkable degree, Lee's fears about political corruption coalesced in a decade-long string of commentary about one person in particular, that flamboyant figure of Louisiana lore, Huey Long.

Lee was obsessed with Long. He first took note of him in 1931 when, as Louisiana's governor, Long thrust himself to the forefront of southern politicians by calling for a regionwide cotton holiday program, a plan for southern farmers to take a year off from planting cotton in order to create scarcity and thereby raise its price. Lee liked the idea, and urged the Alabama governor to call a special session to discuss it. But the cotton holiday gained no traction among Alabama's leaders, and Lee's admiration for Long faded quickly. By the early 1930s, Long was becoming a national phenomenon. In 1930, he had run for the US Senate with two years left on his term as governor. When he won, he let his Senate seat sit empty for over a year until he finished his gubernatorial duties. Lee followed closely reports out of Louisiana of Long consolidating his power and ruthlessly dispensing with political enemies, running roughshod over local officials, legislators, and judges alike. Lee's commentary was so frequent that by February 1935 he acknowledged that "[p]erhaps our readers may grow somewhat weary of our continued discussions of the unusual situation existing in our sister state of Louisiana." But that didn't stop Lee from writing more editorials on Long.

Particularly galling to Lee were Long's increasing attacks on President Roosevelt. Long was an early supporter of the president but broke with him soon into Roosevelt's first administration and quickly emerged as perhaps his staunchest critic on the left. He castigated the president for not doing more to bring economic relief to the masses. For his part, Roosevelt viewed Long as the most likely figure in American life to emerge as a homegrown fascist, a Dixie equivalent of the cult-inducing strongmen then coming to power in Europe. Lee reported on the rumors that Long and Father Coughlin, the Catholic priest from Detroit whose radio broadcasts had won him enormous influence among the northern and midwestern working class, would team up on a "stop Roosevelt" ticket in 1936. In May 1935, Lee concluded that, since Long was such a publicity hog, the best thing to do was to give him the silent treatment. Yet he proceeded to editorialize on Long twice a month in May, June, July, and August, three times in September (not counting front-page coverage of Long's assassination that month), and three more times by year's end.

Lee was too polite to recount for his readers the macabre scene of Long's murder at the Louisiana state capitol on September 8. Long was there to orchestrate another of the special legislative sessions that he instructed his handpicked governor to call. One of the bills under consideration was a redistricting measure, outrageous even by Long's standard, designed to oust a state district court judge, Benjamin Pavy, a longtime political opponent. Long darted about the capitol building, in and out of the legislative chamber and various offices. Aides and politicians trailed behind along with his bodyguards. In a marble corridor outside the governor's office, Long turned to address the crowd following him. From behind a pillar a man in a white suit appeared, walked up to Long, and shot him. Policemen turned on the man and shot him dead. Outraged bodyguards emptied their pistols into the already deceased man, riddling him with some thirty bullet wounds. The assassin was a local doctor, Carl Weiss, the son-in-law of Judge Pavy. Long was taken to a local hospital and treated for his wounds, but he died two days later.

For A. C. Lee, Long's reckless pursuit of power, the riots, the armed guards, the assassination—all of these were the sad emblems of political dictatorship. A. C. recognized Long as "one of the brightest and most resourceful men the world has ever produced." Yet he believed that Long's demise dramatized perfectly the dangers of "iron handed rule." Lee followed closely the fate of Long's political machine in the months that followed. Years after Long's assassination, when Lee wanted to evoke the importance of moral leadership and the dangers of concentrated personal power, he would often recall the tragic example of the Louisiana Kingfish.

THE THREAT OF political dictatorship came home for A. C. Lee in a more immediate way in the spring of 1940. It involved the hotly contested campaign in Monroe County for the office of judge of probate. The seventy-year-old sitting judge, M. M. Fountain, was up for reelection. Fountain had made a name for himself in the county as a young man when he killed an escaped prisoner known locally as "the Negro outlaw, Wyatt Tate," who had been arrested for killing a constable. He used his resulting fame to win election as sheriff, and eventually probate judge. His main challenger was E. T. "Short" Millsap, a forty-six-year-old mule trader who had served a term as state senator from 1931 to 1935 and was currently a member of the Monroe County Board of Education. In Montgomery, Millsap was well-known for applying the tough negotiating tactics he had learned in his business trade to his political work. Though small in stature, he was a presence in town, walking the streets of Monroeville with a whip in his hand. For A. C. Lee, ten years' worth of high-minded editorializing on the responsibilities of self-government culminated in a singular, breathless effort to block Millsap's election as probate judge. Never before or afterward would he support or oppose a candidate for public office as fiercely as he fought to defeat Millsap.

Probate judge was no insignificant office in Alabama politics. In about two-thirds of the counties in the state, the probate judge was the chairman of the governing board, and as such, he was, according to V. O. Key Jr.—author of a classic study of mid-twentieth-century southern politics—the "principal factotum in local affairs." In challenging Fountain, Millsap was vying to become, in essence, the head of Monroe County's courthouse ring, a collection of local officials who used their office to dispense favors and thus consolidate their influence among the rural folk out in the county who almost always comprised the majority of eligible voters. Short Millsap would become one of Alabama's legendary courthouse operatives. Generations of aspirants to statewide office would see it as a rite of passage to stop in at Millsap's mule barn to talk politics. His rural supporters preferred meeting him there, rather than in the courthouse, where they were more likely to have to endure the condescending glances of town folk, some of whom, like A. C. Lee, would have been hard-pressed to conceal their disgust at witnessing Millsap's political machine in actual operation. Late into the evening, country supplicants and hangers-on would gather at the barn, waiting their turn for a few minutes with Short, the little man reared back in his old oak chair, one leg thrown casually over the arm.

Lee's displeasure with Millsap dated to 1932 when, as state senator, Millsap had tried to undermine efforts to reorganize and save the Monroe County Bank. The suspicion was that Millsap wanted to be named the liquidating agent and reap the healthy fee paid for such service. Also, Lee complained that as more people in Monroe County found a spot on public payrolls, relief lists, or lists of old age or farm benefits, Millsap had convinced uneducated, rural voters that Millsap himself had been responsible for their jobs or the checks they had received. This, according to Lee, was how he amassed the political chits that he cashed at election time.

As a newspaper editor, Lee took pride in not telling his readers how they should vote. He believed that his job was to inform them of the relevant facts and issues, and then trust that his fellow citizens would properly dispose of their responsibilities. Such restraint was particularly important in local races, where everybody knew or in some cases was related to everybody else. Only one time did A. C. ever break this rule, and it was with his endorsement of Judge Fountain against Short Millsap.

Lee opened the campaign season in mid-February 1940 with a general disquisition on honesty in government. He followed with several pieces citing the Huey Long example and warning county folks not to fall for politicians who promised them the world. A month out from the election Lee turned up the heat. "[O]ur local county people are face to face with the greatest threat they have ever been called upon to deal with," he wrote in an editorial titled "The Truth Shall Make Us Free." The next week he denounced Millsap by name for the first time, along with "the vicious political system he has built in the county." Nelle Dailey, an unwed forty-two-year-old middle school teacher, wrote a letter to the editor: "More power to you Mr. Editor! Let's have Spring house-cleaning." So, too, did Homer Dees, a fifty-year-old farmer and father of seven. "[F]or the last two or three years you have had a lot to say about the Huey P. Long dictatorship," Dees wrote. "I guess that was O.K. in his day. But as to the men that's running for Judge of Probate, I don't think either of them is related to Huey." Dees said that he had lived in Monroe County all his life, had been a legal voter since he was old enough, and had "never thought I needed the Editor of The Journal to tell me who I should vote for." He asked that his subscription be discontinued.

Thus it began in earnest. A letter to the editor the next week listed five signatories announcing their new *Journal* subscriptions to compensate for Dees's discontinued one. Lee aired publicly his charge that Millsap had tried to undermine efforts to save the county bank, and published a long letter from a member of the County Democratic Executive Committee, who accused the Millsap machine of having stacked the list of officers overseeing election boxes with loyal henchmen.

The night before the election, a crowd packed the county courthouse, the overflow filling the surrounding square, to hear Hunter McDuffie, the third candidate in the race, announce that he was withdrawing his candidacy and throwing his support to Judge Fountain, thus consolidating the anti-Millsap vote. Still, it would not be enough. Millsap prevailed comfortably, winning by a margin of 600 out of some 3,900 votes cast.

In defeat, A. C. Lee was magnanimous, at least at first. "The primary pillar of our governmental structure in this country of ours is majority rule," he wrote. He urged everyone "to remove from their minds any bitterness that may have grown out of the campaign just closed, and present a united front in every effort to promote the welfare of our people upon the proper basis." But it was hard for Lee himself to do so. An editorial the next week commented on the "refreshing" campaign for judge of probate in a nearby sister county. The successful candidate told voters, "I have nothing to offer for your support and vote except faithful, efficient and honest service." Lee was comforted that "there are still some people in public life who seem to properly appraise values."

Harper Lee was fourteen years old when Short Millsap was elected judge of probate. Millsap surely inspired her description in *Go Set a Watchman* of William Willoughby, the Maycomb County political boss who met with his constituents in a hutch, and who sent out his operatives to "drum it into the head of every ignorant hungry wretch who accepted public assistance, whether job or relief money, that his vote was Willoughby's." And in her conception of Atticus's summation in *Mockingbird*—that portrait of an honorable man making a desperate but ultimately futile plea to the better angels of a group of ordinary citizens—she may have drawn upon the memory of her father's noble failure in his stand against the Millsap machine in the spring of 1940.

As UPSETTING AS Short Millsap's victory was for A. C. Lee, developments abroad in the early summer of 1940 were far more troubling. Under Lee's leadership, the *Monroe Journal* followed international matters closely. That wasn't uncommon for rural newspapers of the day. The media landscape in the South was changing rapidly in the 1930s. Improved roads meant that metropolitan dailies started daily delivery in rural areas. As federal electrification programs brought down the price of utilities, more southerners bought radios. Yet the local weekly paper was still the place where the vast majority of rural southerners read the news. Compared to his fellow country editors, A. C. Lee was among the more curious, well-informed, and prolific commentators on the dramatic events unfolding around the world.

The French army's surrender to Germany in June 1940 prompted an editorial from Lee titled "Liberty's Darkest Hour." Not one normally to mix politics and religion, the fall of France led Lee to wonder aloud "why the all powerful God of the universe permits these things to be." He took hope, however, in the resolute leadership of Franklin Roosevelt. A cablegram that Roosevelt sent to the president of France pledging to make available to the Allied army vital war materials received Lee's heartiest endorsement. That same month he applauded Roosevelt's decision to appoint the Republicans Henry Stimson and Frank Knox as secretary of war and secretary of the navy. The move made clear the nation's "united front in our program of preparedness."

Lee, like the great majority of southern editors and politicians, was among the earliest advocates for US intervention against Nazi Germany. In Gallup polls from September 1939 through the bombing of Pearl Harbor, the South ranked first among all American regions in its support for the British, even at the risk of war with Germany. When asked to explain the South's eagerness to get involved in a distant war, southern editors and spokesmen chalked it up to the region's endemic poverty—poor folks had less to lose in a war—or its ongoing dependence on cotton and tobacco, two international commodities sold profitably in foreign markets. Others pointed to the fact that so many southerners—meaning white southerners—were of English stock, and thus connected personally to the fate of Britain. One of the most common explanations concerned the Civil War. "[W]e of the South have once been a defeated and invaded country and we have learned just what this means," said Clark Howell of the *Atlanta Constitution*. Other Americans "have never had the invader set his foot upon their soil and possibly this is why there is not the unanimity among them to defeat Hitler on the other side of the Atlantic rather than wait for him to come over here."

As for A. C. Lee, his interest in foreign matters sprung from his sense of ethnic loyalty with England combined with a genuine curiosity and love of learning. From the early years of his editorship, Lee's *Journal* carried wire service reports on events including the civil disobedience campaigns of Mahatma Gandhi and fighting between communist and nationalist forces in China. Lee himself weighed in with editorials on Japanese imperial ambitions, Mussolini's warmongering in Ethiopia, and, frequently, the rise of Hitler. Throughout the 1930s, Lee's tireless warnings about would-be dictators in Monroe County, Louisiana, or Washington were magnified by the regular reports of portentous events in Germany. As early as August 1934, Lee warned his readers not to believe Hitler's denials of Nazi involvement in the July putsch in Austria. The next year he decried German rearmament, and ran a front-page news item about Nazi persecution of Jews, the forced dissolution of Freemasonry, and ongoing harassment of Protestant and Catholic organizations. By March 1938, he wondered if Germans didn't look back "upon Kaiser Bill as something of a 'piker' as compared with their present-day Hitler."

For Lee, events in Germany were not distant, marginal matters for his Monroe County readership. They dramatized the stakes of free government and the fragility of basic forms of civilized life. In a November 1938 editorial, he expressed his horror over reports of Jewish persecution that emerged in the weeks following *Kristallnacht*, the wave of anti-Jewish pogroms that occurred on November 9 and 10, 1938. Just over a month earlier, Lee had celebrated on the front page the grand reopening of the newly refurbished Katz Department Store on the Monroeville square. The Katz family were the only Jews in Monroeville. Middle-class white families like the Lees took pride in their presence in the community. They noted what a good store Meyer Katz ran, how generous he was in supporting local charities. Townspeople loved to tell the story of how Katz sold to Klan members the white sheets they used to make their robes, a tale Harper Lee would fictionalize in *Mockingbird*. Stories of this sort were common in small towns across the South. The *Journal* was filled with congratulatory advertisements from Monroeville businesses celebrating Katz's refurbished store. The *Journal*'s ad was the largest of them all, dominating the front page. "Your new store is a credit to this progressive community," it read.

Throughout the 1930s, as international agreements crumbled, nationalism reemerged, and fascists marched, Lee regularly evoked the tragic path-not-taken at the end of World War I. He memorialized as the paragon of international statesmanship the southern-born Woodrow Wilson, the previous Democratic president. In his wisdom, Lee believed, Wilson had imagined an international order that could bring an end to ancient rivalries and forge relationships among governments of free people based on order, mutual respect, and justice. Efforts by Republicans to disparage Wilson and the US role in World War I, such as the high-profile hearings led by Senator Gerald Nye in the mid-1930s, disgusted Lee. He was convinced that the world's present troubles could be laid at the feet of the isolationist Republican Congress at the end of World War I, which had foolishly rejected Wilson's leadership and refused to join the League of Nations.

With Huey Long dead, no figures in American life elicited more consternation from A. C. Lee than the isolationist spokesmen who fought to keep the United States out of the European conflict. Colonel Charles Lindbergh, the flying hero of the 1920s, was a figure of great admiration and sympathy, Lee wrote in an October 1939 editorial, but he was "a serious disappointment as a statesman." Lee noted Lindbergh's recent visit to Berlin, which he suggested had muddled Lindbergh's ideas about world affairs. Lindbergh's suggestions, Lee argued, "would play very directly into the hands of Hitler and Stalin, and would insure the destruction of England and France." Henry Ford possessed a "peculiar" mind, Lee believed. Ford auto plants had been turned over to the manufacture of airplanes, yet Ford stipulated that the planes should be used only for home defense, not sold to Britain. Many would rightly question "the complete loyalty of Mr. Ford to the cause of freedom in the world," Lee contended. He applauded President Roosevelt's decision to accept Colonel Lindbergh's resignation as a reserve officer in the US Army in May 1941, as well as the decision not to renew the commission of General Hugh Johnson, another leading isolationist. These were men "who are known to be working at cross purposes with the aims and purposes of [the] government."

The isolationists had already left their mark by that point. Between August 1935 and May 1937, Congress passed a series of laws, the

Neutrality Acts, restricting US involvement in foreign wars. Even after war broke out in Europe in 1939, Roosevelt struggled to win concessions that would allow him to aid Britain and France in the struggle against Germany. Small town lawyer and editor though he was, Lee saw clearly the dangers of international developments and the need for US action years before many of his fellow Americans. Editorializing in September 1937 on Japanese attacks on China, Lee expressed his fear that "this may be the beginning of another world war." It was a prescient statement, as was his March 1938 editorial, in which he explained to Monroeville's citizens that war in Europe between free and fascist nations was inevitable. Better for Americans to join the fight in Europe, when it came, "rather than have the armies of the world invade our own country and let it suffer the extreme devastation that is bound to come."

Lee celebrated Roosevelt's resolute support for the peoples of France and Great Britain. He hailed the president's frank letter to Hitler and Mussolini in April 1939, confronting them on their continued aggressions. "The time is here even now," Lee wrote, "when the 'pussy footer' has no place in this country of ours." Roosevelt's September address opening a special session of Congress to deal with the embargo on war materials was, in Lee's estimation, "one of the outstanding messages of his whole administration." That fall Roosevelt signed legislation that revised the Neutrality Acts, lifting the arms embargo that Congress had put in place at the height of the isolationist frenzy. Critical to the passage of the bill were southern Democrats. In the House they voted 110 to 8 in favor of revision.

For several years Lee had opposed the idea of a third term for Roosevelt. He was reluctant to abandon the two-term tradition established by George Washington. Yet by the summer of 1940, Lee believed that circumstances were extreme and that the moment demanded a man of Roosevelt's experience and wisdom. He eagerly supported Roosevelt for a third term.

The great conflagration to come would leave almost no aspect of the world unchanged. Americans would have to fight to defend freedom around the globe, as A. C. Lee had feared. At home in Monroeville, Lee took it all in, writing his editorials in his *Journal* office, reading his newspapers and magazines at home in the parlor. The world as he knew it was being transformed, as was Lee himself. None of it would be lost on his youngest daughter.

Chapter 2

Jackassonian Democrats

If the impish, inquisitive Scout of *To Kill a Mockingbird* is not an exact autobiographical portrait of Harper Lee, it would seem a good approximation. "The first two-thirds of the book are quite literal and true," Truman Capote, Lee's childhood friend, wrote to mutual friends shortly after *Mockingbird*'s publication. "And yes, my dear, I <u>am</u> Dill." Long summer days spent in a treehouse reenacting adventure stories, gewgaws uncovered from secret hiding places, tall tales and romps to the square: there's no reason to think that these aspects of her book were too far from Harper Lee's actual experience.

In these early days, A. C. Lee recognized the spark of intelligence and creativity in Nelle and her childhood friend Truman, and he encouraged them both. He patiently answered Nelle's questions about the books and newspapers that he read, or Truman's inquiries about the crossword puzzles that he worked. He played little games with them, making up sentences using words that started with the same letter, and gave them one of his old typewriters, an Underwood No. 5. The children hauled it out into the backyard, under the yellow rosebushes, taking turns hammering away at the keys, writing their first stories.

Nelle was purportedly the inspiration for the character of Idabel Thompkins in Capote's debut novel, *Other Voices, Other Rooms* (1948). Idabel is the argumentative tomboy who befriends Joel, the thirteen-year-old protagonist. She bridles at Joel's shyness in washing naked in the creek. "I never think like I'm a girl," she explains, "you've got to remember that, or we can't never be friends." Plaintively she knocks her fists together, murmuring, "I want so much to be a boy: I would be a sailor, I would . . ." Later, she and Joel sneak off to the circus, where Idabel is mesmerized by the tiny, rouged, yellow-haired Miss Wisteria, a midget. Idabel fawns over her, insisting that she share a sodapop with them and ride the Ferris wheel. When Idabel is momentarily distracted, waving at other circus-goers, Miss Wisteria turns to Joel and asks, "Poor child, is it that she believes she is a freak, too?"

How much of Nelle there was in Idabel, or vice versa, is hard to say. Perhaps Nelle felt like an oddity, but it's also possible that by her early teens she was simply the youngest, most isolated member of what had become a rather somber, lonely household. She was a sophomore in high school on December 7, 1941, when the Japanese attacked Pearl Harbor, which marked America's official entry into World War II. All the older Lee children had moved away. Her eldest sister Alice was in Birmingham working as a clerk for the Social Security Administration and attending night school to get her law degree. Louise, ten years older than Nelle, was married with a small child living in Eufaula, with a husband who would soon be away at war. Edwin, a student at Auburn, had left his studies to join the US Army Air Corps.

The presence that would have compounded the sense of absence for A. C. Lee and Nelle both was that of Frances Lee. Back in 1910, the thirty-year-old A. C. Lee had married above his station. Frances Cunningham Finch, nine years his junior, had descended from Virginians who had moved south; her mother's side of the family owned a plantation near Bells Landing on the Alabama River. Gentle and cultured, she had enjoyed a formal education that A. C. could have only dreamed of. At the girls' boarding school in Montevallo, founded by the pioneering feminist leader and penal reform advocate Julia Tutwiler, Frances excelled in music, both as a pianist and a vocalist. She continued to play and sing the rest of her life. Her children recalled her expert musicianship, along with her love of reading, which she shared with her husband. Her aspirations as a mother were reflected in the title of a talk she gave in 1922 at a meeting of the Methodist Church's missionary society, "The Home—a School of Ideals."

Yet relatively early in her motherhood, Frances began struggling with mental health problems that would plague her the rest of her life. The family would always describe it as "a nervous disorder." It began with the birth of her second child, Louise, who had a difficult infancy. The baby was losing weight and constantly crying. Frances couldn't sleep and didn't know how to help her child. A. C. couldn't help his daughter or his wife. They finally found a pediatric specialist in Selma, Dr. William W. Harper, who diagnosed Louise's problem. His aid was so important to A. C. and Frances that they would name their youngest child, Nelle Harper, for him.

The baby improved, but Frances didn't. She lived away from her family for a year, staying with relatives near Mobile, where she received care from a doctor. During that time, A. C. was a single father to his five-year-old daughter Alice and the infant Louise. He was assisted by Hattie Belle Clausell, the family's black servant who lived nearby and was a near-constant presence in the house. The Lee daughters always remained fiercely protective of their mother's reputation, but given Frances's precarious health, it would not have been easy for the teenaged Nelle to have dealt with her mother without her older siblings also around to contribute.

Nelle graduated from high school in 1944, and immediately enrolled in the summer session at Huntingdon College in Montgomery, formerly the Woman's College of Alabama, which Alice had attended for a year. Alice herself had returned to Monroeville earlier that year, her law degree in hand, to join her father's firm, becoming the first female lawyer in Monroe County. Nelle didn't take to Huntingdon, which had too much the air of the finishing school for such an independent-minded young woman. Yet the school's literary magazine, *The Prelude*, was where she would publish her first pieces of writing. The spring 1945 issue carried two short items. Both show that the political and racial themes that preoccupied Nelle's later writing were present from the beginning.

The longer and more polished of the two pieces, "A Wink at Justice," tells the story of a shrewd country judge who presides over the trial of eight black men arrested for gambling. The narrator views the action from the courtroom gallery. The story anticipates the form of *Watchman* in that it concerns a skeptical, uninitiated person learning the wisdom of an elder. The judge has the men hold out the palms of their hands so that he can inspect them. He dismisses three of the men and sentences the others to sixty days in jail. When the narrator asks the judge afterward how he had come to his decision, he explains that the hands of the men he dismissed had calluses, which, for the judge, marked them as farmhands likely to have families to support, whereas the hands of the men he sentenced were smooth, suggesting that they were professional gamblers. "Satisfied?" the judge snaps. "Satisfied," the narrator nods.

The other piece, "Nightmare," only three short paragraphs, describes a traumatic memory that comes flooding back to a daydreaming school girl. Crouching to peer through a broken board in a fence, she hears on the other side a man being lynched. She flees, screaming and sobbing, to her bedroom. Later, as the lynchers walk below her open bedroom window, she overhears their self-satisfied comments on their work.

Nelle only spent one year at Huntingdon. At the end of the school year, she transferred to the University of Alabama, where she planned to study law. Perhaps she would go back to Monroeville and join the family practice, just like Alice. A. C. liked to joke around town that he could re-name the firm "A. C. Lee and Daughters, Lawyers."

BY 1944, TAKING stock of developments in Alabama and around the nation, A. C. Lee found fewer and fewer things to smile about. He was sixty-four years old, and an unmistakable crotchetiness suffused his editorials. A clear divide emerged in his political thinking. Roosevelt, so noble and wise in international matters, had all but ceded his domestic agenda to the liberals and the labor bosses, or so Lee felt. Gone was any effort by the New Dealers to balance the needs of labor with capital. In Alabama, political sentiment ran toward liberal New Dealers like Lister Hill, who had won reelection to the Senate earlier that year, despite Lee's fervent opposition.

Times had been tougher in the 1930s, yet back then everyone seemed to be pulling their oar in the same direction. That's the way A. C. Lee saw it in 1944. Roosevelt's first hundred days were like a dream. Before taking office, Roosevelt had come over from Warm Springs to visit friends in Alabama. In Montgomery, he stood on the very spot where Jefferson Davis had taken the oath as president of the Confederacy to announce the government would take over the Muscle Shoals dam and use it for a coordinated effort in regional development. Roosevelt's critics called him "autocratic," yet for A. C. Lee he was a man with "a keen conception of public duty." For too long the country had been run by the "House of Morgan," Lee believed, and Roosevelt was restoring a measure of balance to the financial sector. Monroe County got one of Roosevelt's forestry camps, and the Civilian Conservation Corps was soon at work creating the Little River State Forest, which ran along the county's southern edge. A. C. was even willing to go along with Roosevelt's controversial National Industrial Recovery Act. True, it allowed for an extraordinary measure of government intervention in private business, yet were they not extraordinary times?

A. C. Lee knew it well. He was a member of the board of directors of the Monroe County Bank when it closed its doors on November 12, 1932, out of fear of a bank run. He published a front-page editorial explaining why people shouldn't panic. Roosevelt had to do a similar thing with the bank holiday he had declared shortly after taking office, when local banks across the country were failing in unprecedented numbers. In the first of his radio addresses to the American people that would come to be known as "fireside chats," the president described in clear, direct language what he had done, why he had done it, and what would happen next. "[T]he God who overrules the universe has raised up the man to lead us in this emergency," Lee wrote in August 1933. "Whether we agree in matters of detail or not, the fact remains that the objectives sought are of the highest order, and marks Franklin D. Roosevelt one of the greatest leaders of all times."

Most essential of the objectives that Roosevelt sought, at least to Lee, was relief for struggling farmers. The Agricultural Adjustment Act was the culmination of decades' worth of progressive thought about how to organize the cotton industry, the lifeblood of south Alabama. It included a cotton allotment program that paid farmers to take land out of cultivation, thereby suppressing supply and raising prices in the way that Huey Long's cotton holiday idea had intended to do. "Never in the memory of man now living have the farmers of the nation had so devoted and loyal a friend in the White House as its present occupant," Lee wrote. Lee was more astute and forward-thinking on agricultural issues than many of his fellow country newspapermen. One study of rural southern editors observed how "badly befuddled" many of them were, lambasting Agriculture Secretary Henry Wallace as "a sinner who wasted the earth's substances in the cotton and tobacco patches, to say nothing of his famous bloodletting at the pigpens."

Lee, by contrast, was infuriated by southern politicians who stoked opposition to Roosevelt's farm reforms. Alongside Huey Long and the isolationists in Lee's hall of villains was Georgia governor Eugene Talmadge, who in 1935 was undermining the cotton allotment program, and, Lee believed, trying to feather his own political nest by urging southern farmers not to sign away their God-given right to plant as much cotton as they well pleased. For Lee, this was the height of irresponsible demagoguery.

Through the entirety of Roosevelt's first term and even afterward, no New Deal policy provoked a quibble from Lee, not even Roosevelt's controversial 1937 plan to restructure the Supreme Court. Yet a turning point in Lee's thinking came that same year. "Much as we have desired to support the present administration in Washington in all its major undertakings," he wrote in June 1937, "the time has now been reached when we find ourselves unable to travel with it on one of its policies."

The policy in question established a minimum wage and set maximum work hours in industries throughout the country. It would eventually come to fruition in the 1938 Fair Labor Standards Act, and it actually had its origins in Alabama. Hugo Black, the Alabama senator whose loyal support of the New Deal led Franklin Roosevelt to reward him with a Supreme Court appointment, had first introduced the legislation in 1932. Many southern laborers supported the bill, but A. C. Lee sided with business interests who argued that it would deal a terrible blow to still-fledgling industries in the South. He was concerned about the small manufacturers in rural areas who would be upended by the law, like the sawmills where he used to work keeping the books. When they shut down, workers would have to flee to urban manufacturing centers. As Lee saw it, only large-scale industries could compete under the new rules.

Yet in the South, even they would struggle, and that was an outcome that the bill's backers knew full well, or so Lee suspected. The recruitment of new factories was critical to the South's effort to balance agriculture with industry, and northerners didn't like the South's aggressive tactics, particularly the confidence with which they assured northern industrialists of a nonunionized workforce. Lee and many of his fellow southerners believed that the wages and hours bill was designed to kill the South's competitive advantage, and they were not alone in this view. The influential journalist Walter Lippmann would describe the Fair Labor Standards Act as "a sectional bill thinly disguised as a humanitarian reform." Just as northern states had been benefiting for decades from differential freight rates applied by the federal government, Lee argued, here again the South would get the short end of the stick.

Lee also fought against the Fair Labor Standards Act because it cut against one of the single most important developments in Monroeville history. In 1937, J. E. Barbey, owner of the Vanity Fair Corporation, a manufacturer of women's lingerie, announced that he was closing down his mill in Reading, Pennsylvania, and building a new plant in Monroeville. Barbey was a trophy catch for the gregarious First District US congressman Frank Boykin, who had an international reputation for hosting powerful politicians and businessmen at his hunting lodge in Washington County. "One deer and three wild turkeys shot by the right people can bring a million or a million and a half dollars to Alabama," Boykin was known to boast, although it was a chance encounter one morning in Washington that sparked the Vanity Fair deal. In his aptly titled memoir, *Everything's Made for Love in This Man's World*, Boykin told the story of inviting a

Vanity Fair official to coffee and hearing his complaints about the horrible winter weather in Pennsylvania. Boykin enlightened him about the ideal climate of south Alabama.

It wasn't the Pennsylvania winters that concerned J. E. Barbey, however. He had watched closely several strikes in the early 1930s in the northern hosiery industry, and he vowed that he would never operate a union shop. What Monroeville offered was a place off the beaten path that union organizers would have a hard time finding, and wouldn't feel terribly comfortable visiting, even with the temperate winters. It was a place with state and local officials eager to provide the financial and tax incentives to make it worth it for Vanity Fair to relocate. The fact that Monroeville had an economically conservative state legislator who happened to own the local newspaper and who could pen a convincing editorial about how labor unions threatened the South's economic future would have been a big mark in the town's favor.

The *Monroe Journal* celebrated the opening of the mill with fanfare equal to that of VE Day, and for good reason. In economic terms, Vanity Fair brought Monroeville into the twentieth century. The town was little different from nearby Jackson, Alabama, where the company built another factory two years after the Monroeville opening, and where, before Vanity Fair showed up, there wasn't a brick building in the entire county. In Jackson, few people had electricity, because hardly anyone could afford the utility bill. Lawyers and doctors were accustomed to being paid in kind, as was the case, of course, with Mr. Cunningham's payment to Atticus in *Mockingbird*. The three hundred employees Vanity Fair hired in Monroeville drew from the almost entirely untapped labor market of women. In a few cases the men stayed home and kept house, but many other households enjoyed dual incomes, dramatically raising living standards. In the decades to come the monotonous work of sewing women's underwear would become a drudgery, particularly as competition from overseas led to speedups and compressed wages (talk of unionization flared up and then mysteriously died out, time and again). But in the 1930s, Vanity Fair was a godsend. The largest and most reliable consumer of gas and electricity in the county, the factory brought about expanded coverage and lower rates for everybody. Vanity Fair had standing orders for paper supplies and other goods among local merchants, allowing them to expand their businesses. It built a park and a lake, where local children played in the summertime. It even renovated the golf course, which A. C. Lee would have enjoyed immensely.

It goes without saying that the park and the lake and the golf course were for whites only, and that the women that Vanity Fair employed in the 1930s were all white. From the plant's establishment until the 1960s, when federal civil rights laws forced the company to open jobs for black workers for the first time, the economic disparity along racial lines in Monroe County, which had already been significant before industrialization, became even more stark. Racial tensions increased in ways that would have been hard to recognize at the time. As the war came, the younger and more ambitious of Monroe County's black community moved to cities, or left the South altogether. Whites in town complained that the rising generation of blacks did not have the same manners as their elders. Commonplace, everyday frictions increased, such as incidents of aggressive driving by local blacks on county roads, a development that in *Watchman* Jean Louise observes upon her return home from New York.

A. C. Lee's souring relationship with the New Deal tracked closely with the emerging fault line in southern politics. White southerners as a whole were largely supportive of the New Deal through 1937 or so, yet political divisions in the region were sharpening. On one side were liberals who wanted to push forward with further New Deal reforms that would truly modernize the southern economy. They took heart from President Roosevelt's much publicized *Report on Economic Conditions of the South*, released in August 1938, in which the president famously described the region as "the nation's No. 1 economic problem." A few months later, a coalition of New Dealers and labor and civil rights reformers met in Birmingham to establish the Southern Conference for Human Welfare, which would be the main voice of progressive reform in the region over the next decade, and the target of countless reactionary attacks.

On the other side were conservatives who felt that the economic emergency was over, that relief efforts should be pulled back, and that government should ease up on business and let the free market do its work. The principal expression of this view was the 1937 Conservative Manifesto, signed by a bipartisan group of senators, but driven mostly by southern Democrats, particularly North Carolina senator Josiah Bailey. It has been called "a kind of founding charter for modern American conservatism . . . among the first systematic expressions of an antigovernment political philosophy that had deep roots in American political culture but only an inchoate existence before the New Deal."

A. C. Lee had always tended toward the conservative side of things. As a state legislator he mostly voted with the Black Belt, the swath of counties in south-central Alabama. This was the area with the richest farmland, the largest planters, and the largest black population; it had been the stronghold of slave owners in the nineteenth century. In the twentieth century, the political leaders of the Black Belt aligned with the "Big Mules" of Birmingham, and the smaller "Mules" of Mobile—the heads of the steel, ironworks, and shipbuilding plants, along with the utility executives who had helped bring them to the state. They comprised the conservative faction in Alabama politics. They joined together to fight labor unions, and they opposed the counties of northern Alabama and the southwestern wiregrass counties, where the black population was much smaller, which meant that politicians there felt a freer hand in backing populist, progressive measures that had the potential of dividing the white community along class lines.

Yet A. C. Lee's conservatism was rooted as much in his religion as in any economic or political philosophy. He strived to live a Christian life, as taught by the Methodist church in which he had been born, baptized, and reared to manhood, and which he served faithfully in adulthood. His idea of a good and moral life was informed, too, by the relationships he made and the responsibilities he assumed as a conscientious member of his community. Being conservative meant that you didn't spend money that you didn't have, you didn't wear flashy clothes or buy expensive cars, you didn't show off, or brag, or gossip, you weren't lazy, you didn't say one thing in town and something else at home, and you were polite, particularly to those less fortunate than you.

These were values essential to a moral life and, Lee was always quick to point out, essential to democracy as well. Free government required elected representatives to be honest, responsible, and trustworthy. For A. C. Lee, a good political representative didn't have to be a self-professed political conservative, but he should be conservative in temperament and habit. In a June 1930 editorial that anticipated an upcoming gubernatorial primary, for example, Lee defined conservatism as "the idea of moderation as distinguished from extremism." The conservative candidate was the person who didn't traffic in negative campaigning, who didn't court votes with extravagant promises. An editorial two months later titled "The Present Need for Conservatism" warned readers against "the glittering appeal of the demagogue."

The Depression tested the small town conservative values of Lee and millions of other Americans in novel ways. It was not just that opportunistic demagogues exploited the fears of desperate, downtrodden people— though that was a concern. Equally ominous was the reality that values of thrift, personal responsibility, and individual initiative, along with traditions of private charity, all seemed like weak medicine for so monumental an emergency. In 1933, when A. C. Lee wrote about God raising up Franklin Roosevelt to meet the present crisis, it wasn't just talk. For him, as for millions of Americans, the New Deal really did seem heaven-sent.

By the late 1930s, however, Lee had slid into the camp of those who felt that the New Deal had done enough. The wages and hours bill was the turning point, but his reaction to it fit with his broader assessment of relief policy. The New Deal had begun to "actually promote the idea of dependence . . . on the part of our citizenship," he wrote in 1938. He lamented the "rapidly growing idea among our people that the government owes them a living." Government debt was growing out of control, he feared. It was time that Americans started "Living within Our Income" once again. As his objections to the New Deal increased, his conservatism became less about personal morality and more of a clearly defined political position. This, it should be noted, was part of a broader change in the New

Deal itself. By the late 1930s, the New Deal, which had begun as a grab bag of old reform ideas that had come out of the Populist and Progressive movements, became more of a unified, coherent liberal program.

Lee's commentary on two high-profile political races in 1938 is revealing in this regard. In both Lee supported the conservative, anti–New Deal candidate. The first involved the campaign for the US Senate seat in Alabama that opened up when President Roosevelt appointed Hugo Black to the Supreme Court in 1937. The White House backed Lister Hill, the congressman from Alabama's second district and a reliable New Dealer. Conservatives in Alabama supported "Cotton Tom" Heflin, who until George Wallace came along was perhaps the most notorious bigot in Alabama politics—no small distinction. Heflin had helped draft the 1901 state constitution that secured black disfranchisement, and had served ten years in the US Senate in the 1920s. He failed to win renomination as the Democratic candidate in 1930 after refusing to support the Catholic Al Smith, the Democratic nominee, in the 1928 presidential race.

In 1930, A. C. Lee, who had only recently taken over as *Monroe Journal* editor, had been an outspoken critic of Heflin. This was of a piece with his conservative, Black Belt inclinations. In the 1920s, Heflin had been a member of the Klan, which at the time had been a favorite organization of Alabama's white workingmen (the future US senator Hugo Black had joined the organization in order to win the loyalties of white laborers). Lee denounced the Klan groups from outside Alabama lobbying on Heflin's behalf. He also criticized efforts by Heflin and his supporters to turn the race into a referendum on Catholic influence on the Democratic party. In a speech in Monroeville, Heflin called out Lee as one of the "Hickory Nut Heads" leading Alabamans astray, a designation Lee proudly publicized on the *Journal*'s editorial page. Seven years later, however, all of that was ancient history. Lee still had no great enthusiasm for Cotton Tom, yet, as he wrote in December 1937, a vote for Heflin was "[t]he only way the people of Alabama can effectively voice their opposition to the pending wages and hours legislation." Lister Hill was too much of a New Deal yes-man, Lee argued. The majority of Alabama voters saw it differently. They sent Hill to the Senate in an easy victory.

The other campaign of interest was in Georgia, where US senator Walter George was up for reelection. In a June fireside chat, President Roosevelt announced that, in his role as leader of the Democratic Party, he would be taking part in a number of legislative races that affected his administration's priorities. Southern liberals had been urging him to leverage his popularity in the region to help unseat conservatives who had opposed the New Deal. Chief among them were George and South Carolina senator "Cotton Ed" Smith, who was also up for reelection that year. In a late summer visit to Warm Springs, Roosevelt traveled to the nearby town of Barnesville for an awkward face-to-face encounter with George. Appearing on the same platform as George and his rival, a young attorney named Lawrence Camp, Roosevelt stunned the crowd by bluntly endorsing Camp. "[O]n most public questions [Senator George] and I do not speak the same language," Roosevelt explained.

In an editorial, A. C. Lee coolly noted the president's flair for the dramatic. Senator George voted with the president 85 percent of the time, Lee pointed out. No president should expect members of his party to rubber stamp every measure. Roosevelt's friends in Georgia would be doing the president a favor, Lee wrote, by sending George back to the Senate: "[W]hen [the president] allows his judgment to lead him astray, his friends should take the situation in hand and set him right again, not leaving this chore to his enemies." The greater fear for Lee was that in trying to turn the Democratic Party into the party of liberalism, Roosevelt was "inviting a storm that may easily sink the ship."

Lee would never go all the way with Black Belt–Big Mule conservatives in actually opposing Roosevelt's third term, yet by the 1940s, his editorial page was filled with anti–New Deal sentiment. Some of the editorials Lee wrote, but some were editorials that he republished that had been circulated by national business organizations mobilizing in new ways to oppose the New Deal. Lee had resisted earlier efforts of this kind, such as the Liberty League, which he denounced in a 1934 editorial. Yet, during the war, business groups were inundating newspaper editors throughout the country with pro-business pamphlets, publications, and ready-made editorials, and A. C. Lee lapped them up. His favorite was the Industrial

News Review, based out of Portland, Oregon, and funded primarily by the utility industry. It sent out for free roughly a dozen editorials each week that editors could use without attribution, although Lee always ran his with the credit line. For much of the 1930s, if Lee ran editorials from other publications, they tended to be from Alabama newspapers, most commonly either the Mobile or the Montgomery papers, and the topics concerned state matters. By the 1940s, however, the Industrial News Review was by far the most frequent source of guest editorials, offering pieces with titles such as "What Is Capitalism?," "Free Enterprise Medicine," and "Planned State Leads to Despotism."

Lee's own writings on domestic politics during the war years took on a decidedly more ideological cast, reflecting the influence of such groups. Labor unions replaced Huey Long as his bête noire. He denounced as selfish and unpatriotic striking workers in the nation's defense industries, such as the dockyard workers in Mobile. Criticism of striking workers was perhaps his most frequent complaint in the early years of the war. In the latter years, denunciations of the Congress of Industrial Organizations, which had broken with the American Federation of Labor in 1938 and represented the more liberal wing of the American labor movement, would take its place. Yet he also wrote on broader economic issues, emphasizing the needs of private industry in the fight against labor and government regulators. A sample of editorial titles during these years gives the flavor of such writings: "Private Enterprise Must Be Saved," "The Great Internal Problem" (which was labor unions), "What We Can Expect of Labor" (Lee's answer: more headaches), "Private Industry at Crossroads," and "Are We Headed for Statism?"

Lee's ideological turn coincided with a broader hardening of attacks on labor and liberal groups in Alabama. Charges of communism or fellow-traveling flew hard and fast in Alabama newspapers, particularly those connected to Alabama industrialists. "Around here," John Dos Passos reported an Alabama farmer telling him in the early 1940s, "communism's anything we don't like. Isn't it that way everywhere else?" Little of that thinking showed up in the *Monroe Journal*. Adamant though he was in his opposition to labor groups, Lee was no red-baiter. He stuck to the dry economic facts to make his case.

Yet the most fundamental threat signaled by the labor agitation, for A. C. Lee and for all Alabama conservatives, was the threat to white rule. Labor politics in Alabama had always been inseparable from racial politics, and because wartime mobilization had opened up new opportunities for employment and military service for black and poor white Alabamans alike, white rule was more tenuous than it had been in decades. In 1941, in response to a nationally organized civil rights campaign, President Roosevelt established the Fair Employment Practices Committee, giving African Americans a toehold to advocate for equality in the workplace. For the first time in Roosevelt's long tenure, he placed the White House clearly on the side of the black community. Three years later the Supreme Court outlawed the white primary, the scheme that denied blacks participation in Democratic primary elections on the grounds that the party was a private organization that could determine its own membership. It had been a pillar of Jim Crow rule, and the decision sparked an increase in black voting in the upper South and in some cities across the region. In the Deep South, though it had little immediate impact, it still provoked tremors.

In the 1930s, it was easy for A. C. Lee to write off racial agitation as the meddling of political radicals from outside the state. That had been his stance during the Scottsboro controversies. But in the 1940s, calls for change were coming from unexpected places. In particular, the assaults on the poll tax, the annual fee required of all registered voters, concerned Lee. Alabama had the stiffest poll tax in the country: $1.50 annually, required regardless of whether it was an election year. The tax was cumulative, meaning that it was due for every year missed dating back to when a person turned twenty-one, the age of eligibility. A. C. Lee defended it as part of a venerable tradition in American politics that could be traced to the nation's founding. Voting was a right of citizenship, but it was also a responsibility not to be taken lightly. He believed that the law helped ensure that vital matters of public concern would be decided by a serious, deliberate, responsible citizenry. Of course, that was how its authors had promoted the poll tax back in 1901 when they passed it as part of a new state constitution, one that effectively disfranchised almost every black Alabaman and a large number of poor whites who had supported Populist candidates in the preceding years.

During World War II, however, when thousands of poor Alabamans were risking their lives to defend democracy abroad, it hardly seemed right that they be taxed in order to exercise the most basic right of citizenship. Labor and civil rights groups, including the Southern Conference for Human Welfare, had been lobbying against the tax for years, but in the 1940s a significant number of white southerners were warming to the idea. Veterans' groups were pushing anti–poll tax measures, and a number of southern states had already dispensed with it. In 1942, Congress passed a law that exempted all veterans from the tax through the end of the war. Later that year, liberals in Congress managed to put forward a national anti–poll tax bill. Lee lauded the southern senators who successfully filibustered it, yet even among the normally unified southern delegation were poll tax opponents, most notably Florida senator Claude Pepper, an Alabama native.

When he wrote about race, A. C. Lee talked about defending the rights of states relative to the federal government. This was the conservative, dignified way to speak about white supremacy. Lee was convinced that the rights of states were among the most fundamental, long-established principles in American governance. Whatever his private racial views might have been, Lee never published any screeds trumpeting white racial superiority or railing against race mixers, as was common in Alabama newspapers. That kind of talk clashed with his paternalistic sensibilities. He saw no profit in inflaming racial passions on either side of the color line. Perhaps he was mindful of people he would have referred to as his Negro friends in Monroe County, people who he knew read his editorials each week, men like Horace James Lamar, the principal of the Bethlehem Industrial Academy, a black school, who wrote letters to the *Journal* requesting assistance from the white community in fundraising efforts.

In the 1940s, as membership in the NAACP grew exponentially and the drive for African American rights took on greater urgency and openness, A. C. Lee valorized an older, more accommodating generation of African American leaders. In an October 1942 editorial, for example, Lee applauded the navy's decision to name a battleship for the late Booker T. Washington, founder of the Tuskegee Institute. "No other colored man has yet appeared," Lee wrote of Washington, "who possesses the ability and the broad understanding of humanity and the relationships between the races." In a similar vein, Lee memorialized George Washington Carver, also of Tuskegee, as "the most eminent negro living" who "occupied a unique place in the scientific world, and in the minds and hearts of the people of America."

Yet the pressures for change were never ending, and they wore on Lee. The energy and optimism of his editorials during Roosevelt's first term had been replaced by gloom and bitterness by the mid-1940s. Fights in Congress like the effort to make permanent the Fair Employment Practices Committee were evidence of "the lengths to which we have gone in recent years toward socializing this fair country of ours." The "political complex" had changed in fundamental ways, he believed, ceding power to those who controlled "a large bloc of the people." Surveying the conditions in the country in November 1945, Lee wondered "if the American people are losing their art of properly appraising values in life." The ideals of America's forefathers had long been abandoned. Selfishness and greed prevailed, Lee believed. "We are traveling the downward road to ultimate destruction."

GIVEN THE DESPONDENCY evident on his editorial page, perhaps the brightest news for A. C. Lee in the fall of 1945 was the fact that his youngest daughter Nelle seemed to be finally hitting her stride in college. The second half of her freshman year at Huntingdon Nelle had spent in practical seclusion. The transition to the University of Alabama had been just what she needed. She was never much of a joiner, so it was a measure of her eagerness to make a new start that Nelle went out for sorority rush.

The Greek scene in Tuscaloosa was legendary, even then. The Tri Delts' rush party adopted a wedding theme, as did the ADPi's, where guests were seated by ushers as they entered and wedding cake was served afterward. The Delta Zetas had an Arabian nights motif where guests rubbed a magic lamp and a genie appeared with gifts. The Chi O's, where Nelle eventually pledged, had a plantation party. Mint juleps were served and a "Negro quartet furnished music Southern style." A southern colonel and his wife met rushees at the door and showered them with hospitality "à la Confederate era."

More exciting to Nelle, however, were the campus publications. Her first semester in Tuscaloosa she started working at *Rammer Jammer*, the monthly student humor magazine. By December she was considered "a valuable regular on the staff." The next year, she would serve as editor-in-chief, leading a staff of sixteen. She also became a contributor to the *Crimson-White*, the student newspaper. During the summer session of 1946, in between her sophomore and junior years when Nelle stayed in Tuscaloosa to take classes, she had a weekly column aptly titled "Caustic Comment." It consisted of mordant, humorous portraits of campus scenes, such as Nelle suffering through the byzantine registration process in the law school, a friend's frustrated attempt to find an unsanitized copy of James Joyce's *Ulysses* in the library, and the pathetic response of campus police to an attempted burglary at a sorority house.

In her June 28 column, Nelle was unusually upbeat. There was a "striking difference," she wrote, between university students in 1946 and those five years earlier. Undergrads used to be interested only in Greek life, debating the merits of Glenn Miller versus Tommy Dorsey, or making sure their clothes were exactly the same as everyone else's. Now, however, the average student "doesn't give a damn what kind of pants he wears to a formal." Students all of a sudden cared about "things that really count." As an example she mentioned the "hell-for-leather" political campaigning on campus during the recent gubernatorial election, and new groups organizing for the upcoming US Senate race. "Young people are at last waking up to the need for good government and are doing something about it," she wrote.

It was true. Tuscaloosa had changed. World War II veterans newly mustered out of the service flooded the campus. Student enrollment that

Nelle, second from left, was designated a "campus personality" in the 1948 yearbook at the University of Alabama. (The University of Alabama Libraries Special Collections)

year had been 6,000, a university record. The next year it would increase to 8,500 students, over half of whom were freshmen. The campus was so crowded that Pug's, the diner on University Avenue that was the preferred student hangout, ran ads in the *Crimson-White* asking students to share booths so that more people could be served. Floated by the GI Bill, some of the veterans on campus treated college like an extended R&R. But a significant number were older, had traveled the world, had fought to save democracy, and were now interested to see how it was operating back home in Alabama. They brought a seriousness and relative sophistication to a campus that was often characterized as the country club of the South.

The new tenor on campus was noticeable in at least two ways. First was the popularity among students of "Big" Jim Folsom and his whirlwind campaign for governor in the spring of 1946. Folsom came by his nick-name honestly. Six feet, eight inches tall, only thirty-seven years old, a strapping, raw-boned country boy from northern Alabama, Folsom advo-cated opening up the franchise and rewriting the state constitution in or-der to break the power of the Black Belt. Knowing how rural people lacked for entertainment, Folsom traveled with a "hillbilly band," the Strawberry Pickers, top-notch musicians who occasionally counted Hank Williams among their members, his schedule permitting. Folsom liked to address his audiences holding a corn-shuck mop. "I'm going to take that mop and scour out the kitchen and open up the windows and let [in] a green breeze out of the north . . . ," he would tell the crowd, "you'll have the freshest, sweetest smell that you've seen in that Old Alabama capitol since it was built." Some of the veterans and other college students might have rolled their eyes at the bumpkinism. Yet Folsom's youth and energy contrasted sharply with his opponents, the same Big Mule stooges and party gate-keepers who acted like state politics was their own private game.

A second indicator was the slate of liberal speakers who appeared on campus in the spring of 1946, toward the end of Nelle Lee's first year in Tuscaloosa. Her conservative father would have been suspicious of the lineup, to be sure. Whether Nelle herself attended any of the lectures is not known, but the events fed the political ferment on campus that she found so invigorating.

In May, Horace M. Kallen, an influential philosopher of cultural plu-ralism and dean of the graduate school at the New School for Social Re-search in New York, spoke to the Alabama student forum. Asked why the South was not more of a leader in education, Kallen answered bluntly: "[T]he disintegration of the economic system following the Civil War and oppression of the Negro are the causes. A society is no stronger than its weakest element." The same group had heard earlier that spring from Myles Horton of the Highlander Folk School, the racially integrated train-ing ground for a generation of labor and civil rights activists in the South, including Rosa Parks and Martin Luther King Jr. "The CIO has done more to solve the problem of race in the South than all the other educa-tional forces put together," Horton told the students. He pointed to Georgia governor Ellis Arnall, the thirty-five-year-old reform candidate who had bested Eugene Talmadge in the Georgia governor's race, as proof that the "reactionary stronghold on the South could be broken."

Arnall himself spoke on campus as well. A *Crimson-White* article announcing the visit noted Arnall's opposition to what the governor called "the moth-eaten doctrine of the states' rights." In office, he had successfully pushed a variety of progressive reforms, including repeal of the poll tax. Three weeks after Arnall's appearance, that other prominent southern liberal who had provoked A. C. Lee's ire in regard to the poll tax, Claude Pepper, a university alumnus, addressed students at the summer convocation.

At the *Crimson-White,* Nelle befriended a tight-knit group of smart, curious nonconformists who all, like her, loved to write. She memorialized each of the staffers by name in an ebullient final column in August. The editor Bill Mayes was a "lanky, Klan-hating six-footer from somewhere in Mississippi." A veteran of the Pacific War, Mayes had led a campaign that summer against Klansmen who had incorporated several klaverns in and near Birmingham with designs on statewide expansion. The real problem, Mayes believed, was not the Klansmen themselves, though they were repugnant, but the fact that "the authorities—that is, the lawmakers—in this state do not wish the activities of the Klan discontinued." An anonymous letter was sent to the *Crimson-White* office the next week. "It would be advisable for you to stop your yankee-inspired propaganda against the Klan," it warned. Mayes reiterated his stand for decency and law enforcement, and mocked the letter writer for being too cowardly to sign his name.

The *Crimson-White* published its last issue of the summer term on August 16. Presumably Nelle Lee went home to Monroeville for a week or two before fall semester began. If so, she and her father might have had some heated political conversation around the dinner table. It's impossible to say for sure, yet, given his usual editorial themes, it was odd that in his August 22 editorial A. C. Lee chose to write about the confusion among contemporary young people about the origins and meaning of liberalism.

Everyone liked the term *liberalism*, A. C. wrote, and liked to think of themselves as liberal. But young people didn't realize that liberalism originally referred to the "broad recognition of the rights of all our people to pursue their own ways and to live their own lives as free from interference from governmental supervision." Yet today, "the word has been appropriated by those who would regiment the American people, bestow special favors upon certain groups and classes, and extend governmental regulation over all the activities of life." Lee implored America's youth to "re-dedicate themselves to the task of studying anew the principles upon which our government was founded."

While the dispute that might have spurred A. C. Lee to write the column can only be imagined, two months later the political differences between father and daughter were made plain in the pages of the respective publications they edited. At issue was the Boswell Amendment, the Alabama legislature's response to the Supreme Court's historic 1944 decision outlawing the white primary. Alabama's conservatives were on the defensive. In Georgia, Ellis Arnall had not only abolished the poll tax but also lowered the voting age to eighteen. In Alabama, Governor Folsom was planning on mirroring Arnall's program. Conservatives warned that these measures could threaten white supremacy. In the years immediately following World War II, however, such fear-mongering didn't have the same traction that it had had historically, and that it would regain in the massive resistance era of the 1950s and 1960s. Without the benefit of the white primary, and given the rising sentiment against the poll tax, the prospect of large numbers of liberal-leaning voters, white and black, registering to vote seemed increasingly likely. Not only that, but blacks had already sued a county board of registrars in Alabama and won relief in federal court. The case came out of the Black Belt county of Macon, home to the Tuskegee Institute and an African American veterans' hospital. Given these developments, the existing property and literacy requirements under current law seemed to Jim Crow's defenders like weak measures indeed. Any person who owned an automobile was exempt from the $300 property requirement, and as for literacy, as Gessner McCorvey, the chairman of the Alabama Democratic Party, put it, "A smart parrot could be taught to recite a section of our Constitution." The key should be whether an applicant *understood* the Constitution, he believed.

This was the thinking behind an amendment proposed by the south Alabama legislator Elmo C. "Bud" Boswell. Under the measure, county boards of registrars would be empowered to test the comprehension of an applicant and, if necessary, "prevent from registering those elements in our community which have not yet fitted themselves for self government." The legislature passed the measure and scheduled a ratification vote for the fall of 1946. The Boswell Amendment split the Alabama Democratic Party down the middle. Almost all of the major daily newspapers in the state, along with Governor-elect Folsom and the state's two senators, opposed it. Supporting the amendment were current governor Chauncey Sparks, former governor Frank Dixon, Democratic chairman McCorvey, and many legislators.

A. C. Lee was among the supporters. He made his case in four ponderous editorials in consecutive weeks in October (the last one began: "It may be that our readers are growing tired of reading about the Boswell Amendment . . ."). The liberals were in favor of universal suffrage; conservatives were opposed to it, but for good reasons, Lee argued. The simple question was "[w]ill our people, as a whole, fare better under the leadership of an intelligent electorate?" The amendment would help protect against political bosses manipulating the votes of the ill-informed, uninterested masses, a widespread problem under current voting rules, according to Lee (his more devoted readers might have recognized this as a veiled jab at Short Millsap). Lee did take a few liberties in laying out his position. For example, he repeatedly implied that opponents of the measure were for complete universal suffrage, opposed even to safeguards against criminals voting, which was not the case. His tone throughout was unapologetically elitist. Yet to a notable degree, he kept the discussion on the high plane of theory and principle: "We believe very definitely in the idea that our people will be happiest under a system of rules and regulations dictated by an electorate that prizes the privileges of citizenship, and who have proven themselves worthy."

Political sentiment at the *Rammer Jammer* ran in the opposite direction. The unsigned introductory column to the October issue included a wry, oblique note: "If the Boswell amendment goes through, the campus liberals are going to petition the legislature to change the state motto from 'We Dare Defend Our Rights' to 'Dare We Defend Our Rights?'" But there was nothing indirect about the parody Nelle Lee published under her own name, "Now Is the Time for All Good Men: A One-Act Play." A precocious piece of political satire for a twenty-year-old college student, it showed not only Nelle's sharp wit and talent for setting a scene, but also her sophisticated understanding of important divisions in southern politics, and her early desire to comment on them in a fictional form.

Scene I opens with the Honorable Jacob F. B. MacGillacuddy, chairman of the Citizens' Committee to Eradicate the Black Plague, sounding forth in the manner of the bumptious Senator Beauregard Claghorn, a popular radio character at the time on the *Fred Allen Show*. MacGillacuddy, known as J.F.B. to his "multitude of acquaintances and one friend," rails against the "goddam yankees" who came to tell folks how to vote, how to run their businesses, and "even influencing our colored friends to turn against their benefactors." A small group of "'Communists from the U. of A.'" stands nearby, holding signs reading "Wallace for President—of the University" (a reference to Henry, the liberal former vice-president and 1948 Progressive Party presidential candidate; not George, the future governor of Alabama) singing Woody Guthrie lyrics to the tune of the socialist anthem "The Red Flag." J.F.B. has worked up a measure that perfectly resembles the Boswell Amendment: a requirement that every "gonna-be voter" would have to interpret passages of "the Yewnited States Constitution." Scene II shows J.F.B. before his local registrar, trying to sign up to vote so as to beat back a liquor referendum. As he interprets the required passage, the local political boss walks behind him and gives a nod to the registrar, who tells him his interpretation is not to her satisfaction. J.F.B. fumes that he wrote the goddam law. He vows to take the issue all the way to the Supreme Court, the site of Scene III. "Of all the cheek!" the justices say upon hearing J.F.B.'s complaint—and this was the best gag in the piece—"How can the state of Alabama be so presumptuous as to require an ordinary voter to interpret the Constitution when we can't even interpret it ourselves?" The justices beg off on deciding the matter, noting that their calendar is full until 1983. The play closes with J.F.B. prattling on in the same manner as in Scene I, only this time he heads the Citizens' Committee to Restore Civil Liberties. The protestors wear signs labeled "reactionaries." J.F.B. tries to rally the crowd to protest their disfranchisement.

The broader debate over the amendment framed the disagreement between A. C. and Nelle Lee. It was neatly summarized in a staged face-off in the pages of the *Alabama Lawyer,* the official publication of the Alabama bar. Richard T. Rives, a Montgomery attorney who represented the boards of registrars in Montgomery and Macon County, and who would eventually serve on the Fifth Circuit Court of Appeals, where in the 1950s he joined in historic decisions that desegregated public transportation and public education in Alabama, argued against the amendment. Rives was no proponent of black voting, but he objected to the arbitrary power given to registrars. Not only could it be abused by "an unscrupulous political boss or machine," as Nelle suggested in her play, but it also amounted to legislative overreach that could invite federal interference in Alabama voting law, also a possibility Nelle evoked in the scene before the Supreme Court.

Arguing in favor was Horace Wilkinson, a Birmingham judge and longtime Alabama politico. His article was breathtaking in its unabashed appeal to white supremacy; Nelle's caricature of the Committee to Eradicate the Black Plague seems tame by comparison. "I earnestly favor a law that will make it impossible for a Negro to qualify [to vote]," Wilkinson wrote. Given that that was unlikely, the Boswell Amendment was for him the next best thing. "[N]o Negro is good enough," Wilkinson claimed, "and no Negro will ever be good enough to participate in making the laws under which the white people in Alabama have to live." The amendment could be used to keep some whites from the polls, he admitted, but that was "a small price to pay . . . to keep this inferior, unreliable, irresponsible, easily corrupted race from destroying the highest civilization known to man."

Such beliefs were common among the amendment's conservative supporters. J. Miller Bonner, a prominent Black Belt planter, told the Montgomery Civitan Club that if the Boswell Amendment failed to pass, whites would have only three choices: "leave their homes, submit to Negro domination, or engage in inter-racial conflict resulting in extermination of one or the other races." Outgoing governor Sparks campaigned for the amendment around the state, telling crowds that "around 2,000" blacks had shown up on registration day in Macon County, a wildly exaggerated number. Pro-Boswell forces ran newspaper ads evoking the specter of county courthouses ringed by throngs of Negroes demanding registration.

The Boswell Amendment was approved by a narrow margin, but it wouldn't last long. A federal court struck it down only three years later. Yet the contentious debate over its passage, and the Lee family's contrasting contributions to it, suggest something important about the nature of both the political and the emotional rift developing between father and daughter.

Compared to the racist demagoguery of other conservatives, A. C. Lee's editorials were notably restrained. He defended old-fashioned republican ideals of meritocracy in an age in which modern fashions demanded an absolute and indiscriminate leveling. Yet Lee's conservative ideals did not exist in a vacuum. For him as for everyone, the political was shaped by the personal. Lee would have known how his daughter was repulsed by the pro-Boswell Negro haters. Perhaps that was one of the reasons that he went to such pains in those overwrought editorials to articulate the principled defense of the amendment. It was to prove to his daughter, and maybe to himself, that there was one.

But Nelle wouldn't have seen that. She would have seen a man willfully obtuse, disingenuous even, cloaking the sordid sentiments of Black Belt elites in abstract theories. Everybody in Alabama knew what was at stake in the Boswell debate. "Let us be frank and honest with ourselves," Richard Rives wrote in the *Alabama Lawyer*. "You and I know that the people of our State are expected to adopt this Amendment in order to give the Registrars arbitrary power to exclude Negroes from voting." Yet A. C. Lee would admit no such thing. It must have been maddening to his daughter. Her father was no Horace Wilkinson, no J.F.B. MacGillacuddy. Yet, in the end, what difference did his precious principles really make?

THE TIGHTER A. C. Lee clung to his principles, the looser his hold became on his youngest daughter. Nelle Lee's college writings provide more than just traces of their row. There were direct slights, too, or at least they were likely to have been read that way in Monroeville. The February 1947 issue of the *Rammer Jammer* included a spoof on "[t]he country weekly," which Nelle wrote was "as much a Southern institution as grits and gravy." The piece captured well the hokey, oddball notices that often appeared in small town southern papers, some of which she stole straight from the *Monroe Journal*. A small item in the *Rammer Jammer* spoof, for example, notes a prize turnip had been brought to the editor's office, where it would be kept on display for interested townspeople. Something very similar had run in her father's newspaper back in January 1941. Perhaps it was all in good fun and no one at home thought anything of it, if they even read it at all. But if Nelle ever did send copies of her publications to her family, there was a biting line introducing the satire that was likely to have raised eyebrows in Monroeville. "All in all, [the country weekly] reflects the opinions of the minute section of the country it represents," it read. "It is gossipy, sometimes didactic, and always provencial [sic] in its outlook."

It seems to have been a calculated dig. Gossipy and didactic were easy to toss off, but provincial? The *Monroe Journal* may have been small in readership but it was large in outlook. Each night A. C. Lee religiously read state and national publications after dinner so that he could bring to his readers important matters concerning the nation and the world. If A. C. Lee noticed the line, he might have advised his daughter that if she was going to call someone provincial, she should at least spell the word correctly. The title of this mock weekly, however, would have been hard to miss: "The Jackassonian Democrat." One Harper Lee biographer suspects that at some point A. C. Lee might have tried to persuade Nelle to come home to take over the editorship of the *Monroe Journal*. If true, the February *Rammer Jammer* would have provided Nelle's answer.

Perhaps it was just a coincidence, but around this same time, A. C. himself started losing interest in his newspaper. That spring he began hearing rumors that two newspapermen from out of town, Jimmy Faulkner and Bill Stewart, were scouting out Monroeville to start a rival weekly.

Lee went straight to them and offered to sell them the *Journal* for a song. They leapt at the chance. Lee published his last issue on June 26, 1947. The editorial page included one final reprint of an Industrial News Review editorial and words of thanks to his loyal readers. He was proud to say, looking back on the many years of his editorship, that "we are unable to recall any position we have previously taken on any important question that we would wish to change."

That summer, when she was home for the wedding of her brother Edwin, Nelle made it plain to her family that her heart wasn't in the law. Years later she would say that she had pursued it as "the line of easiest resistance." She went back to Tuscaloosa in the fall, giving it one final go, but nothing was the same. She stopped hanging around the campus magazine crowd that had sustained her in her first two years. At her sorority and in her law school classes she was a spectral presence. Only a handful of young women were enrolled in the law school at Alabama in those days, yet few of them would even be able to recall Nelle Lee years later. Those who did remembered her as defiantly dowdy—long skirts, baggy blouses, plain flats, no makeup—and intensely reclusive, saying as little as she possibly could when called upon in class, scurrying out afterward with her head down.

The political climate on campus had changed as well. The heady days of lectures by Ellis Arnall and Claude Pepper had come and gone in a flash. So, too, had the student editorials castigating the Birmingham Klan. All those veterans who had flooded campus as freshmen two or three years prior were now juniors and seniors, crowding campus organizations that during the war had enjoyed ample co-ed participation and leadership. On campus, as in national politics, the optimism of the postwar years had given over to loyalty oaths and subversive investigations. One of the few things that could provoke Nelle enough to crawl out of her shell that year was the red scare showing up in the pages of the *Crimson-White*.

In February 1948, student columnist Jim Wood began with a simple question: "Is there any Communism on the University of Alabama campus?" Without offering any facts as evidence, the answer he came to quickly was yes. Universities were fertile ground for "communistic conquest," as everyone knew. "There are numerous persons on campus who are professed communists," he wrote, "either trying to be shocking or by actual belief."

Trying to be shocking was Nelle Lee's specialty, if not in class then at least in print. It's almost impossible to find anything she published in college that didn't include at least one four-letter word, which in Baptist-soaked Alabama in the 1940s still had the power to scandalize. But she provoked readers in other ways as well, such as her line in the *Crimson-White* a year and a half earlier that for her "Utopia is a land with the culture of England and the government of Russia." The comment was another of Nelle's acts of rebelliousness—of a piece with her refusal to wear shorter skirts and makeup to class—rather than any sincere admiration for communism. Yet it surely would have marked Nelle as part of what Jim Wood called "the 'intellectual' group," the ones who are "aware of the faults in our democratic system, yet overlook the faults of the Communistic system." Perhaps that is why Nelle was one of the earliest and harshest critics of Wood's column. In a letter addressed "My Dear Young Man," she called Wood's article a "horror," nothing more than "fallacious propositions illogically strung together." She challenged him to name names. "You do us conservatives no good by propounding such idiotic generalities," she wrote.

Nelle's critical letter was one of several. A small tempest brewed in the pages of the *Crimson-White*. Wood, for example, responded that the real horror was Nelle Lee's editions of the *Rammer Jammer*. Interestingly, one of the questions raised was about the conservatism of Ms. Lee. "Are you a conservative?" a friend of Wood's wrote in, addressing Nelle directly. "That is a conservative radical—or am I too harsh in my interpretation." A friend of Nelle's responded that Lee was in fact a good conservative, but one who objected to the shabby, indiscriminate smearing of broad swaths of the university. "Let me assure [you] that far from riding the pink horse, Nellie is hanging onto the extreme tail (right) end of the very black donkey!" her friend wrote. "In fact, on most any afternoon you may find her gazing with hard eyes toward the White cliffs, sipping her daily tea, and lustily singing, 'God Save the King.'"

This was calculated to confound Jim Wood and his friends, which it surely would have. The comment spoke to Lee's Anglophilism, to which she would gesture frequently in interviews in later years, and which she was able to indulge that summer in a study program at Oxford. When she got back from England, she would manage only one more semester in Tuscaloosa before giving up the law for good. Her childhood friend Truman Capote had been urging her to come to New York for years. He had made a name for himself with his short stories, and his debut novel had been published earlier that year. Nelle decided to take the leap. She came home for Christmas in 1948, worked a few weeks waiting tables at the Monroeville golf club to save money, and in early 1949 headed to New York.

As for Nelle's conservatism, though it ran more toward the cultural traditionalism of Chesterton rather than the more narrow-minded racial and economic interests of the Alabama Black Belt, the fact that she would put herself in the company of Tuscaloosa's conservatives is notable. Even in those years when she was pulling hard against the reins of family and tradition, she remained her father's daughter. Her conservative inclinations could be seen in her irritability over what she saw as the melodrama, licentiousness, and opportunism of the southern gothic novels so lauded by the New York literati. In a 1945 essay lampooning modern writers, she mocked the trend toward writing about small southern towns with their "annual race riot full of blood and gore which cause violent reaction in [the author's] sensitive soul." The southern writer has the opportunity to "expose to the public the immoral goings-on in an out-of-the-way village . . . and instigate a movement which would do away with small towns forever." In a review of a novel published by an Alabama faculty member, Nelle noted how "[t]he South has been repeatedly embarrassed by the [Lillian] Smith, Faulkners, Stowes, et al, who either wrote delicately of the mint julep era or championed the dark eddies of 'niggertown.'"

In the end, however, it's a fool's errand trying to pin down Nelle Lee too precisely on any political spectrum. She relished, above all, the role of the iconoclast. Unlike her father, she would never have a side, liberal or conservative. What she had, and this is no small irony for the woman who would create one of the quintessential figures of American liberal mythology, was an instinctive sense for gauging the amount of hot air in any particular literary or political idea, and a compulsion to poke a hole in it.

THE HANDFUL OF writings Nelle Lee published in college did not exhaust her efforts to work out her differences with her father. Her first novel, *Watchman,* continued that work both literally and figuratively. Yet after college, and before she would take up her writing career in earnest, tragedy struck the Lee family. It would only deepen her sympathies for her father and make any genuine break with him all but unimaginable.

Though Nelle's mother Frances had struggled with her health for some time, nothing seemed particularly ominous in late May of 1951. She was sixty-two years old and still suffered from her "nervous disorder." That month, when she told her doctor that she had been feeling ill, he sent her to Vaughan Memorial Hospital in Selma for tests. A. C. dropped his wife off for a couple of days of examinations on a Wednesday, and headed on to the annual Methodist conference, an early summer ritual for him given his longtime status as a lay delegate. When he returned on Friday to pick up his wife, he received the bad news. Frances had late stage malignancies in her liver and lungs. She wasn't expected to live more than three months. A. C. went home to Monroeville to tell Alice and call the other children. They told Nelle not to come home from New York just yet. The family was going back to the hospital the next day, and they would know more then about what she should do. But on that Saturday afternoon, June 2, 1951, while the family went out to get food, Frances suffered a heart attack. She never regained consciousness and died later that evening.

The death of Frances was compounded beyond measure the following month. A. C. was in his law office, just weeks after burying his wife, when a phone call came from the commandant at Maxwell Air Force Base in Montgomery. His only son Edwin was stationed there, having been called back to duty with the outbreak of the Korean War. The commandant had no explanation, only the grim news that Edwin Lee had been found dead in his bunk that morning. An autopsy would reveal that he had died of a

A. C. Lee, his arm propped on the train, included his granddaughter Molly Lee in a photo with the crew and staff of the Manistee & Repton Railroad. Molly's father, Ed Lee, along with A. C.'s wife, Frances Lee, had passed away the year before. (Aaron White)

cerebral hemorrhage. He was thirty years old. Left behind was his wife of four years, Sara Ann, the couple's three-year-old daughter Molly, and a nine-month-old son, Edwin Jr.

The sorrow the Lees experienced in the summer of 1951 drew an already close-knit, private family even closer. Not long after Edwin's funeral, A. C. sold the family home on Alabama Avenue and bought a small brick house in a new neighborhood development carved out of the pine forest behind the Monroe County High School. He and Alice would live there on West Avenue, and it was where Nelle stayed when she came home from New York, even after the phenomenal success of *Mockingbird* would have allowed the family to move to a more spacious home. Whether the move was to distance A. C. from old memories or simply to get away from the commercial blight that had encroached on South Alabama Avenue is anyone's guess. Nelle wrote about the move in *Watchman* as an emblem of Atticus's determination to soldier on despite the sadness. "He is an incredible man," Jean Louise thinks, after Atticus loses his wife and son. "A chapter of his life comes to a close, Atticus tears down the old house and builds a new one in a new section of town. I couldn't do it." In the book, the old family home is replaced by an ice cream parlor, which was also true to life.

On holidays the extended Lee family packed into the small house on West Avenue. A. C.'s grandchildren recall the lively exchanges among the three sisters—Alice, Louise, and Nelle—who, despite the spread of their ages (Alice was five years older than Louise, who was ten years older than Nelle) and the distance between them (Alice in Monroeville with their father; Nelle in New York; Louise in Eufala with her husband and two sons), remained extremely close the rest of their lives. Each of them had her distinctive role: Alice was the mother hen; Louise was the pretty one; Nelle was the cutup. Local gossip, family lore, and English history were common topics of conversation, and laughter abounded. "Opp," as his grandchildren called A. C., listened to the sisters' gabfest, smiling at witty or well-turned comments, until called upon by one of the daughters to weigh in on, and thereby resolve, an issue under debate. When not conversing, the family was reading, grandchildren too, everyone silently absorbed in a book—a work of history or biography for A. C. and Alice; fiction more likely for Louise and Nelle. The only allowance for modern entertainment was when Nelle, or Aunt Dody as her nieces and nephews called her, put on a record, carols at Christmastime; Handel, Elgar, or Gilbert and Sullivan year-round. Even in their music the Lees loved all things English.

In the early 1950s, a controversy developed at the Monroeville Methodist church that shows the intensity of Nelle's loyalty to her father, and how fiercely she would defend him. Reverend Ray Whatley was a thirty-one-year-old minister who came to Monroeville in June 1951, just after Frances Lee's death. Edwin Lee's funeral the next month was the first that he performed in Monroeville. Whatley had known when he went to Monroeville that the church had requested another pastor, the minister at the smaller of the two Methodist churches in Selma, a man well-known in the regional Methodist conference for his dynamic, evangelical preaching. But that man still had another two years in his term in Selma. By his own admission years later, Whatley was young and inexperienced when he went to Monroeville, and he was taking over a church with a number of prominent families who were accustomed to running things as they wished. This was a common problem for Methodist ministers, who rotated among churches every four years—how to impose their own vision for the church without alienating the men and women who had their own pet projects, Sunday School classes, or committees that they ran like their own little fiefdoms. Whatley recognized this pattern in Monroeville, and moved quickly, perhaps presumptuously, to put his stamp on the church. He asked a talented churchwoman to take a step back from her frequent public speaking. The choir director pulled double duty as the chairman of the finance committee, a responsibility that Whatley believed was getting short shrift. When Whatley asked the chairman for regular committee reports, it was like lighting "a fuse onto dynamite."

None of it might have mattered had Whatley not been such a bore as a preacher. That would be the knock on him that survived in the Lee family's account of things. In *Watchman*, Harper Lee imagined a young minister at the church in Maycomb who seemed modeled on Whatley, "a young man . . . with what [Uncle Jack] called the greatest talent for dullness he had ever seen in a man on the near side of fifty . . . he possessed all the necessary qualifications for a certified public accountant: he did not like people, he was quick with numbers, he had no sense of humor, and he was butt-headed." This fictional preacher also "had long been suspected of liberal tendencies."

Those liberal tendencies were what was really at issue in Monroeville, or so Whatley believed. In no sense was he an agitating preacher from the outside. He was born and reared in the tiny village of Whatley, named for his family, some thirty miles west of Monroeville. He tried sincerely to fulfill the duties of his calling as he understood them. When it was Race Relations Sunday he preached on race relations. On Labor Day he preached on labor. The handful of notes and sermon transcripts that survive from his tenure in Monroeville reveal a young minister struggling to apply the wisdom of scripture to the problems of the day. Whatley received his divinity degree from the Candler School of Theology at Emory University in Atlanta, the most progressive Methodist seminary in the South. There he became absorbed with the Old Testament prophets, Amos in particular. In 1946, when he was in Atlanta and had charge over three rural churches south of the city, in the heart of Eugene Talmadge country, he had given a sermon in the midst of the contentious gubernatorial campaign, when Talmadge inflamed racist reaction in opposition to the liberal administration of Ellis Arnall. Talmadge rode that reaction to victory. Before the election, when Whatley told his congregants that it was both undemocratic and un-Christian to deny a person the right to vote because of his race, attendance the following week dropped by roughly half, and did not improve from there.

In Monroeville, only a few weeks after Edwin Lee's funeral, Whatley preached a Labor Day sermon quoting from Isaiah about workers enjoying the fruits of their labor—"They shall not build and another inhabit; they shall not plant and another eat"—applauding gains won through collective bargaining, which helped protect workers, he said, from the lures of communism. Whatley wouldn't have known about the dozens of editorials that A. C. Lee, his pastoral relations committee chairman, had written in the 1940s decrying the undue influence of labor unions, nor the efforts that A. C. and other locals had taken to ensure that Vanity Fair, the economic lifeblood of Monroeville, didn't unionize. The preacher gave what he felt was a fair account of Christian principles applied to industrial relations.

From the pews, however, his sermon would have come across very differently. A. C. Lee would have heard a young man moralizing about complex matters with which he had no practical experience. If A. C. Lee wanted to hear political speeches, he'd have gone to the courthouse. He came to church to do as the apostle Paul had admonished the Philippians, to think on those things that were true, noble, right, pure, lovely, and admirable. His favorite hymn, "Dwelling in Beulah Land," which he would sing in his bumblebee bass, captured the vision of God's reward for the faithful. His Sunday mornings were a little slice of that, a place where "doubt and fear and things of earth in vain to me are calling, none of these shall move me from Beulah Land."

The next year Lee gave a speech at a Methodist conference gathering that reflected his views on the intersections of church and politics. He emphasized how God had created man in his own image, with free will. The system of government in the United States, Lee argued, protected the individual exercise of freedom to an unprecedented degree in human history. But those protections were imperiled in numerous ways: by the decline of statesmanship, by the philosophy that government exists not for the public good but to allow politicians to win spoils for their favored groups, by the selfishness that had infected politics, symbolized by labor bosses, by the usurpation of basic freedoms, symbolized by the FEPC, and by the subtle, gradual, creeping spread of philosophies that led toward communism. All of these were pet themes from the last several years of Lee's editorship. So if Ray Whatley didn't know about his pastoral relations chairman's politics before, after this speech he knew.

Yet Reverend Whatley stayed the course. He was not unduly concerned with A. C. Lee. He forged ahead with his ministry and continued to deliver sermons similar to his Labor Day address. A sermon on Race Relations Sunday, the Sunday once a year designated by the Methodist Church to collect offerings for Methodist-sponsored black colleges, noted that white people made up only one-third of the world's population, and reflected on how acts of discrimination in Alabama could be used "to try to convince yellow and brown people of Asia and black people of Africa that injustice to minorities is the rule in America."

It was in his role as pastoral relations chairman that A. C. Lee eventually requested a meeting with Whatley. He advised him that his committee, representing the congregation as a whole, felt that Whatley should "'preach the gospel' and stay off social issues." Relations between pastor and congregation deteriorated. In 1953, before the next annual conference meeting, two years before Whatley's regular term ended, the pastoral relations committee petitioned that Whatley be reassigned, and that the preacher in Selma, who the church had initially requested and was now available, be sent to Monroeville. Whatley believed that Chairman Lee had violated church procedure in making this request without first consulting him. He explained this to the committee, in rather heated fashion. Lee became rather heated himself, and defended his committee's actions. The two men eventually cleared the air in an exchange of letters. They saw each other not too long afterward at a meeting of the conference pension board, on which they both served. When some of the board members went out to lunch after the meeting, Lee made a point of paying for Whatley's lunch, which Whatley appreciated as a gesture of reconciliation.

Ray Whatley left Monroeville for St. Mark's Methodist in Montgomery. He would go on to play a minor role in one of the great moral and political dramas of twentieth-century America. In early 1955, in an effort to help establish communication between the white and black communities in Montgomery, Whatley helped organize a Montgomery chapter of the Alabama Council on Human Relations. He was elected president. Serving as vice-president was a young black minister new to town who had just taken over the pastorate of Dexter Avenue Baptist Church. In December a local black seamstress refused to give up her seat to a white passenger, sparking a bus boycott among Montgomery blacks. Whatley's vice-president, Martin Luther King Jr., became head of the organization coordinating the boycott. As president of the Human Relations Council, Whatley issued a number of public statements recognizing the just demands of the boycotters and urging city leaders to negotiate. Again he found himself in hot water with his congregation. He was reassigned to a small church in the Black Belt town of Linden, which proved more hostile even than Montgomery and Monroeville. Martin Luther King Jr. informed his former professor, L. Harold DeWolf at the School of Theology at Boston University, of Whatley's ordeal, and DeWolf wrote with offers to help get Whatley assigned to a church in the North. But Whatley declined. He moved on to a church in Mobile, where again he lent controversial public support to efforts to desegregate the city buses, and eventually, to a position on the Methodist General Board of Pensions, headquartered in Evanston, Illinois, lending some credence perhaps to *Watchman*'s fictional evocation of a man possessing "all the necessary qualifications for a certified public accountant." Yet it must be said, though Harper Lee herself never seemed to recognize it, that Ray Whatley was a genuine, true-life example of the heroic figure that *Mockingbird* would eventually evoke to such everlasting fame: the principled white southerner who made a public stand for racial decency and fairness and suffered because of it.

Whatley continued to see the Lee family on trips back to Monroeville, where he visited his brother Joe, who worked at a bank on the square. The Whatleys and the Lees remained friends, in all of the complicated ways that people did in small towns. One of Ray Whatley's prized possessions was his copy of *To Kill a Mockingbird*, which Harper Lee signed to him and his wife "with admiration and affection." Whenever she went to New York, Nelle left her car in the large driveway of Ray's brother Joe, so that Alice would have more room for her car in the narrow driveway of the Lee home on West Avenue. In 1981, at the Methodist annual conference, it was Alice Lee, having taken over her father's role as a regular lay delegate from Monroeville, who presented Whatley with a plaque honoring him for his long service on the pension board.

The entire quarrel between Reverend Whatley and A. C. Lee would have been lost to history had not Harper Lee's biographer, Charles Shields, stumbled upon Whatley in 2004 while cold-calling names from a list of Huntingdon College alumni who were in school the same year as Nelle Lee. Whatley had completed his undergraduate degree at Huntingdon after the war through a special program that allowed men to attend. Whatley told Shields that he didn't have any memories of Nelle from college, but he did know the family from his time serving the church in Monroeville. When Shields's book was published in 2006, with the revelations about Whatley's run-in with A. C. Lee, Nelle vented privately in a letter to a friend. "Rev. Ray Whatley . . . thinks my father got him fired because he was 'liberal' at the wrong time," she wrote. "He may have been but what got him fired—and this doesn't seem to have occurred to him—was that he was a lousy pastor, totally unsuited for the ministry, who belonged at a desk—where he spent his career, serving his Lord working with pension plans and doing a great job." More than fifty years after the events in question, old grudges died hard for Nelle Lee, particularly when they involved a slight to her father.

PART II

ATTICUS IMAGINED

Chapter 3

Setting a Watchman

Nelle Harper walked around the block twice before entering the building. That's how nervous she was the first time she visited the office of Maurice Crain and Annie Laurie Williams. Yet in only a matter of weeks, as Nelle started dropping by at regular intervals with new manuscript pages, it seemed like they were all old friends. Crain and Williams were the first people outside of Nelle's tight circle to read her stories and affirm her talent. Both native Texans from farming and ranching communities, they had been charmed by the "nice little Suth'n gal—from Alabama" who "says Yes, Mam and No Mam." In the years to come Nelle would decamp for long stretches to their stone cottage in Connecticut to write. Crain and Williams hosted Nelle and her sisters there, and even accompanied them on one of their annual sisters' trips, a steamboat cruise on the Mississippi River.

Because *Watchman* is not nearly as well-known as *Mockingbird,* a brief description of the novel that she was writing in early 1957 is in order. The book opens with the twenty-six-year-old Jean Louise Finch, a struggling writer in New York, on the train home to Maycomb. She is met by Henry Clinton, a childhood friend and suitor, who has risen above his station by getting a law degree and joining the firm owned by her father.

Jean Louise's aunt, Alexandra, has moved in to help with Atticus, who has become enfeebled by arthritis and other ailments. She is the same grating presence, only older, that she is in *Mockingbird*. A sense of loss pervades the home after the recent, unexpected death of Jean Louise's older brother Jem. Atticus, though physically weakened, is still wry, lively, and loving. The novel turns when Jean Louise discovers a racist, right-wing book among his reading materials. She heads immediately to the county courthouse where Atticus and Henry had gone to a meeting. Looking on from the balcony, she discovers that it is a gathering of the White Citizens' Council. The rest of the novel tracks her outrage and disbelief that her wise and loving father would take up with such bigoted malcontents. She has a series of contentious conversations with, first, her uncle Jack—a doctor who is a more loquacious, outlandish version of Atticus—then Henry, and, finally, Atticus himself. Each man explains to Jean Louise the impossible position in which the reasonable, decent white southerner has found himself. She remains furiously unsympathetic until another turn at the end of the novel forces her to reconsider her views.

Nelle started writing *Watchman* after the Browns' 1956 Christmas gift, which came on the heels of a long stretch that she had spent at home in Monroeville helping to care for A. C., who had had a heart attack. It was his first major health crisis, and his recovery was painful and slow. The cortisone injections that he had been taking for over a year for his arthritis had caused internal bleeding. The doctors stopped the injections immediately, which left him terribly weak and in great pain. On top of that, he developed a stomach ulcer, which limited him to small meals every two hours. The medicines he had to take ruined his appetite and sense of taste, so that he ate mostly baby food. He required constant care, and was only able to get out of bed and shuffle to the living room a few times a day, where he typically would work a crossword puzzle. He didn't have the strength to hold a book.

The handful of letters that survive from this period suggest that the portrait of the emotionally torn Jean Louise in *Watchman*—she feels guilty about not being home enough to help with Atticus, yet is frustrated by small town life—is pretty close to how Nelle herself felt at the time.

Nelle wrote to friends in New York that it was "excruciating" to sit through an hour of conversation with old high school acquaintances, an experience that she would fictionalize in *Watchman*. Yet her father's illness, and her willingness to forgo the pleasures of New York to stay in Monroeville to help care for him, gave Nelle a seriousness of purpose and brought a new level of maturity. "I've done things for him that I never remotely thought I'd be called upon to do for anybody, not even the Brown infants, but I suppose there is truth in the adage that you don't mind it if they're yours," she wrote. In another letter she described "staring at his handsome old face, and a sudden wave of panic flashed through me, which I think was an echo of the fear and desolation that filled me when he was nearly dead." To her friends she recounted a humorous story about A. C. sneaking out to check the gas meter, falling over on the grass, and crawling to a tree to pull himself up. He was "so charming in the telling of it that I did not have the heart to fuss at him," she wrote. Solving a crossword puzzle perhaps, he quizzed her one afternoon, asking who Josip Broz was. Nelle said she didn't know. "Tito, hah," he answered. She had not lived with her father on a day-to-day basis in years, she observed in one letter. "These months with him have strengthened my attachment to him, if such is possible."

Racial politics at the time were important as well in shaping the novel that Nelle was writing. 1956 was the year that massive resistance began in earnest in Alabama. The Supreme Court decision in *Brown v. Board of Education* two years earlier had prompted immediate, outraged commentary throughout the state, but organized resistance to *Brown* emerged more slowly. It originated in the Black Belt, and its engine was a new organization, the White Citizens' Council. In early 1956, during the Montgomery bus boycott, the number of Council chapters in that city exploded. Most pivotal in stoking militant resistance in the state, however, was the desegregation of the University of Alabama. When Autherine Lucy enrolled in February 1956, riots broke out on campus days later. Their size and vehemence shocked the nation. University leaders, receiving no help from either state or federal officials, suspended Lucy, ostensibly for her own safety. Yet the message to the militant mob was clear: violence and intimidation worked. There would be much more to come.

Students at the University of Alabama burn desegregation literature to protest the enroll-ment of the school's first black student, Autherine Lucy, February 6, 1956. (Associated Press)

These developments drew intense media coverage, and one need not have been a white militant in 1956 to be defensive about the bad press white Alabamans received in the nation's newspapers. In the first conver-sation between Atticus and Jean Louise in *Watchman*, before leaving for his law office, Atticus asks abruptly, "[H]ow much of what's going on down here gets into the newspapers." Jean Louise acknowledges the negative coverage in the *New York Post,* which suggests that Nelle had been reading the *Montgomery Advertiser* while home in Monroeville in 1956. In the spring of that year, a friendly rivalry developed between *Post* reporters and *Advertiser* editor Grover C. Hall Jr., the dandyish, bachelor son of A. C. Lee's fellow newspaperman and occasional antagonist, Grover C. Hall Sr. Hall, whose newspaper office was inundated by national and international reporters setting up shop to cover the bus boycott, was convinced that white southerners weren't getting a fair shake in the stories being written. He voiced these concerns frequently, and even began a series of editorials on racial disturbances in northern cities, a campaign that actually provoked an introspective series of articles at both the *Post* and the *New York Times.* Setting straight "the North" about what was really going on down South would be a major theme of *Watchman* as well. Nelle wanted to explain to readers of newspapers like the *New York Post* why they shouldn't write off men like Atticus Finch.

IT'S NOT SURPRISING that in January 1957, when thinking about how to dramatize the politics of the small town South, Harper Lee would ground her story in the rise of the Citizens' Council. For the past year, the organization had been at the center of a political struggle taking place among whites in Alabama. Rival factions vied for control of the Councils, and thereby for the leadership of the massive resistance movement.

The Citizens' Councils originated in the Mississippi Delta, but they spread quickly to neighboring states, including Alabama. Sometimes they advertised themselves as the White Citizens' Councils, to make clear that local blacks were not invited, but some members frowned on that qualifier as unnecessary and uncouth. Journalists, eager to make things plain for their readers, spread the name White Citizens' Councils. From the start, Citizens' Council leaders were obsessed with what the young David Halberstam called "an almost self-conscious desire for respectability." They were determined to distinguish themselves from the Klan. "None of you men look like Ku Kluxers to me," a founding Council member proclaimed to an audience in late 1954. "I wouldn't join a Ku Klux—I didn't join it—because they hid their faces; because they did things that you and I wouldn't approve of." Another founder warned that if "our highest type of citizenship" didn't take the lead in maintaining segregation and "the integrity of the white race," then the wrong crowd would, and "violence and bloodshed" would ensue.

Violence was something the responsible men who now flocked to the Citizens' Councils frowned upon. But economic intimidation of black families who joined desegregation lawsuits was another matter. As a Council leader in Selma put it, "We intend to make it difficult, if not impossible, for any Negro who advocates de-segregation to find and hold a job, get credit or renew a mortgage." So too was the silencing of white moderates whose independence of mind might threaten the perception so critical to resistance leaders that the white South was united in the fight against integration. These ends the Citizens' Councils pursued with vigor. Influential southern newspaper editors dubbed the organization the "white-collar Klan."

At the beginning of February 1956, the Citizens' Council chapter in Montgomery had expanded from just five hundred members the previous November to over six thousand. By the end of that month, membership was twelve thousand. Within two weeks of Autherine Lucy's entry at Alabama, Council leadership announced the formation of a new statewide organization, the Alabama Association of Citizens' Councils, headquartered in Montgomery and boasting a membership of forty thousand.

The state association was dominated by the conservative leadership of the Alabama Black Belt. Their leader was Sam Engelhardt, a young, balding, bespectacled planter and state legislator from Shorter. A graduate of Washington and Lee, Engelhardt owned 6,500 acres of prime Black Belt farmland that had been in his mother's family for four generations. His entry into politics in 1950 had been on a pledge to preserve white rule in his native Macon County, which had the highest ratio of blacks to whites of any county in the United States. It was also home to the Tuskegee Institute. Middle-class, college-educated African Americans in Tuskegee had been quietly mobilizing black political power for years.

In *Watchman,* Harper Lee fictionalized Macon County as Abbott County, where, Atticus ominously reminds Jean Louise, the "population is almost three-fourths Negro" and "the voting population is almost half-and-half now, because of that big Normal School over there." In a detail Harper Lee took directly from the newspapers, Atticus notes that "the county won't keep a full board of registrars, because if the Negro vote edged out the white you'd have Negroes in every county office." This was exactly what was happening in Macon County. As the *New York Times* reported in March 1956, the board of registrars there had met only once that year. Afterward, a board member had resigned and another refused to accept her appointment, denying the board the necessary quorum of two out of three members.

Engelhardt and the Councils claimed to be the spokesmen for respectable resistance in Alabama. Engelhardt brought in the US senator from Mississippi James Eastland, a fellow planter, to address a Council rally in Montgomery in February 1956 that drew over ten thousand people. Eastland talked about coordinating a regionwide campaign that would take the South's case to the nation. Above all, Engelhardt emphasized that resistance to the *Brown* decision would be through lawful, legal means. The day after a bomb exploded at Martin Luther King's home in Montgomery in 1956, Engelhardt announced rewards totaling one thousand dollars for information leading to a conviction. It was a savvy move. The Councils were booming in Montgomery thanks to the bus boycott, and violent actions might have jeopardized the establishment support the Councils were enjoying in that city.

Yet a rival faction in the Council movement was emerging that would have no such compunction. Their leader was a dark-haired charismatic former gas station attendant named Asa "Ace" Carter. During World War II, he had received training in radio broadcasting in a navy school in Colorado, expertise that he would put to use for a variety of far-right, racist causes in the postwar years. He worked for a time for the professional anti-Semite Gerald L. K. Smith, and moved to Birmingham in 1954 to become the spokesman and radio voice of the American States Rights Association. He was forced off the air in February 1955 for denouncing the

National Conference of Christians and Jews, which actually had a strong following among influential citizens of Birmingham. Carter was quickly reassigned to head up the newly founded North Alabama Citizens' Council, which drew much of its membership from the working-class, industrial neighborhoods in and around Birmingham.

Whereas Engelhardt strove for the image of buttoned-down, respectable, lawful resistance, Carter's group fought a shrill, red-faced culture war against the forces of racial integration. In *Watchman*, Harper Lee may have used Carter as the basis for the figure of Grady O'Hanlon, the firebrand extremist that Atticus introduces to the Maycomb Citizens' Council. Carter regularly denounced southern elected officials as weak-willed accommodators. He called for a ban on rock-and-roll music in southern juke boxes, attacking it as an attempt by the NAACP to infiltrate the minds of southern whites with integrationist ideas. And he linked the North Alabama Council with Klan movements of old by requiring that "members believe in the divinity of Jesus Christ." Jews should fight integration through other organizations, he said. Engelhardt's group, by contrast, issued a statement declaring that it was "not interested in religious bias or prejudice, but is concerned only in maintaining segregation."

Most importantly, however, Asa Carter and the North Alabama Citizens' Council were behind a number of high-profile incidents of racial violence. The most outlandish occurred in April 1956 when six white men attacked Nat King Cole, the famous African American singer and television star, during a performance in Birmingham. All six were members of the North Alabama Council, and Carter refused to repudiate their actions. Later that year Carter addressed one thousand people on the courthouse lawn in Clinton, Tennessee, during a protest over school integration. After Carter's speech, a mob of whites blocked Main Street and attacked two cars with black passengers. Carter went on a speaking tour with John Kasper, a Council leader from Washington, DC, and instigator of much of the violence in Clinton. In 1957, Carter's North Alabama Council became all but indistinguishable from the Birmingham-area original Ku Klux Klan of the Confederacy. Some of his followers would be responsible for a heinous Klan initiation rite in which an elderly black man was abducted and castrated. Carter himself was arrested in January 1957 for shooting two Klansmen during a dispute at a Klan meeting in Birmingham. Everyone present was robed and hooded, so Carter's identity could not be definitely proven and the charges were eventually dropped.

In November 1956, the Supreme Court ruled that segregation laws governing Montgomery city buses were unconstitutional. It was a signal victory for the Montgomery bus boycotters, and, in the long run, would be seen as a turning point in the modern civil rights movement. In the short term, however, the court's decision enflamed the forces of white extremism in Alabama like nothing else before. Asa Carter called for "minute men" to enforce segregation on Birmingham buses. A civil rights leader described racial tension in that city as like "a lighted stick of dynamite with a short fuse." White and black leaders both feared widespread violence on buses throughout Alabama between African Americans intent on testing the court's decision and vigilante whites determined to maintain segregation. On Christmas Eve 1956, the night before Harper Lee received the Christmas envelope from her friends that allowed her to start drafting her novel, a shotgun blast tore through the front of Martin Luther King Jr.'s home in Montgomery. It came just hours after he had announced an accelerated campaign to secure black access to municipally owned recreational facilities in Montgomery. Six days later, while King addressed a mass meeting, a bomb exploded on the front porch of his home with his wife and daughter inside. White policemen and the Montgomery mayor hurried to King's home, as did an angry crowd calling for retribution. One of the white policemen on the scene would later claim that he never would have made it out alive had it not been for King, who went out to the front porch to quiet the crowd, his hand raised high, evoking to many who saw him the scene of Christ calming the troubled waters.

HARPER LEE WITNESSED the Council's rise firsthand during her extended stay in Monroeville in 1956. On March 5, 228 men gathered at the courthouse to establish the Monroe County Citizens' Council. Nothing happened in Monroe County that Short Millsap didn't put his stamp on.

He had inspected the Councils and found them useful, as shown by the fact that the group's president was Harry Lazenby, the Monroe County tax assessor and one of Millsap's chief henchmen. In one of her letters to New York friends, Nelle, in a humorous description of her family's efforts opposing Short Millsap's candidate for local elections, described Lazenby as "a singularly spineless creature all his life."

The purpose of the Council, as reported in the *Monroe Journal*, was to preserve the "legal, moral, and ethical separation of the races," and "to engender and promote good feeling between the colored and white people." The friendly talk about good feelings was in part an answer to the strong skepticism about the organization already voiced on the *Journal*'s editorial page. Bill Stewart, the newspaperman who had bought the *Journal* from A. C. Lee in 1947, was the publisher of the paper in 1956. For months he had been hearing about how Monroe County needed a Citizens' Council, and he addressed the rumors in a brief paragraph that ran in February 1956. "Certainly there is no hint of any type [sic] racial problem existing in our county," he wrote, "and the formation of such a group could possibly create such an unwanted situation." The paper repeated the warning of Governor Jim Folsom, that "nothing based on hate can exist for any length of time in a Christian Democracy." Two weeks later, the *Journal* elaborated on its position. A Citizens' Council in Monroe County would be both "hazardous and needless." Recent racial "situations," meaning primarily the Montgomery boycott and the Lucy controversy, had been "instigated by anti-South agitators," the editorial held. "The majority of the people in our county and state should be credited with enough basic intelligence to keep their feet on the ground."

Black Monroe Countians objected to the formation of a Council as well. In March 1956, Reverend G. H. Brown, pastor of three black churches in the county, in Finchburg, Beatrice, and Monroeville, wrote a letter for publication in the *Journal*. "I can hardly see where an organization that adopts the program which it has adopted can rightly assume the position to work toward the end of peaceful relationship," Brown said. A much better way forward, he suggested, would be an interracial committee to discuss community problems, a suggestion uniformly ignored by whites in Monroe

County. Brown would go on to play a leading role in civil rights advances in Monroe in the 1970s and 1980s. He was one of five plaintiffs in a case challenging the county's shift to at-large county superintendent districts, a common tactic used by southern counties after the 1965 Voting Rights Act to dilute black voting strength. He would later become the first African American countywide elected official in Monroe in the twentieth century.

Despite these complaints, or perhaps because of them, whites in Monroe County flocked to the Councils. The first full meeting in late March drew 1,500 people to the county coliseum. Sam Engelhardt was there, one of four state senators present. He addressed the denizens of Monroe County like a time traveler who had come back from the future, warning them that what had happened in Macon County—Negroes demanding the vote, filing suit in federal court when denied it, planning a boycott of white merchants—would be visited on them soon enough. His loudest ovation came at the end of his remarks when he declared that "no Negro Congressman in the future will ride in Alabama's Cadillac number one," a reference to a recent incident in which Governor Jim Folsom had adhered to the custom of extending to visiting congressmen use of a state automobile—only in this instance, the visiting congressman was Adam Clayton Powell, the African American representative from Harlem. By May 1956, the Monroe Council claimed over seven hundred members. Over the next several months, many of the arch-segregationist luminaries would make their way to Monroeville, including Georgia Speaker of the House Roy Harris, the former State Department official Hugh G. Grant, and Mississippi judge Tom Brady.

The *Journal*'s editorial opposition to the Councils died off quickly, suggesting that Bill Stewart and other Council opponents adopted the logic of Atticus in *Watchman:* If you can't beat 'em, join 'em. Harper Lee adorned her manuscript with real-life details to signal the distinction between the decent and the dangerous Citizens' Councilors. "The Maycomb council's not like the North Alabama and Tennessee kinds," Atticus explains to Jean Louise, referencing Asa Carter's organization and the violent school desegregation protests in Clinton, Tennessee, that he had helped incite. Atticus rejects violence or intimidation in favor of a strategic paternalism toward the black community, with an eye toward undermining the influence of civil rights groups like the NAACP. In a detail that Harper Lee might have borrowed from Selma in 1953, where the NAACP represented a young black man accused of an assault against a white woman and thereby stirred the local white community toward formal organization, Atticus agrees to defend the grandson of the Finch family's maid after the young man runs over and kills a white man. "[I]sn't it better for us to stand up with him in court than to have him fall into the wrong hands," Atticus explains to his junior partner, Henry Clinton. The wrong hands, of course, would be the "NAACP-paid lawyers" who were "standing around like buzzards down here waiting for things like this to happen." At the Council meeting that Jean Louise observes from the courthouse balcony, Atticus provides an ostentatiously curt introduction of the Asa Carter–esque Mr. O'Hanlon, the fiery main speaker. "I hope you noticed my brevity in introducing him," Atticus says to Jean Louise later in the book. "Baby, Mr. O'Hanlon's not, I'm happy to say, typical of the Maycomb County council membership."

The typical Maycomb County Citizens' Councilor was someone like Henry Clinton, Atticus's junior partner and Jean Louise's would-be beau. Henry tells Jean Louise that the Maycomb Council was nothing more than "a protest to the Courts, it's a sort of warning to the Negroes for them not to be in such a hurry." Like Atticus, Henry participates in the Councils out of a sense of civic duty. It was the same sensibility that one of the real-life Council founders described, how the "highest type of citizenship" had to take the lead of the resistance movement, otherwise the wrong crowd would.

Henry Clinton wasn't from the higher social rungs, but he aspired to them. There was in the Council movement a class distinction, one that Harper Lee would have understood. Sam Engelhardt and the Council movement headquartered around Montgomery were intent on recruiting the planters, doctors, lawyers, bankers, and businessmen. Asa Carter saw the people that Engelhardt was signing up and felt that the common man was being left out. He went after the small farmers, mechanics, store-keepers, and small clerks. In *Watchman*, Henry Clinton came from the common folk who lived out in the country. He had a no-account father, and entered the orbit of the Finches only as the young boarder at a neighboring house. He lived in town so he could attend high school, his room paid for by a mother who worked long hours at a crossroads general store. He understood his precarious position in the Maycomb social structure. "[A] ny deviatin' from the norm" and the folks in Maycomb would write him off. Yet Henry had gone to war, gotten a law degree, and won a plum job in Atticus Finch's law office. The Citizens' Councils, for him, represented a means of social advancement. "[M]en, especially men, must conform to certain demands of the community they live in simply so they can be of service to it," Henry explains to Jean Louise. Being of service to the community was important to Henry Clinton, just as it was to Atticus.

IN *WATCHMAN*, ATTICUS FINCH is not merely a town father performing his civic duty; he is also a shrewd lawyer with a jaded view of the role that the law and the courts have played in shaping the South's political crisis. Harper Lee shows us this side of him when Jean Louise finally confronts Atticus directly about his Citizens' Council membership. Like any good lawyer, Atticus, when called on to defend himself, instead goes on the attack: "Jean Louise, what was your first reaction to the Supreme Court decision?" We know from an early scene in the novel that Atticus is contemptuous of the decision; he refers to it as "the Supreme Court's bid for immortality." As it turns out, this is a "safe question" for Jean Louise to answer because she and her father share similar views about the court's reasoning in *Brown*. It's a surprising turn given not only Jean Louise's fury at other aspects of the segregationist position, but also how confident she is in her political opinions in other parts of the novel. Yet when discussing *Brown* with Atticus, Jean Louise turns into a slump-shouldered, diffident little girl as Atticus smugly leads her through the particulars of the case.

Jean Louise admits that upon reading the *Brown* decision she was so furious that she had to stop at the first bar she saw for a drink. "[T]here they were, tellin' us what to do again," she complains. In trying to satisfy the Fourteenth Amendment, which provided for equal protection under the law, the court "rubbed out" the Tenth Amendment, as Jean Louise put it, which reserved to the states the powers not explicitly delegated to the federal government. "It's only a small amendment, only one sentence long, but it seemed to be the one that meant the most, somehow," she says to Atticus, her gee-whiz tone evocative of how Scout would speak of Boo Radley in *Mockingbird*. As Atticus goads her, Jean Louise stumbles through half-formed claims about the separation of powers. An activist Supreme Court, no matter how well-meaning, represents "something that could be truly dangerous to our set-up." The federal government is to her "one small citizen," mostly "dreary hallways and waiting around." Yet, by the end of this impromptu lesson in constitutional theory, she manages a succinct summary of the danger of *Brown* for American democratic traditions: "[I]nstead of going about it through Congress and the state legislatures like we should, when we tried to do right we just made it easier for them to set up more hallways and more waiting." Atticus sits up and laughs. "Sweet, you're such a states' rightist you make me a Roosevelt Liberal by comparison."

However ham-fisted the scene is, Harper Lee was evoking a substantial debate that the *Brown* decision raised about the law, the courts, and social change, one in which the segregationist position was more formidable than is often remembered. *Brown* prompted a storm of criticism, not merely for outlawing state-mandated segregation, but for *how* it outlawed it. The criticisms were not limited to southern segregationists. Writing in the *New York Times* the day after the decision, for example, James Reston, the paper's chief Washington correspondent, called *Brown* a "sociological decision" based on "hearts and minds rather than laws." Chief Justice Earl Warren's unanimous majority opinion read "more like an expert paper on sociology than a Supreme Court opinion," Reston wrote. In outlawing segregation in public schools, the court "rejected history, philosophy and custom as the major basis for its decision and accepted instead Justice Benjamin N. Cardoza's test of contemporary social justice."

What Reston didn't say was that the court's reasoning in *Brown* was closely connected to the precarious political position in which it found itself. There was no perfect way to outlaw southern school segregation. The court was going to provoke outrage in most quarters of the South no matter what it said. Earl Warren wanted to communicate the court's ruling as reasonably and nonconfrontationally as possible. The sociological evidence was used to buttress the decision's central moral claim that legally mandated segregation damaged the hearts and minds of black schoolchildren. Only eleven pages long, Warren wanted it to be short so that newspapers would reprint it in its entirety. Importantly, the court provided no implementation order, and it wouldn't until the following year, when, in a seven-paragraph statement, it remanded the cases to the district courts and ordered them to proceed "with all deliberate speed." The court was signaling its patience. The hope was that reasonable, responsible white leaders in the South would come to the fore and lead the region through a difficult but necessary transition.

Atticus Finch loathed the Supreme Court's decision in *Brown*, yet Harper Lee believed him to be the kind of reasonable, responsible southerner that the nation needed if the South was going to adapt to it peacefully. Harper Lee knew that white southerners were not united in how they should respond to it. A good example of the division that soon appeared was the behind-the-scenes struggle that took place among southern senators over the drafting of a statement of southern resistance. The March 1956 "Declaration of Constitutional Principles," more commonly known as the Southern Manifesto, was signed by nineteen senators and eighty-two congressmen and was the blueprint for the discussion between Atticus and Jean Louise.

With the *Brown* decision, the court substituted "naked power for established law," the statement began, before moving quickly to a review of the Constitution's checks and balances. *Brown* was the climax of a trend of the court "undertaking to legislate, in derogation of the authority of Congress." Neither the Constitution nor the Fourteenth Amendment mentioned education, the statement observed, and the same Congress that proposed the Fourteenth Amendment later provided for segregated schools in the District of Columbia. The statement recapitulated the long history of the court's sanctioning of segregated education. No constitutional amendment or act of Congress had challenged this established legal practice. Instead, the court "undertook to exercise their naked judicial power and substituted their personal political and social ideas for the established law of the land."

The Southern Manifesto reads today like the embittered gasp of a dying political class, but at the time it represented the triumph of those who were considered the measured, responsible segregationists of the Senate. One of their more strident colleagues, Strom Thurmond of South Carolina, originally drafted an incendiary statement around which he hoped to rally southern senators. At the center of it was the doctrine of interposition, an antiquated political idea dating back to James Madison's Virginia Resolution of 1798, which held that states had the right to intercede when the federal government exceeded its enumerated powers. Interposition was all the rage among segregationists in 1956, owing mostly to the efforts of James J. Kilpatrick, the arch-segregationist newspaper editor at the *Richmond News Leader* and a close advisor to Virginia senator Harry Byrd. Thurmond, who had been the 1948 presidential candidate of the "Dixiecrats," the third-party group that abandoned the Democrats in protest of Harry Truman's civil rights proposals, worked closely with Byrd in pushing the idea of interposition. Byrd gave a Senate speech in February 1956 advocating the theory as a "perfectly legal means of appeal from the Supreme Court's order."

Not all the southerners in Congress were convinced, particularly Richard Russell of Georgia, dean of the Senate's southern caucus. In the 1950s, Russell was perhaps the single most respected member of the US Senate. His protégé, Lyndon Johnson, often spoke of how Russell had the learning, temperament, and wisdom to occupy the White House, yet was hamstrung politically by his southern origins. Russell knew in detail the political situations of all his fellow senators, and they would regularly pull him aside to ask for his advice. Yet they also would have known of his unalterable commitment to racial segregation. In a speech opposing the 1957 civil rights bill, Russell spoke of how he "would gladly part with what remains of [this] life if this would guarantee the preservation of a civilization of two races of unmixed blood in the land I love."

Russell had a frosty relationship with Thurmond, whom he distrusted as a self-interested grandstander. He gave Thurmond's draft statement to a committee of southern senators of greater legal expertise and more even temperament than the South Carolinian. They excised the interposition sections and came up with the final language that stuck to the legal and historical aspects of the case. Russell even used the announcement of the manifesto to tweak another opportunistic southerner riding the wave of massive resistance. Herman Talmadge, son of Eugene and a distant cousin of Thurmond, not to mention the author the previous year of the hastily written volume *You and Segregation* (1955), was challenging Walter George for his Senate seat. Russell had Walter George read the statement into the record as a sign of his smart, tough-minded defense of segregation in opposition to the loudmouth Talmadge.

Smart, tough-minded, politically astute, suffering the hotheads so that he could temper them: This is the Atticus Finch of *Watchman*. His discussion of *Brown* with Jean Louise is interesting as much in what it does *not* say as in what it does. There is no mention, for example, of the doctrine of interposition, nor of nullification, another obscure constitutional theory popular among segregationists at the time. Atticus Finch was too level-headed to tilt at such windmills.

In *Watchman*, Atticus is a pragmatic segregationist, but he's also a principled southerner. He describes himself as a "Jeffersonian Democrat." Jefferson believed that citizenship and suffrage should not be privileges granted to every man, Atticus explains to Jean Louise, but only to those responsible enough to use them wisely. His political philosophy is most fully elaborated by his brother Jack, who shares his views completely and whom Jean Louise had visited earlier to try to make sense of what she had observed at the Citizens' Council meeting. Uncle Jack explains how he and his brother represent a worldview under attack, one that includes "some good things in it."

Among those good things is a "mistrust of paternalism and government in large doses." Uncle Jack articulates the despair of the principled

Jeffersonian in mid-twentieth-century America. He decries the loss of the yeoman ideal, one rooted in "[t]he time-honored, common-law concept of property—a man's interest in and duties to that property." New ideas about government had emerged that were raising up the "have-nots" while restricting the "haves." The South was industrializing, an ominous development that saw tenant farmers-turned-industrial workers become the coddled, unthinking masses manipulated by a federal government consolidating its power. The government "lends them money to build their houses," Uncle Jack observes to Jean Louise, "it gives them a free education for serving in its armies, it provides for their old age and assures them of several weeks' support if they lose their jobs." The fear was of a federal government become "monstrous," one that would destroy the liberty and individual initiative that had defined America. "The only thing in America that is still unique in this tired world is that a man can go as far as his brains will take him or he can go to hell if he wants to."

Harper Lee could have drawn this portrait of Jeffersonianism from a variety of sources, but the most obvious and direct was her own father. Invoking the Jeffersonian ideal in his editorials, A. C. Lee had encouraged tenant farmers in Monroe County to buy their own land as soon as they could, which would be good for them economically and good for the community. "[T]he happiest people are those who own their own homes and farms, and who are largely independent," he wrote. "[T]he contented man or woman is necessarily the most valuable citizen to the community. . . . They are the ones who are free to think carefully, and to pursue their duties as citizens and as members of society fearlessly." In July 1939 he warned about the "rapidly growing idea among our people that the government owes them a living," an idea detrimental to "the American spirit of independence and self-reliance." And in an August 1946 editorial, "What Is Liberalism Today?," the one written in response to the liberal friends and perspectives that his daughter Nelle seemed to be embracing in Tuscaloosa, he reminded readers that liberalism, originally understood, meant "the rights of all our people to pursue their own ways and live their own lives as free from interference from governmental supervision," an idea he attributed to Thomas Jefferson, "the Great Democrat."

A. C. Lee likely took inspiration from the Southern Agrarians, the collection of scholars and poets affiliated with Vanderbilt University who in 1930 published the collection of essays *I'll Take My Stand: The South and the Agrarian Tradition.* That book, though put out by a group of intellectuals representing a diverse set of motivations, opinions, and ideas, was an attempt to combine an artistic aesthetic with an economic strategy. The authors criticized the sources of modernity and industrialization that they believed were undermining the conditions that made true art possible. Yet agrarianism was wrapped in a romantic defense of an idealized southern tradition. The failure to grapple with the legacies of slavery and segregation would lead a number of the original contributors to distance themselves from the initial project. One who would not was Donald Davidson, the poet, essayist, and longtime faculty member at Vanderbilt, who provided the most highbrow, real-world equivalent of the political views of Atticus and Uncle Jack.

Davidson's signature collection of essays, *The Attack on Leviathan* (1938), encompasses most aspects of the conservative worldview that Harper Lee sketches in *Watchman.* The ideas of Uncle Jack are all there: the learned references, the esteem for the Founding Fathers, the pointed comments on New Deal policies. "The greatest present threat to the Federal Union," Davidson wrote, "comes . . . from the advocacy and the more than incipient growth of a Leviathan State." No such state could ever "abolish sectionalism," he warned, "unless like Tamerlane it proposes to rule from a pyramid of skulls." Davidson revered Jefferson, of course, and took umbrage with southern liberals who tried to appropriate him for their cause. He mocked Virginius Dabney's history of southern liberalism in which "Jefferson becomes the spiritual grandfather of the swashbuckling idealists who want the government to guarantee everything from bank deposits to tonsillectomy for the mountain whites." As Davidson put it, "Above all things Jefferson feared the Leviathan state and denounced the tendencies toward 'consolidation' that Hamilton and Marshall were busily forwarding."

Davidson was in the midst of reinterpreting Agrarianism to meet the needs of a burgeoning mid-century conservative intellectual movement.

One of the key figures in that movement, Russell Kirk, called *The Attack on Leviathan* "the most important neglected book of this century." Davidson was an esteemed southern contributor to the *National Review,* the magazine established in 1955 by William F. Buckley to serve as the organ of the conservative movement. An essay he published there gives a sense of how southern Jeffersonians were merging with a nascent national conservatism. As the historian George Nash has observed, in the 1950s *National Review* was "one of the very few journals receptive to the viewpoint of conservative white Southerners." In his essay, Davidson decried the assault on southern tradition represented by *Brown.* It was an attack on the southern social order, one founded on the "sense of kinship and the importance of family," a condition reinforced by the fact that "the white population is largely descended from the original colonial stock" (a point that Uncle Jack stresses to Jean Louise as key to understanding the heated response of the Citizens' Council movement). With *Brown,* the court had overstepped its bounds and plunged the nation into constitutional chaos. "[O]nce more," Davidson wrote, "the Negro question is most confusedly mixed up with large and general constitutional questions far more important to the nation than the special matter of how the reasonable aspirations of the Negro minority or any other racial minority are to be satisfied."

This racially condescending tone—the "special matter" of the Negroes—was a staple of conservative political rhetoric in that era. It came from both North and South, and eased the regional integration of conservative thought that would be essential to a national mobilization of the right. A *National Review* editorial titled "Why the South Must Prevail" that appeared during the debate over civil rights legislation in 1957 reflected a patronizing, racist view that black southerners were not yet ready for full integration into white southern society: "The central question that emerges . . . is whether the White community in the South is entitled to take such measures as are necessary to prevail, politically and culturally, in areas in which it does not predominate numerically? The sobering answer is Yes—the White community is so entitled because, for the time being, it is the advanced race." Atticus Finch expresses a very similar view in *Watchman.*

Davidson longed for a cross-regional effort to "revive the old American conviction that a government which is not firmly kept in the position of a servant of society will inevitably become a tyrant over society." His hope, and the hope of Buckley and other early leaders of conservative revival, was that the true Jeffersonians from below the Mason-Dixon line could join with the libertarians, the cultural traditionalists, and the fervent Cold Warriors of the North to form a new alliance in American politics. This merging would require that white southerners abandon their traditional loyalty to the Democratic Party. Davidson himself had already done that. He was an enthusiastic backer of Strom Thurmond's Dixiecrat campaign in 1948.

Harper Lee gives no indication of how Atticus might have voted in that historic election, but we do see him break ranks with the majority of his fellow white southerners in voting for the Republican Dwight Eisenhower. Whether this was in 1952, when a fellow Alabaman, US senator John Sparkman, was the vice-presidential candidate on the Democratic ticket, or in 1956, or both, is unclear. Eisenhower won significant southern support in each election, the first time in the twentieth century that a Republican candidate had really competed in the South. Atticus's vote for the GOP was rooted in his individualist, small-government political philosophy. Jean Louise is clueless as to how Atticus could call himself a Jeffersonian Democrat and vote for a Republican. It's intended as another sign of her callowness in comparison to the learned, principled politics of her father.

NELLE HARPER MAY or may not have read Donald Davidson, but there is no doubt that she read and was deeply influenced by the most prominent southern writer of the day, William Faulkner. Awarded the 1949 Nobel Prize for Literature, in the 1950s Faulkner was without equal as the internationally recognized authority on the racial ferment in his corner of the world. Already by the late 1940s, he was out in front of most of his fellow white southerners in accepting the inevitability of Jim Crow's demise. He dramatized this view in the lawyer figure Gavin Stevens in his novel *Intruder in the Dust* (1948), a character and a book that Harper Lee borrowed from in her own fiction. But it also came through clearly in a number of high-profile public statements. In 1951, for example, he protested the conviction and sentencing to death of Willie McGee, a black man accused of raping a white woman in Laurel, Mississippi. McGee's case approximated the Scottsboro trials of the 1930s as an international cause célèbre, and Faulkner's comments provoked outrage among his fellow white Mississippians. The district attorney in the McGee case said Faulkner was either a fool or had "aligned himself with the Communists."

In the year and a half following the *Brown* decision, Faulkner became an important voice of white southern moderation. To a Memphis reporter, he defended desegregation as a commonsense proposal; opposing it was "like living in Alaska and saying you don't like snow." He was in Rome on a goodwill tour sponsored by the American government when the press called for his reaction to the murder of Emmett Till. "If we in America have reached that point in our desperate culture when we must murder children, no matter for what reason or what color," he declared, "we don't deserve to survive, and probably won't." In the fall of 1955 he participated in a panel discussion at the Southern Historical Association, where he issued perhaps his most indelible quote about the southern racial crisis: "We speak now against the day when our Southern people who will resist to the last these inevitable changes in social relations, will, when they have been forced to accept what they at one time might have accepted with dignity and goodwill, will say, 'Why didn't someone tell us this before? Tell us this in time?'"

With such statements, Faulkner cultivated what a biographer would call "the role of artist as savant, a capability he so much admired—indeed, even idolized—in several French writers." But the public pronouncements obscured his private ambivalence. His fame and the accompanying pressures of the public spotlight also exacerbated personal crises, including his alcoholism, poor health, and an affair with a woman less than half his age. In early 1956, as he followed the protests in Tuscaloosa surrounding Autherine Lucy's admission to the University of Alabama, Faulkner became convinced that someone was going to shoot Lucy, and that chaos would ensue. Both sides were digging in and something had to give. Faulkner felt compelled to adjust his public stance on racial matters. He would do so in ways both serious and absurd.

The serious part came in his "Letter to the North" published in *Life* magazine in March 1956, one week before southern senators released the Southern Manifesto. It was perhaps the most concise statement of the political concern at the heart of *Watchman:* the defense of the white southerner caught "in the middle of a revolution," as Uncle Jack would call it, or, as Faulkner put it, the man "present yet detached, committed and attainted neither by Citizens' Council nor NAACP." This position, Faulkner's position, was being made untenable by an overbearing Supreme Court, he argued; the decision in *Brown* was "the first implication, and—to the Southerner—even promise, of force and violence." The mayhem in Alabama, as well as the Emmett Till lynching and the failure of state officials to convict his murderers, Faulkner laid at the feet of the court. The North would have to learn again a lesson it should have learned in the Civil War, Faulkner wrote. The South, which he imagined as "a white embattled minority who are our blood and kin," would "go to any length, even that fatal and already doomed one, before it will accept alteration of its racial condition by mere force of law or economic threat."

The absurdity came a few weeks later with the publication of an interview Faulkner gave to a British reporter. Faulkner pledged that "if it came to fighting I'd fight for Mississippi against the United States even if it meant going out into the street and shooting Negroes." He was drunk at the time of the interview, a fact he implied the following month in a public letter disputing the comments attributed to him.

Harper Lee would have recognized Faulkner's bombast for what it was, yet certainly she sympathized with his notion that "the rest of the United States knows next to nothing about the South." In a sense, *Watchman* was her own letter to the North. That's how Maurice Crain tried to pitch the novel to potential publishers, as a book with important lessons for readers above the Mason-Dixon line. "Well, to hear the *Post* tell it, we lynch 'em for breakfast," Jean Louise informs Atticus when he asks how the newspapers up North covered southern racial matters.

The ambition to correct pat northern assumptions is why Lee gives so much of the argument in the novel to Atticus and Uncle Jack. In an internal dialogue Jean Louise has with an imagined northern audience, she thinks to herself that "New York has all the answers." New York knows who Jean Louise is, knows what kind of people she comes from. "Please believe me," Jean Louise imagines herself saying, "what has happened in my family is not what you think. I can only say this—that everything I learned about human decency I learned here." Atticus she defends as a "man who could not be discourteous to a ground-squirrel," a man who waited in line behind Negroes, a man who had raised her not to despise, fear, or mistreat Negroes. "Look sister," the voice of New York says to her, "we know the facts: you spent the first twenty-one years of your life in lynching country. . . . So drop the act." But it wasn't an act, not for Atticus and not for Jean Louise. Or at least she had always believed it wasn't— that is until the day she spotted Atticus at the Council meeting.

HARPER LEE MAKES clear by the end of *Watchman* that Jean Louise wasn't, in fact, mistaken, that Atticus really was a decent man. Yet for all of Jean Louise's confusion, she has her moments with her father and her uncle both. She may struggle to follow Uncle Jack's explanation of southern politics and history, yet she's smart enough to suspect that he's dissembling, and her conversation with him ends with Uncle Jack placing a worried phone call, presumably to his brother, to warn him that Jean Louise had seen him at the Council meeting and was incensed. With Atticus, though Jean Louise can't rebut him point by point, she responds with an emotional appeal that manages to unsettle her father. "Atticus, the time has come when we've got to do right," she says. The imputation of immorality stings Atticus. "Have you ever considered that you can't have a set of backward people living among people advanced in one kind of civilization and have a social Arcadia?" he asks her. He and Jean Louise descend into a shouting match in which Atticus is "[d]esperately trying" to make her understand his position. The argument lays bare the ugliest aspects of his views.

This is the passage that received the greatest attention in 2015, when *Watchman* was published for the first time. "Do you want Negroes by the carload in our schools and churches and theaters? Do you want them in our world?" Atticus asks Jean Louise. He talks of schools being "dragged down to accommodate Negro children," of government run by incompetents, as was allegedly the case during the first Reconstruction. "[T]he Negroes down here are still in their childhood as a people," Atticus explains. "They've made terrific progress in adapting themselves to white ways, but they're far from it yet."

Yet what stands out to modern readers—Atticus's racism—would not have seemed so scandalous either to Harper Lee or to many readers in the 1950s. Such racist views were a common part of American political discourse at the time. They showed up without comment or apology in major newspapers, opinion journals (and not just the *National Review*), and the *Congressional Record*. Men of achievement who enjoyed great esteem in American life—Georgia senator Richard Russell for example—expressed them openly. Non-southerners who may not have shared such views exactly conveyed their sympathy with them privately. This was the case reportedly with President Dwight Eisenhower, who, not long before the court issued its decision in *Brown*, buttonholed Supreme Court Chief Justice Earl Warren at the end of a White House dinner. Southerners were not "bad people," Eisenhower suggested to Warren. "All they are concerned about is to see that their sweet little girls are not required to sit in school alongside some big overgrown Negroes." For years southern politicians had sought and found political friends from other regions who could appreciate what they would have described, and what would have been understood by sympathetic northern whites, as their region's peculiar difficulties.

That Harper Lee did not intend Atticus's racist remarks as any kind of final judgment on his character is indicated by what comes next. Atticus, not his daughter, is the one who maintains his dignity and sense of propriety in the midst of the heated exchange. Jean Louise shouts Atticus down, furious that he would raise her to believe in justice knowing full well he didn't practice it himself. She calls him a coward, a snob, a tyrant, a son of a bitch. She compares him to Hitler. As her fury devolves into hysteria,

Jean Louise cedes the moral high ground. Atticus, meanwhile, has come back to himself. He assures his daughter of his love. She is merely a young woman beyond reason. She has idolized him for too long, and now she has to grow up and realize that he is mere flesh and blood.

The chapter resolves this way because Harper Lee is intent on balancing the scale: Atticus's racial conservatism on one side, Jean Louise's moral condemnation of Jim Crow on the other. The critical scene in *Watchman* involves a similar sort of accounting, one that pulls Atticus back from the brink of moral condemnation. Jean Louise goes to visit Calpurnia, her beloved African American maid, her only true mother, to assure her that Atticus would represent her grandson in court. It is one of the few times that Harper Lee manages to dramatize, rather than merely ventriloquize, the novel's political ideas. A veil has come down between the two women. Jean Louise knows when Calpurnia is putting on company manners for white folks. She recognizes it as Calpurnia mouths pieties about what a good man Mr. Finch is, how he always does the right thing, all the while her eyes show "no hint of compassion." "Tell me one thing, Cal," Jean Louise asks as she stands to leave, "just one thing before I go—please, I've got to know. Did you hate us?" Calpurnia sits silent, Jean Louise suffering the agonizing moments, until finally Cal shakes her head. Here, as it so often was in the stories that white southerners told about themselves, it is the loyal black servant who provides the essential testimony as to the decency of the good white southerner.

In the end, the most erratic character in *Watchman*, Uncle Jack, conveys the novel's real message. There are "meaningful things" that will be lost when men like Atticus are tossed on the dust heap of history, he says, things that "the North" doesn't understand and that the editorial page of the *New York Post* refuses to see. It is Uncle Jack who will resolve the novel's central conflict with a violent *deus ex machina*, a "savage" backhand slap of Jean Louise as she is packing the car to leave. It literally knocks her to her senses. A stiff bourbon soothes the pain, and, as Uncle Jack imparts final words of wisdom—including a bizarre non sequitur that he was secretly in love with Jean Louise's mother—Harper Lee does some last-minute scorekeeping: Jean Louise has been bigoted against the South;

she's convinced finally that Atticus really would stop the Klan if it came to that; it takes maturity and humility to live in a region in the midst of political revolution. Jean Louise goes to see Atticus, they reconcile, and she drives him home, remembering to duck her head getting into the car, a sign that she is learning not to be so hardheaded.

The limitations of *Watchman* as a work of fiction were clear to those who read it at the time. The editors at G. P. Putnam's Sons and Harper & Brothers, where Maurice Crain sent the manuscript in March and April of 1957, both turned it down, citing the lack of story and suspense. For readers today, the limits of the novel as a work of political critique are clear as well. The white South's principled conservatives would not be the ones who guided the region through its social and political crisis. Writing nearly four decades later, Eugene Genovese, one of the most distinguished historians of the antebellum South and one of the fiercest theorists and defenders of the southern conservative tradition, frankly criticized that tradition in the civil rights era. "The responsible, humane, decent conservatives of the South did almost nothing to lead their people toward a well-ordered, locally guided integration," Genovese wrote. "They could not do so. For they have always stood for the rights of the community, and their particular communities, which embraced all social classes among whites, were implacably hostile to black demands."

Completing a draft of "Watchman" in late February 1957, however, Harper Lee didn't have the benefit of hindsight, and she wasn't looking backward anyway. She was already on to a new novel, one that drew on the childhood short stories that she had first shown Crain a few months earlier. Meanwhile down South, the honorable white southerners—the Sartorises of Faulkner's world whom she valorized in *Watchman*—were either being swept up in the madness of segregationist militancy or slinking into a cowering silence. Maybe a letter to the North wasn't what she needed to write after all.

Chapter 4

The Boiling Frog

The pages flew out of Nelle's typewriter in ribbons. In late May 1957, she gave Maurice Crain 111 pages of her second novel, which she had titled "The Long Goodbye." A little over two weeks later she had a finished version of it. Crain immediately sent the novel to Lynn Carrick at J. B. Lippincott. A month earlier he had given Carrick "Go Set a Watchman," hoping that the third submission would be the charm. But Carrick set aside "Watchman" to focus on this second novel, which Harper Lee continued to work on during the summer. She sent Lippincott a revised version of the manuscript in July, and then another in August. By October, the Lippincott editors had seen enough to know that they wanted Harper Lee under contract, even though there remained work to be done, as suggested by the fact that Lippincott dropped the title "The Long Goodbye." On the contract that Lee signed on October 17, 1957, the work was untitled.

The project was assigned to Tay Hohoff, the formidable, silver-haired publishing veteran then in her late fifties. With a throaty voice made deeper by near-constant cigarette smoking, Hohoff, fiercely independent, was known to scoff at recently married women in the office who had taken their husband's name. She would edit an impressive array of writers over her long career, including Zora Neale Hurston, Thomas Pynchon, and

Nicholas Delbanco. In Nelle, Hohoff found an eager young writer, lacking in experience but with genuine storytelling talent. Yet, upon signing Nelle, "[t]he editorial call to duty was plain," Hohoff wrote years later. "She needed, at last, professional help in organizing her material and developing a sound plot structure." An editorial assistant had reported to Hohoff that the manuscript was "diffuse," "autobiographical," and far too long. It's not surprising that a novel that grew out of several short stories might read like "a series of anecdotes," as Hohoff put it, or that a manuscript that Harper Lee had told Maurice Crain could go "on and on" might in fact do so. Revisions were expected to take six months. As it turned out, they took over two years.

Set in the Depression-era South, the novel follows the adventures of three precocious children as they try to unravel the mystery of the town recluse. The story unfolds through the perspective of the smallest of the children, the puckish, irresistible Scout Finch. Lee switched between the childhood voice of Scout and the adult Jean Louise in ways that some critics hailed as brilliant and others dismissed as amateurish and utterly implausible. But most readers hardly noticed or cared, so charmed were they by Scout, Jem, and Dill and the colorful characters that populated Maycomb. When her classmate Cecil Jacobs announces at school one day that Scout Finch's daddy "defends niggers," she fights him. Only when she gets home does she learn what he meant, that her father, Atticus Finch, would take the case of a black man, Tom Robinson, who had been accused of raping a white woman. Thus begins the children's initiation into the world of adults, a story that plays out in parallel with their growing realization that things with Boo Radley, their mysterious, reclusive neighbor, are not as they seem.

In *Mockingbird*, the character of Atticus is conceived from a very different point of view than the character in *Watchman*. He offers no ruminations on the nature of racial difference, no warmed-over defenses of Lost Cause dogma, no diatribes against the dictates of the Supreme Court. Gone is almost any detail that would identify Atticus with the more distasteful or impolitic orthodoxies of his region. The few that remain are studiedly indirect, such as his uncharacteristically peevish aside to the

jury about the "distaff side of the Executive branch in Washington" hurl-
ing Jefferson's words on equality in the face of southerners, or his response
to Scout who, when prodded by an annoying question from Cecil Jacobs,
asks Atticus if he is a radical. "You tell Cecil I'm about as radical as Cotton Tom Heflin," he chuckles.

These were shorthand ways for Lee to make the case that, yes, Atticus was of his time and place, despite holding some views not commonly
associated with white southerners. Most readers, if they had heard of Tom
Heflin at all, would have known him from his rabid justifications of lynching as a means of defending white southern womanhood. What could Atticus have meant by that? Harper Lee is content to leave the reader as
confused as Scout. They wouldn't have known Cotton Tom as Lee herself
knew him, refracted through her father's evolving politics in the 1930s,
as a Klansman-turned-handpicked candidate of the Black Belt–Big Mule
coalition, the avatar of white racial populism that economic conservatives
backed against the liberal Lister Hill. Heflin was a flawed vessel by A. C.
Lee's lights, no doubt, but still the best chance by the late 1930s of beating back the radical New Dealers ascendant in Washington.

Yet Harper Lee was moving away from any overt engagement with
politics. With Hohoff's guidance, she was learning how every element of
the novel must be in service to the story. In *Mockingbird* the particulars
of Atticus's politics would muddy his essential nobility, which is critical to
the novel. His politics could only be implied, and only sparingly at that.
This not only streamlined the narrative, it also gave Harper Lee a slyer,
more implicit way to make one of her central arguments. *Watchman* hits
the reader over the head with the idea that a segregationist like Atticus
could be a principled man. *Mockingbird* presents readers with a principled
man who—oh, by the way—sees things pretty much eye-to-eye with Tom
Heflin.

The most straightforward explanation for the altered view of Atticus is
that it was dictated by Lee's change in narrative voice and temporal setting. In *Mockingbird*, readers see Atticus through the eyes of Scout, and so
through the limited experience, knowledge, and perspective of a child. Yet
it's not *only* through Scout that we see and hear the story. The novel opens

in the adult voice of Jean Louise, and conceivably it could have ended that way, with Lee inserting some reflective qualifying comment about the limits of Atticus's example, some more detached version of the criticisms that Jean Louise gives in *Watchman*.

That, however, could have unraveled *Mockingbird* entirely. What would Harper Lee have had the adult Jean Louise say exactly? There was nothing detached about Jean Louise's criticisms of Atticus in *Watchman*. She rages at her father and his politics, and her reaction to him is of a piece with her disillusionment with and alienation from Maycomb. In *Mockingbird* it is only through Atticus's goodness that the reader is assured that Scout and Jem will be all right in the end, and that Maycomb will be all right, too.

Perhaps Tay Hohoff was instrumental in helping Harper Lee craft the idealized view of Atticus. At the same time she was editing Lee, Hohoff, who had grown up in Brooklyn in a multigenerational Quaker home steeped in tradition, was finishing up a book of her own about an idealistic man. In 1959 she published an admiring biography of John Lovejoy Elliott, a familial descendant, though not blood relative, of the famous abolitionist martyr Elijah Lovejoy, and an important figure in the settlement house and ethical culture movements in turn-of-the-century New York. In the book's epilogue, Hohoff imagined Elliott himself viewing the motley group of rich and poor, uptown and downtown, who had gathered at his funeral. "[H]e would have been pleased that his death had broken down all the barriers, even for so short a time," she wrote; "to have no barriers ever any more between different sorts of people had been the dream and the work of his whole life." This would not have been an unreasonable description of the Atticus of *Mockingbird*. The Quaker influence could be seen in at least one of the early reviews of *Mockingbird*, which described Atticus Finch as "simply the man of conscience who must obey his inner light."

Yet it may have been that the process for Nelle of drafting her first novel, and putting down on the page the roiling mix of emotions that she had felt toward her father, had brought her new perspective, independent of Hohoff's guidance. Nelle had been writing practically her whole life, but mostly short works, some of them satirical, pieces that were funny or that vented about some absurdity. She had never sat down to compose an extended piece of writing in which she was forced to develop and sustain the point of view of a character that didn't come out of her own experience. Perhaps Lee was able to write the Atticus of *Mockingbird* only after having written the Atticus of *Watchman*. Late in *Watchman*, the narrator explains that Jean Louise "did not know that she worshiped" her father, but now, as she was writing and revising *Mockingbird*, Lee knew that she herself had. The words she puts in the mouth of Uncle Jack in *Watchman* are words she might have spoken to her younger self: "[Y]ou confused your father with God. You never saw him as a man with a man's heart, and a man's failings. . . . You were an emotional cripple, leaning on him, getting the answers from him, assuming that your answers would always be his answers."

WHATEVER THE ARTISTIC and personal concerns that led to the new portrait of Atticus, the politics of the day would have influenced his transformation. The founders of the Citizens' Councils had a theory, one that Atticus, Uncle Jack, and Henry Clinton subscribed to in *Watchman*. The Councils were the responsible element that calmed the racist hotheads. Violence and terrorism of the Klan only fueled the forces of change by inviting federal interference and alienating would-be white moderates. Strong leadership from the Councils would sap the momentum of the Klan while also providing firm direction for weak-willed whites, particularly those business and financial leaders whose eagerness to recruit new industry could cloud their thinking. In the process, the southern white community would speak with a single voice, and act with a unanimity of purpose, repelling the outside forces that threatened the southern way of life.

That was the idea. But in truth resistance politics unfolded very differently in Alabama in the more than two years it took Harper Lee to write *Mockingbird*. Indeed, it's possible if not likely that the new Atticus was, at least in part, a consequence of the amount of time Lee needed to write her new book. For while she was working with Hohoff, and writing and rewriting, the Councils were not moderating the Klan, as they claimed they would. Rather, the Klan was radicalizing the Councils. In 1957, whatever white moderation existed in Alabama came not from within the Councils, as *Watchman* implied that it would, but in opposition to them.

An example that Harper Lee was unlikely to have missed was that of Buford Boone, editor of the *Tuscaloosa News*. In May 1957, by which time two houses had already passed on *Watchman* and Lee was hard at work on "The Long Goodbye," Boone was awarded the Pulitzer Prize for editorial writing. Amid the hysteria surrounding Autherine Lucy's enrollment at the University of Alabama the previous year, Boone had written calm, measured editorials calling for law and order and respect for individual rights. Boone was no liberal. He, like the vast majority of white people in Alabama in the 1950s, was an avowed segregationist. Yet the backlash against him was fierce. Threats poured in, and many readers canceled their subscriptions. Windows in his house were broken. The family phone rang so frequently through the night that he had to get an unlisted number. Boone became the bane of the local Citizens' Council, which tried to start a rival newspaper to compete with the *News*. A former FBI agent, Boone benefitted from confidential reports from Bureau contacts about various Council members, yet he had to face the public barrage by himself. That's what he did in January 1957 when he accepted an invitation to speak before a tense, jam-packed Council meeting. During the question-and-answer session, Boone was asked what the university should do the next time a black student tried to enroll. Someone shouted "kill him." Another said "hang him." To some in attendance, it was unclear whether they were talking about Boone or the hypothetical black student.

In the late 1950s, militant segregationists waged war on white moderation. The fight against black activism did not slacken, but Council leaders were confident that economic intimidation could repel those threats. The thing that caught their attention, the thing they worried about at night, was the existence of moderate segregationists like Buford Boone, along with business leaders intent on wooing outside industries. It was not merely that in their pragmatism and profit-mindedness these people might compromise on racial matters, so that little by little segregation would be chipped away. The fear went deeper. White moderates represented an existential threat to the foundational myth of the militant segregationists: the idea that all white southerners, united by the blood of their Scotch-Irish forebears and the tragic history of their fathers and grandfathers, were uniformly devoted to racial segregation. A fixed, invariable, unyielding response was essential for holding the line against the forces of change.

In his exhaustive history of civil rights politics in Montgomery, Birmingham, and Selma, Mills Thornton showed how in Alabama in the period from roughly 1957 to 1961, militant segregationists effectively silenced any dissent in the white community. Moderate, interracial political projects that in the early 1950s had provided encouraging signs of progress in Montgomery and Birmingham were anathema by the decade's end. In Montgomery in 1953, for example, voters elected a liberal police commissioner and the city voluntarily desegregated its police force, putting it in the vanguard of cities in the Deep South. In Birmingham in 1950, city leaders created an interracial committee in response to Klan bombings that had worked throughout the first half of the decade as a source of goodwill. Yet as the Citizens' Councils spread and new Klaverns were formed across the state, all such efforts came to an abrupt halt. These were surreal days in Deep South politics. Views once thought extreme became mainstream. Any hint of deviation from segregationist orthodoxy could bring harassment or ostracism. Fairness, moderation, and patience became dirty words.

The best indicator of the radicalization taking place in the white community was the 1958 Alabama governor's race. Political experts handicapping the race identified two front-runners, one of whom, Jimmy Faulkner, was a well-known figure in Monroeville and a good friend of the Lee family. Faulkner was the editor and publisher of the *Baldwin County Times* in Bay Minette who, along with his business partner Bill Stewart, had bought the *Monroe Journal* from A. C. Lee in 1947. A former state senator, Faulkner had run for governor in 1954 and was now on his second try. His political advertisements soft-pedaled the segregation issue, highlighting his pledge to win more "pocket dollars" for Alabamans. His political style was suggested in the name of the singing group that accompanied him on campaign stops, The Statesmen Quartet.

The other front-runner was also considered a racial moderate, although it's easy to forget given his later exploits. George Wallace had served two terms in the state legislature and had been elected circuit judge. He had been at the 1948 Democratic National Convention in Philadelphia when most of the Alabama delegation had bolted to form the Dixiecrat Party, but Wallace refused to join them. An ardent backer of Jim Folsom, he had built his political career as an economic populist. His reputation statewide was based largely on the Wallace Act of 1951, which enabled cities to issue revenue bonds to attract new industries.

Front-runner status would matter little, however, because the 1958 race defied all political prognostication. The lesson of that election would be of the power of the militant segregationist vote. The candidate who learned it before any other was Attorney General John Patterson, who despite holding statewide office was relatively young and inexperienced. He had been elected in 1954 after taking over the candidacy of his father Albert, who had won the Democratic nomination only to be assassinated soon afterward by gambling interests that he had cracked down on in his hometown of Phenix City, Alabama. Outrage over the incident thrust young John to victory. In 1958 he campaigned for governor on the motto "Nobody's for Patterson but the People." The people, in this instance, meant primarily the Citizens' Councils and the Klan, with whom the Patterson campaign allied in ways both covert and overt. It was Patterson whom the decent-minded Jimmy Faulkner would have had in mind in a speech he gave in Monroeville denouncing "[s]ome of the Johnny-come-latelies who, for personal or political reasons, are stirring up the racial issue unnecessarily." Faulkner declared that "there is no room under the bright Alabama sun for demagoguery."

But in fact there was plenty of room. Patterson shocked everyone by winning the initial round of balloting by nearly thirty-five thousand votes. In the runoff, George Wallace tried to attack Patterson for his ties to the Klan, but the charge fell flat. A north Alabama businessman and Citizens'

Council member captured the majority white sentiment well when he told a Birmingham reporter that while he himself would never join the Klan, the organization did necessary work. "I'd rather have Attorney General Patterson attacking the Communists in the NAACP than running down an organization devoted to maintaining our way of life," the man said. In the end, Patterson won the runoff easily. Afterward he paid off a conspicuous campaign debt by appointing Citizens' Council leader Sam Engelhardt to the powerful position of state highway director. He also backed Engelhardt in his successful race for state Democratic Party chairman. George Wallace might have been late in recognizing the power of the militant vote, but it was a lesson he would never forget. After his loss to Patterson he famously vowed that "no other son-of-a-bitch will ever out-nigger me again."

Patterson's election fit a pattern of white radicalization across the Deep South. In every southern state at the time politicians raced to the right. In Arkansas, extremist agitation had pressured Governor Orval Faubus into a remarkable metamorphosis. His entire career had been spent as an Ozark populist with little concern about racial matters, yet in the Little Rock crisis of 1957 he spied the opportunity for political immortality as the champion of the bitter-enders. Mississippians elected a clownish character, Ross Barnett, who had lost two previous races for governor. In 1959, he rode radicalization to victory, giving the Citizens' Councils in the state effective control over the governor's mansion for the next four years.

Militant segregationists truly believed that they could stop integration, and history had given them little reason to doubt themselves. Their elders had stood firm against the race-mixers during the first Reconstruction. Or at least that is what they had been taught, and what they believed—that a valiant generation of whites had restored sanity to the postwar South by overthrowing Reconstruction-era Republican governments. This version of the past—history written by the losers of the Civil War—had become the standard narrative, not only for white southerners but for the great majority of the American public. Now the modern-day southern militants intended to do the same during the "second reconstruction." That was actually the term they liked to use, since it signaled that whatever troubles they would have to endure, they would again emerge victorious. "When the history of the second reconstruction is written," a resolution passed by the Alabama Citizens' Council in 1959 read, Montgomery would be recorded as the place where "integration efforts were stopped cold."

IN MONROE COUNTY, militant racism showed up in late 1957 in the form of the Ku Klux Klan. Klansmen burned crosses in fields throughout the county. Night caravans of men in robes and hoods, the license plates on their cars obscured by adhesive tape, paraded through Monroeville. Klansmen met three times with *Monroe Journal* publisher Bill Stewart, who by that time had bought out Jimmy Faulkner to become the sole publisher. The future of the *Journal* could be in danger if the paper opposed the Klan, the men warned. That only infuriated Stewart. In December, the *Journal* ran an editorial written by Stewart and signed by him along with the paper's manager, Tom Gardner. "There is no place in Monroe County for a branch of any organization that is steeped in racial violence, whose trademark is fear," it read. The job of maintaining segregation would be hard enough without "misguided zealots" burdening the county with unwarranted acts that would only "hurt the legal fight of thoughtful people to preserve segregation."

The column won first place in the better newspapers contest sponsored by the Alabama Press Association. Yet it did nothing to stop the spread of the Klan in Monroe County. The periodic reports of Klan activity published in the *Journal* over the course of 1958 and 1959 hint at the pressure and intimidation Klansmen exerted in Monroe. Conspicuous Klan barbecues held at prominent county crossroads became regular occurrences. So, too, did Klan caravans around town. During one of them, Klansmen fired shots into a black-owned business. A dozen robed and hooded Klansmen marched into revival meetings at rural churches. The Klan held a public screening of the film *Birth of a Nation* at the county coliseum. This was a common Klan recruitment tactic; an advertisement for the event carried the headline "Attention All White People." The Klan held a district meeting at the coliseum a few months later, which they capped off with a parade around the courthouse square. Robed and hooded Klansmen stationed at each corner of the square directed traffic. Klansmen burned a cross in front of the Hi-Ho, a local restaurant, where a group of liquefied petroleum dealers had had a luncheon training meeting for employees, a few of whom were black. They even put up a sign on the south end of town welcoming motorists to Monroeville. At the bottom was the name of the sponsoring agency, "Realm National Alabama U.S. Klans, KKKK Inc., Monroe County Klaverns 46-202."

This kind of thing was not supposed to be happening in Monroeville, not with the respectable members of the Citizens' Council organizing the white community. But in truth what constituted respectable resistance in Alabama in the late 1950s was hard to say. The decent white folks in the state had become like the proverbial boiling frog. As the Klan raised the temperature of white resistance, they lost sense of just how hot the water had become.

Consider the editorial page of the *Monroe Journal*. The anti-Klan editorials were written and signed by the paper's publisher, Bill Stewart, but regular editorials were written by Riley Kelly, a childhood friend of Nelle Harper's, who in these years was a full-throated reactionary. Kelly and Harper Lee were the same age, and they shared literary ambitions (Kelly was an aspiring poet). On Harper Lee's trips home from New York, she and Kelly would visit on the side porch of the Lee home, Kelly filling Lee in on Monroeville scuttlebutt and Lee telling Kelly stories about her novel and the New York editors with whom she worked. "They couldn't believe the stories and situations in the book were really the way things were—and are—down here," Kelly recalled years later. "She would have them call Alice or A. C. to verify that something she wrote could have happened that way down here."

In their stridency and anger, some of Kelly's editorials would have fit comfortably in any Klan publication in the state. He praised Orval Faubus for standing up to "the Hitlerite appearance of federal soldiers and bayonets in public schools." The lynching of Mack Charles Parker in Mississippi in 1959 Kelly blamed, remarkably, on an activist federal bench. "The Southern people have begun to lose their respect for their federal courts and the widespread compulsion is to lose respect for law and order," he wrote. "Much of the mob action can be blamed directly on the U.S. Supreme Court." He even reprinted a scurrilous editorial from the far-right newspaper *Montgomery Home News*, a suspected Klan organ, that urged the "do gooders" pushing civil rights to seek reforms in "the bushes of Darkest Africa" with "their buck dances, their rock and roll jungle rhythm and the good old fashioned native pastime of trading 'mates' and carving up on each other."

Never in his nearly eighteen years publishing the *Journal* had A. C. Lee run anything like the repugnant *Home News* piece. It's impossible to say for certain how much Nelle herself registered the hardening of racist sentiment in late 1950s Alabama. She had felt alienated from home folks on racial issues for several years. In a letter she wrote from Monroeville to her New York friend Hal Caufield in 1956, she reported that the local Presbyterian minister wanted to date her, and that she just wasn't up for it. "I don't trust myself to keep my mouth shut," she wrote. "It will get out all over Monroeville that I am a member of the NAACP, which God forbid."

The best evidence that she noticed the changes in the South was her fiction. In writing *Mockingbird*, she had no interest anymore in publishing a book full of righteous indignation in which Jean Louise tells off her racist, hypocritical father. By the late 1950s, she could never have published that kind of thing and then come back to Monroeville for Christmas, or summer vacation, or her father's funeral (given his health troubles, it was bound to happen soon enough), and expect her family and friends to just act like everything was normal, that nothing had changed. *Watchman*, had it been published then, would have been a slap in the face to all of them.

The trick for Harper Lee in writing this new childhood novel was how to speak about racism and hypocrisy in a way that she could be heard. And what would have been clear by the late 1950s was that the people who needed to hear her most urgently were not northerners, as she had imagined in *Watchman*, nor the Klan, whom she knew didn't read books anyway, nor Negroes, as she would have called them then, who it wouldn't have occurred to her might be an audience for her stories. The people who needed to hear her most were her own tribe, the otherwise decent white folks like Riley Kelly, or the Presbyterian minister, the people who were boiling in the waters of militant resistance and had no clue that their time was almost up.

WHATEVER ELSE CAN be said about Atticus Finch, he's a good father. That is clear in *Watchman,* but in *Mockingbird* it's the preeminent theme of the book. His unconventionality, the fact that his children call him by his first name, and that he reads to them not from children's books but from the Alabama legislative code or Palgrave's *Golden Treasury* only

Mary Badham as Scout with Gregory Peck. (Getty Images)

add to his charm. Atticus benefits, too, from the cultural tendency to turn single fathers into martyrs. Whereas single mothers tend to be viewed with suspicion, their single-parenting seen as the product of bad choices, it is often assumed that single fathers would rely on female caregivers, and therefore when they raise children by themselves they take on a role they've chosen, and it becomes a heroic choice. Atticus is the ideal parent in that he is both protector and nurturer. He is the expert shot who can kill the rabid dog, but also the loving bedside attendant who keeps watch over his injured son throughout the night.

Atticus's parenting, much more than his lawyering, is crucial to his politics. Atticus agrees to take Tom Robinson's case not out of a sense of duty to help legitimate Alabama courts in the eyes of powerful outside interests, which likely would have factored into the equation for A. C. Lee back in 1919 when he took the Ezell case; that was a familiar, self-serving calculus of the Jim Crow elite that Harper Lee evoked in *Watchman*. He does what he does in order to set an example for his children. He has to save them from the prejudice that infects so many folks in Maycomb. Atticus's preoccupation with the moral education of his children, more so even than his racial politics in *Mockingbird*, is the most anachronistic thing about him.

It's not that Americans in the 1930s didn't care what their kids learned, but in the 1950s they were obsessed with the question. One reason was that there were so many children around who needed to be educated. The baby boom was in full swing. Young families moved to new suburbs where they had few friends. Life was so much different from the world in which they had grown up. The one thing everyone had in common was kids. This reality was apparent in popular television shows of the era, a number of which revolved around the figure of the wise and loving father: *Father Knows Best, Leave It to Beaver, Ozzie and Harriet*. At least some parents in the early 1960s read *Mockingbird* as a kind of parenting guide, no doubt alongside that other publishing blockbuster of the era, Dr. Benjamin Spock's *The Common Sense Book of Baby and Child Care*. Such was the case with four suburban Chicago couples who gathered on a Saturday night in 1962 for a dinner party and a discussion of *Mockingbird*.

A *Chicago Tribune* reporter wrote about the gathering as a window onto young suburbanites. The couples lamented that their own children's lives were so structured and unadventurous; the suburbs afforded few vacant lots or haunted houses. Atticus, of course, was their role model. "We all agreed he's such a masculine image, a marvelous father," one mother recalled. "He stands for integrity, for justice regardless of race, religion, or anything. And the way his example molded the characters of that little girl and boy! It's great."

Concerns about the moral education of children played a central role in the racial politics of the era. The impact of segregation in shaping the character of black children worried parents and policymakers alike. The best example is the signature document of mid-twentieth-century racial liberalism, Earl Warren's 1954 unanimous opinion in *Brown v. Board of Education*. Perhaps the most quoted line from Warren's decision was his assessment of how *de jure* segregation generated in black children "a feeling of inferiority as to their status in the community that may affect their hearts and minds in a way unlikely ever to be undone." Among the evidence that Warren cited for this conclusion was a study by Kenneth B. Clark, the African American psychologist. Clark's findings were based on a series of tests in which black schoolchildren were presented with a white and a black doll and asked a series of questions—which did they like best, which would they like to play with, which was "nice." The frequency with which the black children chose the white doll Clark took as evidence of how black children had internalized the racial hierarchy of the larger society. The notion of the psychologically threatened black child appeared again and again in these years, notably in another iconic document of the era, Martin Luther King Jr.'s "Letter from Birmingham Jail." King evoked the image of a young girl learning that the local amusement park was closed to black children, and the agony of her parent witnessing the "ominous clouds of inferiority beginning to form in her little mental sky," and how the girl began "to distort her personality by developing an unconscious bitterness toward white people."

Black children were endangered by segregation, the thinking went, but so, too, were white southern children. One person who had written much on the subject, and whom Harper Lee very likely read and was influenced by, was Lillian Smith. As a student journalist at Alabama, Harper Lee had written a book review that lumped Smith in with William Faulkner and Harriet Beecher Stowe as writers who had "embarrassed" the South. No doubt she had in mind Smith's controversial 1944 novel *Strange Fruit,* which depicted an interracial love affair in small town Georgia. Smith's most celebrated work, however, *Killers of the Dream* (1949), would seem to have informed some of Harper Lee's later writing. That book opens with the image of anxious children in a crumbling society. "Even its children knew that the South was in trouble," Smith wrote. "No one had to tell them; no words said aloud. To them, it was a vague thing weaving in and out of their play, like a ghost haunting an old graveyard or whispers after the household sleeps." Smith came from a prosperous family in north Florida that fell on hard times and moved to their summer home in the north Georgia mountains. There they started a summer camp for girls that Smith herself eventually took over. One of the most powerful passages in *Killers of the Dream* involves an idealized conversation that Smith has with a high school camper who, after seeing a fable-like play put on by the younger campers, is suddenly awakened to the immorality and hypocrisy of her family and the South writ large.

The conversation bears some resemblance to the one that only a few years later Harper Lee would write between Jean Louise and Atticus in *Go Set a Watchman.* Both books depict a sheltered young southern white woman, the daughter of a loving, respectable father. Smith's camper had "never seen Daddy do an unkind thing in all my life." For Jean Louise, Atticus was "the only man she had ever known to whom she could point and say with expert knowledge, 'He is a gentleman, in his heart he is a gentleman.'" Both Jean Louise and Smith's young camper lash out at the adults in their life—for Jean Louise it is Atticus; for the camper it is Smith herself—who had taught them to love virtues that they could never live by in the segregated South. "I think you have done a terrible thing to children," the camper tells Smith. "[Y]ou have made us want to be good. . . . You made us think of ourselves as no better than other people. . . . You've unfitted us for the South. And yet, this is where we shall

live. Unless we run away." Near the end of *Watchman,* as all of Jean Louise's anger at Atticus comes rushing forth, she fumes, "I'll never forgive
you for what you did to me. You cheated me, you've driven me out of my
home and now I'm in a no-man's-land but good—there's no place for me
any more in Maycomb, and I'll never be entirely at home anywhere else."

In *Mockingbird,* however, Harper Lee abandons her earlier condemnation of the segregated South's respectable white fathers while maintaining her evocation of children as the conscience of the white South. The
unconventional Dolphus Raymond confides in the children because they
haven't yet been hardened by the prejudices of the town. Atticus laments
that it is only the children who weep at the unjust fate of Tom Robinson.
Atticus, in schooling his children in the injustices of Maycomb, does not
ruin them for their future lives as Jim Crow white southerners. Rather he
models for them how one could be *in* Maycomb without being *of* it. Here
Harper Lee dramatizes what the moral education of white children in the
segregated South might look like. They could learn to be tolerant and em-
pathetic without having to stop being southerners. It was surely one reason
that the novel was so popular among white southern audiences, despite its
controversial racial theme.

The politics of Atticus's parenting are seen most clearly in the light
of the ongoing crisis of the *Brown* decision. In *Watchman,* Harper Lee's
take on *Brown* was essentially a vindication of segregationist defiance.
Atticus patronizingly walks Jean Louise through the critique of the court's
legal reasoning, at the end of which she can muster only a lame, emotional
response, further evidence of her "feminine reasoning." "I'm trying to say
that I don't approve of the way they did it," Jean Louise says of the court,
"that it scares me to death when I think about the way they did it, but
they had to do it. It was put under their noses and they had to do it." But
she's never able to convince Atticus of this, and, by the end of the novel,
it's Jean Louise who has come to see the logic of Atticus's position, not the
other way around.

In *Mockingbird,* because the action takes place in the 1930s, Lee
can evoke only indirectly the crisis of *Brown.* She does so through Atticus's parenting. His concern about the moral education of his children

expresses the anxiety at the heart of *Brown*. If the South was going to become an integrated, democratic society, it would have to begin with the rising generation.

Harper Lee captured the spirit of the *Brown* era in the scene that she conjured in front of the Maycomb County jail. Atticus goes there to head off the lynch mob. Yet it is not Atticus who saves Tom, but Scout. Her innocent, unknowing exchange with Mr. Cunningham stops the man in his tracks. Atticus makes sense of it for them all over breakfast the next morning. "So it took an eight-year-old child to bring 'em to their senses, didn't it?" he says. "That proves something—that a gang of wild animals can be stopped, simply because they're human. Hmp, maybe we need a police force of children. . . . you children last night made Walter Cunningham stand in my shoes for a minute. That was enough."

The scene of a child stopping a lynch mob in the 1930s South was, by any historical standard, an absurdity. It mocked the gruesome record of southern lynch mobs that had occurred in Harper Lee's own lifetime, like the Claude Neal lynching that had taken place in her father's home county when she was nine years old, where it was reported that among the mob that gathered were children who stabbed Neal's corpse with sharpened sticks. The discrepancy between the historical record and Harper Lee's neat resolution of the scene was perhaps one of the aspects of the novel that led Flannery O'Connor to dismiss *Mockingbird* as "a child's book." Harper Lee herself would observe to a friend late in her life that she was glad that the Young Adult category did not exist at the time that *Mockingbird* appeared, because it probably would have been categorized as such and might have lost the adult audience that it enjoyed.

Scout turning back the lynch mob reflected the politics of the late 1950s, not the realities of the 1930s. Yet as Harper Lee wrote her novel, no one knew how *Brown* would be resolved in the South. Segregation had existed in southern public schools for as long as there had been southern public schools. In the years since the court's ruling, the only things that had changed in Alabama were the volume and the virulence of organized militant resistance. "Atticus, the time has come when we've got to do right," Jean Louise pleads with her father in *Watchman*. Yet how would it happen? How would the law be upheld in southern public schools? How could the South do right?

And a little child shall lead them. . . . It was as though the prophecy of Isaiah, the wolf dwelling with the lamb, the leopard lying down with the goat, had been summoned in the dramatic confrontations outside southern schoolhouses in the late 1950s as black schoolchildren faced down white mobs. The first incident was in Clinton, Tennessee, where in the fall of 1956 twelve black students desegregated the public school. The governor eventually had to call out National Guard troops for two months to protect the students from riotous white protestors. Harper Lee tracked these events, we know, because in *Watchman* Hank assures Jean Louise that the Maycomb Citizens' Council is not like the one in Tennessee (the Citizens' Council in Clinton had led the protests that had turned violent).

She surely followed the travails of the nine black students in Little Rock, which transfixed the nation in September 1957, the month before she signed her contract with Lippincott. Photographs from Little Rock captured one of the protestors, Elizabeth Eckford, walking alone, her eyes downcast, her notebook clutched in her left hand, surrounded by whites. The mob's rage is distilled in the snarling face of Hazel Bryan, the white girl who marches close behind Eckford, hounding her, yelling God-knows-what. Who taught Hazel Bryan to hate like that? No one had been there to save her, as Atticus saves Jem and Scout, from "catching Maycomb's usual disease," from the hysteria that made "reasonable people go stark raving mad when anything involving a Negro comes up."

IN EARLY NOVEMBER 1959, Harper Lee delivered to Annie Laurie Williams the final, revised version of *Mockingbird*. Soon afterward, Truman Capote contacted her about accompanying him on a research trip. He had come across a brief news item about a mysterious murder in rural Kansas. The Clutter family, the father Herbert, his wife, Bonnie, and two of their children, Nancy, sixteen, and Kenyon, fifteen, had been found murdered in their home outside the small farming community of Holcombe. Capote thought that the story of a small town upended by inexplicable violence could make for an appealing piece of writing. "He said it would be a tremendously involved job and would take two people," Nelle recalled later. "The crime intrigued him, and I'm intrigued with crime—and, boy, I wanted to go. It was deep calling to deep." In mid-December, the two of them boarded a train for Kansas.

Thus Nelle was not at home to experience firsthand the events that upended Monroeville that Christmas, and that would summon a bit of the decency in her hometown that she had been trying to imagine in her fiction. The annual Christmas parade had been organized as usual by members of the Kiwanis and Civitan clubs. As they had done for the last seven or eight years, civic leaders had invited the band from Union High School, the local black public school, to march. This meant, of course, that the Monroeville Christmas parade had been racially integrated. Nobody had thought too hard about it—until the Klan did. They paid a visit to the organizers and tried to pressure them into disinviting the Union High band. When the organizers refused, the Klan went directly to the school's principal. Faced with the prospect of Klansmen assaulting his students on the Monroeville square, he promptly pulled his school's band out of the event.

Over the past several years white leaders in Monroeville had sat on their hands as the Klan had paraded through black neighborhoods and intimidated white organizations that had included blacks at their meetings. But the idea that the Klan would try to push the town's leaders around over something as innocent as a Christmas parade was galling to many people. On December 17, the *Monroe Journal* ran a front-page editorial denouncing the "race hate mongers." It reflected the racial paternalism that continued to characterize Monroeville's white elite. "The Negroes can't fight back," the *Journal* noted, "but this newspaper can." It challenged the Klan to "pick on somebody your size." Yet it also revealed the consensus that had emerged among Monroe County's town folk. Civic leaders decided that if the black school's band couldn't march, then no one would. They canceled the parade, and began a public relations campaign against the Klan in the pages of the *Journal.*

The Kiwanis and Civitan clubs published a full-page statement explaining their decision, signed by the membership of both organizations.

They thanked their fellow citizens for the outpouring of letters, commendation, and good wishes that they had received since the cancellation. Dozens of Monroe citizens wrote letters supporting the decision. The *Journal* published photographs of some of the scrawled, misspelled, scurrilous hate mail it had received in response to its editorial, mocking the letter writers for not having the courage to sign their names. Civic leaders hoped to "arouse the indignation of the citizens of the county . . . and properly impress upon them that we should not tolerate the actions of the Ku Klux Klan . . . in seeking to create racial discord." The statement, published on Christmas Eve, closed with a prayer that Monroe County might stand "as a Christian bulwark for all the world," recalling the words of the apostle Paul to the Galatians: "For as many of you as have been baptized in Christ have put on Christ. There is neither Jew nor Greek, there is neither bond nor free, there is neither male nor female; for ye all are one in Christ." Years later A. B. Blass Jr., president of the Kiwanis Club, would remember seeing A. C. Lee, a longtime club member, after the cancellation had been announced. A. C. put his hand on Blass's shoulder and said, "You did right, son."

According to the *Monroe Journal,* the Christmas parade was the tipping point that roused decent white folks to stand up and assert their proper leadership role. The moral of the parade incident was very much like the moral of *Watchman.* When the time came for it, the decent white folks stood up. "Good grief, baby, people don't agree with the Klan, but they certainly don't try to prevent them from puttin' on sheets and making fools of themselves in public," Uncle Jack explains to Jean Louise at the end of the novel. "[T]he Klan can parade all it wants," he says, "but when it starts bombing and beating people, don't you know who'd be the first to try and stop it?"

Yet Uncle Jack's rationalizations in *Watchman* didn't quite square, and neither did the triumphalism of Monroeville's civic clubs. A line from their open letter was revealing. "Let us resolve as sensible, law abiding citizens, to make our views on this clear to everyone . . . public officials and private citizens alike." Public officials in Monroe County weren't necessarily on the same page as civic leaders. If they had been, then civic groups wouldn't have canceled the parade; they would have held it as planned, with the Union High band included. Yet civic leaders knew that throughout Monroe County the Klan had many sympathizers, as suggested in a letter to the *Journal* that complained of how "some officials high in our county government have joined hands with some of the mental giants in the KKK." Even beyond Monroe County, the Alabama Klan had support at the highest levels of state government, including in the governor's mansion. Governor Patterson had appointed one of Monroe County's best-known Klansmen as one of the county's three jury commissioners. Another of the governor's appointees in the county was widely suspected of being a Klansman.

Letters and comments in the *Journal* implied that the Christmas parade controversy ended the Klan's influence in Monroe County, but that wasn't true. In fact, if anything, it was the Klan that could have claimed victory. For some seven or eight years, white folks in Monroe County had been mindlessly consenting to racial integration in the annual Christmas parade, and now the Klan had put an end to the whole thing. One of the letters that the *Journal* reprinted boasted that the parade cancellation had boosted applications for membership by "1,000 percent." The group held public rallies in Monroeville in January and March 1960. In the latter case, several hundred Klansmen paraded around the Monroeville square in cars decked in Confederate flags. Regardless of what the *Monroe Journal* said, militant segregationists were alive and well in Monroe County. And throughout much of Alabama they were still in control.

Yet the best decision that Harper Lee ever made as a writer was to put all that aside. She stopped trying to use her fiction to gauge the political winds in Alabama. Instead, in *Mockingbird* she crafted a fable about racial violence, the white mob, and the visceral, deep-seated fears that underlie both, fears that seem to close people off from any understanding of those different from them, and, yet, when confronted in the light of day, are as frivolous as a child's fear of the bogeyman in the haunted house next door. In the process, she wrote one of the most popular and enduring novels in American literary history.

No one could have seen it coming, least of all the Lee family. They were just thrilled that Nelle Harper had finally finished her book. A. C. Lee received a copy in the mail and sat down to read it. It took him three days. After the first day, he sent his daughter a note: "I am reading it. I think it is very good." After the second, "I have not yet finished it. I don't read as fast as I used to." After the third, "You'll have to go some to beat this on your next one." Of course, there wouldn't be a next one, but no one could have guessed that at the time either. A. C. was surprised when folks around town started greeting him as Atticus. He hadn't recognized himself in the book at all. His main concern had been the news that Ernestine's Gift Shop, Monroeville's lone bookstore, had organized a book signing for Nelle Harper, and, in anticipation of the big event, had bought one hundred copies. He assured the owner that he would buy whatever books were leftover.

PART III

ATTICUS IN THE WORLD

Chapter 5

The Noble Man

The consensus among the Hollywood types was that Harper Lee's book wasn't really movie material. Before publication, when movie rights were typically sold, none of them paid much attention to her quiet little novel. It was understandable given industry convention. The book had little dramatic or violent action, no love interest, no female lead. The plot was carried largely by children, who were difficult to cast and rarely came with star power. And then there were the racial politics. At the heart of the novel was an interracial rape trial in a southern courtroom. How could filmmakers dramatize the scene without alienating southern theatergoers? Boycotts, pickets, letter-writing campaigns could surely ensue.

Only when *Mockingbird* started showing up on best-seller lists in the late summer and fall of 1960 did Annie Laurie Williams begin to receive some tentative inquiries. One proposal pitched the idea of filming the movie on location in the South with an unknown cast. Explaining his cautious strategy, the producer James P. Yarbrough noted *Mockingbird*'s similarity to *The Member of the Wedding*, the Carson McCullers novel, which had bombed at the box office. Also of concern for Yarbrough was "the ever-present Southern problem." Williams politely declined the offer and suggested that Yarbrough consider finding a well-known star to play Atticus.

Williams herself had already begun a search. If she could get a leading man interested in playing Atticus, then the rest would fall into place. In August she sent a copy of the book to Spencer Tracy's agent, along with a handwritten note from Harper Lee to the movie star. "Frankly, I can't see anybody but Spencer Tracy in the part of Atticus," Lee wrote. Tracy, however, was in the middle of filming *The Devil at Four O'Clock*. His agent reported that he could read nothing until filming was over, so Lee would have to wait. Other names tossed among Lee's inner circle included Gary Cooper and John Huston.

Eventually, however, a young producer-director team came along with an offer and Williams took it. The thirty-three-year-old producer, Alan Pakula, had grown up in the Bronx, the son of a successful printer of Polish Jewish ancestry. A Yale graduate with a drama degree, he had gone immediately to Los Angeles after graduation and landed a job reading scripts and working as an assistant producer. He teamed with the thirty-six-year-old director Robert Mulligan, a fellow Bronx native from an Irish Catholic family. As a young man Mulligan had briefly studied for the priesthood, but he found his vocation in the 1950s in the burgeoning field of television, and he went on to direct a number of successful live dramas. Pakula and Mulligan had made one film together, *Fear Strikes Out* (1957), based on a memoir by the major league baseball player Jimmy Piersall. Pakula, who had considered studying psychiatry before turning to film, was drawn to the story of Piersall's difficult relationship with an overbearing, psychologically abusive father.

Once the filmmakers had the rights to *Mockingbird*, they needed three things—a script, a star, and money. The script they would get from Horton Foote, a successful playwright and television writer. The star was the key to getting the money; no studio would bankroll a movie without a big-name actor to fill theater seats. Bing Crosby's agent got in touch with Annie Laurie Williams to make a late bid for the role. Maurice Crain quipped that Crosby "should be made to promise not to reverse his collar, not to mumble a single Latin prayer, not to burble a single note."

Pakula and Mulligan settled on Gregory Peck, who in 1961 was among the small handful of Hollywood's iconic leading men. Each of them had a distinctive quality. Cary Grant was effortlessly charming; Marlon Brando was dark and brooding; Rock Hudson was the quintessential hunk. Peck's calling card was his decency. In his most memorable performances he was the embodiment of earnest integrity: a missionary priest in *Keys of the Kingdom;* a loving, understanding father in *The Yearling;* or a crusading reporter exposing anti-Semitism among the patricians in *Gentleman's Agreement.* He had been nominated for best actor for each of these roles, as well as for his portrayal of a demanding Air Force officer in *Twelve O'Clock High,* but he had never taken home the Oscar.

Pakula sent Peck a copy of Lee's novel, which he read in one sitting, staying up late into the night to finish it. He called Pakula first thing the next morning to tell him he wanted to do it. Peck would later recall for reporters how aspects of the novel reminded him of his own childhood growing up in La Jolla, California: the houses with no numbers; children going barefoot all summer long; the odd characters who everyone knew. He even remembered how the Ku Klux Klan once burned a cross on a hill behind the town.

Peck liked the story so much that he decided to put his own money behind it. With Peck's production company committed, Universal Pictures agreed to handle distribution. Peck included an unusual provision in his contract with the studio, requiring that Pakula and Mulligan be given control over the final cut. He wanted the most important artistic choices in the hands of the filmmakers themselves, not the studio executives distributing it, whose interests would naturally run to the commercial. But given the relative inexperience of Pakula and Mulligan, and the influence that Peck, the film's major star and primary financier, had over them, it also meant that Peck himself would have significant say in the film's final shape. This would prove important late in the process as Peck pushed for recuts that emphasized a more heroic vision of Atticus than Horton Foote, or Harper Lee, initially imagined. Over time, it would be Peck's version of Atticus that predominated in popular culture, one that differed from the character in the novel in subtle but significant ways.

TWO EVENTS IN May 1961 raised the profile of the project considerably. The first was when *Mockingbird* won the Pulitzer Prize. Harper Lee heard the news on a dreary Monday morning in Maurice Crain's office. She was in low spirits for no particular reason when Crain's phone rang. "What have you got to be worried about?" he told her, putting down the receiver; "you've just won the Pulitzer prize." Lee immediately called Monroeville, and A. C. picked up. "Dad, I got the Pulitzer Prize," she told him. He already knew. Riley Kelly had read it on the AP wire and had driven straight over to tell him. The press and publicity events that Harper Lee had done up to this point had been nothing next to what she would be asked to do as a Pulitzer Prize winner. When the prize was announced, her picture ran in the New York papers, and for the first time ever she was stopped on the street in Manhattan and asked for an autograph. When she went to the bank to cash a check, they didn't ask for identification. Yet the publicity for the Pulitzer would pale in comparison to the circus surrounding the movie. Harper Lee was becoming a celebrity, and she wouldn't like it one bit.

The second important event that month could be connected to Harper Lee's novel only in retrospect. On May 4, a group of thirteen civil rights activists, seven black and six white, led by James Farmer, the forty-one-year-old director of the Congress of Racial Equality, boarded buses in Washington, DC, bound for New Orleans. The trip, dubbed "Freedom Ride 1961," was designed to challenge southern laws segregating interstate travel, which the Supreme Court had outlawed the previous year. The group made it through Virginia and North Carolina with little incident. In South Carolina, the future US congressman John Lewis was attacked in Rock Hill, but they passed through Georgia peacefully. In Atlanta, Martin Luther King Jr. met the riders for dinner, building up their spirits, shaking hands with each one. His organization had received rumors of a violent plot in the works, which he passed on to trip organizers. To a journalist traveling with the group, King predicted privately, "You will never make it through Alabama."

He was only half right. In Anniston, Klansmen attacked a group of riders at the Greyhound bus station. The mob followed the bus out of town, forced it to the side of the road, and firebombed it. The riders only barely escaped with their lives. Meanwhile, another group of riders made it to Birmingham on a Trailways bus only to be greeted by a mob of Klansmen armed with lead pipes and brass knuckles. In an agreement between Klan leaders and Birmingham police commissioner Bull Connor, a deal to which the FBI was privy but did nothing to stop, local police gave the Klan fifteen minutes to assault the riders. A melee ensued, sweeping up Freedom Riders, reporters, and innocent bystanders alike. With no drivers willing to take them to their next stop, Montgomery, and reports of another mob lying in wait there, the Freedom Riders opted to take a flight directly to New Orleans.

Reinforcements flocked to Birmingham to finish the ride. Greyhound agreed to provide a bus and driver only after intense lobbying from the Kennedy administration. When the new group of riders arrived in Montgomery, another white mob was given free rein by local police. Among those beaten and left unconscious was Justice Department official John Seigenthaler, who had been dispatched to negotiate with Alabama governor John Patterson ("There's nobody in the whole country," Patterson told Seigenthaler in their first meeting, "that's got the spine to stand up to the goddamned niggers except me"). The next night, at a gathering to honor the Freedom Riders at First Baptist Church, some three thousand rioters surrounded the building, held back by a contingent of only several hundred US marshals. Inside the church, Martin Luther King provided updates on the mob's activities to Attorney General Bobby Kennedy via telephone. As the situation worsened, Kennedy prepared to send in federal troops, which prompted Governor Patterson to finally take action. He declared martial law, and called up the National Guard.

A Gallup poll taken the following month showed that 63 percent of Americans disapproved of the Freedom Rides. Harper Lee was part of that majority. "I don't think much of this business of getting on buses and flaunting [sic] state laws does much of anything. Except getting a lot of publicity and violence," Lee told a reporter in March 1963. She contrasted the Freedom Riders with Martin Luther King and the NAACP, who were "going about it exactly the right way. The people in the South may not like it but they respect it."

Lee was wrong about the impact of the Freedom Rides. More than anything up to that point in the civil rights struggle, they made plain the crisis in the Deep South, crystallizing for the nation and the world that there were Americans who were willing to die for the cause of civil rights, and that there were other Americans who were willing to kill them. In between the two groups was an abyss of resentment and misunderstanding. There wasn't a single political leader in the state of Alabama who was willing or capable of bridging the divide.

The Freedom Rides brought an unprecedented amount of negative attention to Alabama. As a consequence, a number of business and political leaders in the state finally began to take a hard look at the militant segregationist movement, and the degree to which it had dictated politics in the state. The chairman of the Birmingham Chamber of Commerce, for example, Sid Smyer, first learned of the violence in his city when he saw a picture of Klansmen assaulting a Freedom Rider on the front page of the newspapers in Tokyo, where he had gone for a convention of the International Rotary Club. When he returned home, he created a "study group" composed of some of the city's most powerful figures to examine Birmingham's racial problems. It was the first time since the outbreak of militant resistance that local leaders in the Deep South's largest, most intractable city took some form of progressive action. The effort culminated two years later in the ousting of Bull Connor, the kingpin of Birmingham's militant segregationists. A similar story played out in Montgomery. Mob violence against the Freedom Riders in that city marked a turning point. Extremists who had dominated public discourse in Montgomery since the bus boycott finally began to get some pushback from other white leaders.

None of this amounted to any magic resolution of Alabama's racial crisis. So much hatred and violence were still to come. But the extremists who had dominated the state's politics since the Autherine Lucy crisis in 1956 would increasingly be denied what one historian has called "their essential comforting myth, that they spoke for an undivided white community."

But if you had gone looking for quiet dissenters in the summer of 1961, it would have been almost impossible to find them. Sid Smyer and his study group were deep undercover. They weren't about to invite the calumny of the Klan and Bull Connor. The same was true in every city and town across the state. People who publicly identified as moderates were rare birds indeed. Perhaps the best place to spot one, and thereby gain some glimmer of hope that there might be a solution to the South's racial crisis short of outright military occupation, was not in any newspaper; it was in the pages of Harper Lee's novel.

Countless people did just that. By August 1961, the book had sold two and a half million copies. By May 1962 it had been on the *New York Times* best-seller list for ninety-two consecutive weeks, with three million copies sold in hardback, and one million paperbacks sold the first week they were offered. A reviewer described it as "a comparative oddity among contemporary fiction works—one you can enjoy tremendously yet need not apologize for if your maiden aunt (we assume she comes from Dubuque, like most maiden aunts) happens to leaf thru it." A sign of the novel's phenomenal, cross-cultural popularity was that it could be enjoyed by not only the executive secretary of the Chicago District Golf Association, Carol McCue, who was so taken by the book that she gave up her weekend on the links just to finish it (reportedly a "feat only one step this side of miraculous"), but also Roy Wilkins, executive secretary of the NAACP. Wilkins paid a visit to James Farmer in jail in Mississippi, after the Freedom Rider was arrested in Jackson. Nearly two decades later, in an oral history interview for the John F. Kennedy Presidential Library, Farmer would talk about how his former mentor brought him two books as gifts to help pass the time. One of the titles he couldn't recall, but the other, he distinctly remembered, was *To Kill a Mockingbird*.

EVERY ADAPTATION OF a novel into a film is a creative act that involves myriad choices that can alter the ideas and emphasis of the original work. Screenwriters must reduce the complex, detailed events that novelists develop over hundreds of pages into the conventional running time of a major motion picture, ideally no more than two hours (*Mockingbird* is two hours and ten minutes). The major action has to be compressed. Important characters have to be left out. Subplots are condensed or eliminated.

For a brief time, Harper Lee considered doing the work herself. Maurice Crain wrote to her in late January 1961 with a "brainstorm" about how the screen story might go. His suggestions reveal how he thought about the potential political message for the movie. Crain recommended establishing Tom Robinson in the film early on, to "fatten up the part a little, so that the audience reaction would be a little stronger when he is tried." He imagined a scene in which the children see Tom helping Zeebo, Calpurnia's son, collect garbage. Tom and the children exchange playful birdcalls. Crain, who himself had deep southern roots—his grandfather had been a field officer in Lee's Army of Virginia—also suggested that in the lynch mob scene in front of the jail, not only should the newspaper editor let Atticus know that he had had him covered the whole time, but Crain had Link Deas walking out of the alley, shotgun in hand, announcing his presence as well. Atticus would call up to the jail window: "Tom, it seems you've got more friends around here than you know about." Crain thought the addition of Link to the scene would "stand for the southerners whose hearts are in the right place, but who rarely speak out."

Crain had not put this idea on the page, however, before giving up on it. He realized that it would have been exactly the kind of didacticism that the filmmakers hoped to avoid. Harper Lee had already tried to write a novel that spoke directly to the southern racial crisis, and it hadn't even found a publisher, let alone a movie studio eager to produce it. Pakula and Mulligan wouldn't have known about that, but they knew that what made *Mockingbird* so compelling was that it could inform the current political moment without preaching. "The big danger in making a movie of *To Kill a Mockingbird* is in thinking of this as a chance to jump on the segregation-integration soap box," Mulligan told a reporter. "The book does not make speeches. It is not melodramatic with race riots and race hatred. It deals with bigotry, lack of understanding and rigid social patterns of a small Southern town."

When Harper Lee dispensed with the idea of writing the screenplay herself, Pakula moved quickly. In early February 1961 he had contacted Horton Foote to see if he would do it if Lee opted out. Foote would go on to become one of the most distinguished American dramatists of his generation. Like Lee, he was a product of the small town South. His work often dealt with quiet family dramas in southern locales. One of his early successes, *The Trip to Bountiful* (1953), is the story of an elderly woman living with her son and daughter-in-law in a cramped apartment in Houston who is determined to take a trip to her hometown. His adaptation for television of two William Faulkner stories, "Old Man" and "Tomorrow," so impressed Faulkner that he agreed to split the publication royalties with Foote.

Foote and Pakula worked together closely on the script. Pakula would drive up from New York each day to the rambling white Victorian home in the Hudson Valley where Foote lived with his wife and four children. Pakula thought the screenplay should condense the action in the novel, which takes place over three years, into one, and Foote readily agreed. When the two had a version of the script that they were happy with, they flew to Hollywood to discuss it with Mulligan. He felt that their adaptation too often lost "the point of view of the children." Foote and Pakula agreed, and undertook another revision. "[T]he spine of the story should be the awakening of the children to their father as a man and to his values," Pakula wrote in notes from the meeting, "and the year in which we see the development of their inheritance from him."

Maintaining the children's perspective throughout the film would not be easy. The movie never would have been made, at least not in the way and on the scale that it was, if Atticus remained as he was in the book, a supporting figure to the children's experience. From the very beginning of Annie Laurie Williams's campaign to sell the film rights, the pitch was that a leading man could play Atticus, and with a leading man in place, a studio deal could be had. Shortly after Gregory Peck was signed, a rumor started that Peck wanted to change the title to "Atticus." Pakula batted it down as quickly as he could.

Whatever truth there was to the rumor, with Peck in place, and with considerable financial resources committed to the film, it was all but inevitable that it would become a vehicle for a heroic Atticus. Inevitable, too, was that Atticus would be shaped into the image of Gregory Peck. The actor saw much of himself in the character. "I felt I could climb into Atticus's shoes without any play-acting," he would say of the role, "that I could *be* him." A father of five children, Peck was roughly the same age as the character. Atticus was a deep reader, a student of history, and a sharp observer of politics, as was Peck himself, who, like A. C. Lee, loved history and biography, particularly books on Abraham Lincoln and the Civil War. Peck's personal library would eventually include over a thousand books on those two topics alone.

Peck was also one of Hollywood's leading liberals. He took the part because he believed that Atticus was a character who could speak to the current racial crisis. "I think it's the first time that the enlightened, liberal Southerner has been put on the screen," Peck said. "I think it's the point of view of the fair-minded Southerner that will provide the solution to this thing with the help of fair-minded Northerners and people of good will." Notes that Peck made on the script in preparation for shooting suggest his ambitions for the role. In the scene on the front porch where Atticus tells Scout not to fight at school, Peck wrote, "NO FIGHT—peasants fight—big principle in my life—tell audience—it's not the way to help the South! Atticus and his family won—fight on this point—Southern view—problem must be solved by decency—not violence." When reading Atticus's summation to the jury, he left another marginal note: "A fight for justice 30 years ago—a pioneer—Atticus was hidden in a backwater."

In the novel, more than seventy pages pass before the reader learns, as Scout does from the schoolyard bully Cecil Jacobs, that Atticus would defend Tom Robinson. Yet only fifteen minutes into the film we see Atticus accepting Judge Taylor's request to take the case. Foote dramatizes the scene, whereas in the book we learn only in passing that Judge Taylor assigned the case to Atticus. In the film, as Judge Taylor builds up to his request, he pauses, stumbles over his words—"I . . . er . . . was thinking"—aware of the burden he was placing upon this man already loaded down by his law practice and children who "need a great deal of [his] time." In Foote's screenplay, Atticus "reflects thoughtfully" before agreeing to take on Tom Robinson's defense. Peck's actual performance isn't so subtle. In fact, he hardly reflects at all. Atticus knows why the judge has come to see him, and he responds eagerly. "Atticus is a fighter," Peck wrote in his script notes on this scene, "be alive with the problem . . . energetic . . . Atticus is aroused."

Foote joins this scene with the one immediately preceding it, which, taken together, establish Atticus's internal, emotional struggle, professionally and personally. As Atticus puts Scout to bed she asks to see his watch and reads the inscription, "To Atticus, my beloved husband." Here Foote makes literal the matter of the children's inheritance. Jem will receive the watch, Scout her mother's pearl necklace and ring. There is not much else of material worth for him to pass on, Atticus says. The implication is that for the children of a noble man like Atticus Finch, their inheritance will not be measured by a material standard anyway. Atticus walks outside to sit on the porch swing. Through the open window he overhears his children quietly discussing their deceased mother. "How old was I when Mama died?" Scout asks Jem.

Foote invented other scenes that not only flesh out Atticus's character but also distill his heroism. Early in the film Atticus encounters Robert E. Lee "Bob" Ewell outside the courtroom. Ewell, assuming an easy familiarity with Atticus as a fellow white man, all but apologizes for not killing Tom Robinson himself. "That would have saved you and the sheriff and the taxpayers a lot of trouble," Foote has him say, evoking the white taxpayer, whom since Reconstruction southern states had used to justify white rule. Foote also reconfigures the episode in which Bob Ewell spits in Atticus's face. In the novel, the children learn from Miss Stephanie, the town gossip, that after the trial Ewell had confronted Atticus on the post office corner. It was the most public of places in a town without home mail delivery. Ewell had cursed Atticus, spat in his face, and threatened to kill him. Atticus "didn't bat an eye." He took out his handkerchief, wiped off the spittle, and later, to his family, got in one of his dry one-liners, "I wish Bob Ewell wouldn't chew tobacco."

In the film, however, the incident takes place outside Tom Robinson's home, and the audience views it along with Robinson's family and Jem. The script says only that "Ewell spits in Atticus's face. Atticus stares at him, wipes off his face, and starts to get into the car." In his interpretation of the scene, however, Peck elaborates on the interaction and heightens Atticus's physical bravery. After Ewell spits in his face, Atticus doesn't just stare at him. He moves in closer, not turning the other cheek so much as daring Ewell to do it again. Ewell backs away, and only then does Atticus pull out his handkerchief.

Poor Bob Ewell. It's a shortcoming of the film that the white cracker is practically the sole representative of white racism. The rest of Maycomb whites seem so neighborly and reasonable by comparison. The novel itself has been criticized for shortchanging the racism of southern whites, but the book is clearly different from the film on this score. In the novel, for example, Tom Robinson is killed by prison guards whose prejudice and capacity for racial violence are signaled by the seventeen bullet holes found in the dead man's body. "They didn't have to shoot him that much," Atticus observes. Tom's death evoked the brutality of mob violence that was all too common in the Jim Crow South. Yet in the film, Tom is killed by a single shot from a bumbling deputy who fires merely to wound Tom, but misses his aim.

Also, the film cuts out the subplot involving the Finches' elderly neighbor, Mrs. Dubose, which in the novel is important in establishing the depth and the pervasiveness of racism in the white community. Foote preserved it in his original draft of the screenplay. The scene comes after the one in which Atticus shoots the rabid dog. Mrs. Dubose sees the children heading downtown and yells at them, asking if they are proud of their father. When Jem answers yes, Mrs. Dubose smirks that no one else is proud of him. "Old, ugly, nearsighted thing," she says. "What's he done to be proud of except defend black trash that ought to be. . . ." Jem interrupts her, but Mrs. Dubose finishes her thought. "Watch out he's not shot down in the street one of these days, the way he shot that dog." In anger, Jem takes a stick and cuts off the tops of Mrs. Dubose's prized camellia bushes. As punishment, he has to read to Mrs. Dubose after school and on

Saturdays. The children learn from Atticus, only after Mrs. Dubose dies, that Jem's reading had helped her kick her morphine addiction, which the doctor had prescribed to her because of severe arthritis. She was determined to "leave this world beholden to nothing and nobody." Atticus was glad that his son got to see "what real courage is."

The storyline involving Mrs. Dubose serves an essential purpose in the novel by helping the reader imagine the bitter gossip and harsh words spoken against Atticus behind closed doors by members of Maycomb's established families. Mulligan filmed all of the scenes involving Mrs. Dubose that Foote adapted. It was said that Ruth White, an experienced New York stage actress, gave a stellar performance as Mrs. Dubose, and that the scenes with Phillip Alford, who played Jem, were among his strongest. But the scenes didn't survive the film's final cut. The filmmakers felt that they bogged down what by Hollywood standards was already a slow developing movie.

Film audiences would see Mrs. Dubose only as the cantankerous old lady next door who keeps a Confederate pistol under her shawl. She becomes merely the brief subject of Atticus's gallantry, as he compares her flower bed to the gardens at Bellingrath, and thereby models for the children a quintessential lesson of small town southern life—how to kill 'em with kindness. But without the other scenes with Mrs. Dubose, the film loses the sense that the hardened, racist opposition to Atticus comes not only from white trash like Bob Ewell, but also from the older generation of Monroeville's established families, those with a living memory of the Civil War and the alleged tragedies of Reconstruction. They, too, despise Atticus for taking on Tom Robinson's case.

Yet Atticus remains undeterred, and in a moral lesson essential to the novel, he explains to his children how Mrs. Dubose could still be a person of courage, deserving of admiration and respect, despite her prejudice. It is the closest Harper Lee comes in *Mockingbird* to one of *Watchman's* central preoccupations: defending proudly conservative segregationists from the facile condescension of the liberal North. In the film, it falls out entirely.

PAKULA AND MULLIGAN initially hoped to film in Monroeville, but one visit made clear that plan wouldn't work. The town was no longer the quaint, isolated village of Harper Lee's youth. Modern glass storefronts dotted the Monroeville square, and TV antennae sprouted on various homes and buildings. South Alabama Street, which fronted the old Lee family home, had fallen victim to commercial sprawl, and, of course, the Lee home itself was no longer there, torn down and replaced by Mel's Dairy Dream.

Peck also made the trek to Monroeville to soak up the atmosphere and meet the man who had inspired Harper Lee to create Atticus. Lee family members recalled the quiet, focused intensity of Peck as he spoke with A. C. Lee, studying closely his every mannerism. Amused and bemused in equal parts, A. C. politely abided all the Hollywood folks parading into his hometown, as they made careful studies of the curve of the courtroom bannister, or fussed over how he fiddled with his watch fob. Press accounts of the visit added another layer to the fast-developing mythology of Atticus. To reporters, Peck described A. C. Lee as "a fine old gentleman of eighty-two and truly sophisticated although he had never traveled farther than a few miles from that small Southern town." A. C. would have chuckled over this, if he ever read it. He wasn't *that* big of a rube. His legal and political work had taken him to principal cities throughout the country, including New York; Washington, DC; New Orleans; and Atlanta. But Peck and his fellow Hollywood types were on a mission to bring to the largest popular audience the image of the rural, southern-born sage, a man whose broad-minded probity resulted from nothing more than his own curiosity, conscience, and good sense. As to the particulars, who was A. C. Lee, or his daughter for that matter, to quibble?

The shoot took place in Los Angeles in the spring of 1962. *Mockingbird* shared the sprawling lot at Universal with two other productions, *The Ugly American* and *If a Man Answers*. Art directors Henry Bumstead and Alexander Golitzen created a Maycomb streetscape using clapboard cottages salvaged from Chavez Ravine that had been scheduled for demolition to make way for Dodger Stadium. Peck made an effort to spend lots of downtime with the child actors, Phillip Alford and Mary Badham, who played Scout, so that they would grow comfortable with him. He had both of them and their families over for a cookout before filming started, and played chess with Alford during breaks. Mulligan had the children rehearse scenes on set casually, and then would slowly, quietly have the cameras moved into position to start filming. Everything seemed to be going swimmingly, the only note of discord being when Pakula had to ask Alford and Badham not to fish in the pond on the back lot.

As the icon of the liberal white Alabaman was being crafted on a studio lot in California, back in Alabama, two men who a decade earlier represented the closest thing to pass for liberalism in state politics battled it out for governor. So much had changed in the intervening period. George Wallace, the second-place finisher four years earlier, had learned his lesson in his loss to John Patterson. He had discovered that, given the current state of affairs in Alabama and the country, white identity politics was the quickest way for him to get to 51 percent. That had never been the case when he was coming up in Alabama politics. Ever since the Depression helped get Franklin Roosevelt elected, it had been the Black Belt politicians, the handpicked mouthpieces of the Big Mules, who hit the race issue hardest, trying to stir up common folks to vote against the New Deal, which the Mules hated because it buttressed labor unions while increasing their taxes and the regulations on their businesses. But outside of the Black Belt it was hard to get a majority of the vote through racism alone. Most of the whites in these areas were desperately poor, and the New Deal had brought revolutionary changes to their lives. And besides, in north Alabama there weren't that many black folks around to get stirred up over. It was much better for a politician to talk about what government should be doing for the little guy.

Yet the importance of civil rights in national Democratic Party politics had been building for years. Wallace had stuck it out in 1948, refusing to bolt the convention in Philadelphia with the Dixiecrats. Yet northern Democrats in Congress continued to push race issues to win votes from southern blacks who had moved into their districts. And then the Supreme Court had changed everything. There looked to be no end to the agitation that black preachers were stirring up in places like Montgomery and

Birmingham. And as long as that was the case, there would be no end to the Citizens' Councils and the Klan.

"I started off talking about schools and highways and prisons and taxes—I couldn't make them listen," Wallace would explain years later. "Then I began talking about niggers—and they stomped the floor." Wallace made headlines in 1959 as a circuit judge when he refused to turn over Alabama voting records to the US Civil Rights Commission. Facing contempt charges from District Court Judge Frank Johnson, an old friend from his law school days, Wallace paid Johnson a midnight visit, explaining how he planned to run for governor again. He asked if Johnson could

George Wallace walking with supporters and his wife Lurleen in 1959, when he plotted his political comeback from his loss in the gubernatorial race the year before. (Getty Images)

give him ten days or so in jail. "That would help politically," he said, but "if you send me for any length of time, it'll kill my mother; my wife won't care." Johnson promised to "pop [him] hard" if he didn't hand over the records. Wallace persisted in his public defiance, all while quietly allowing two federal officials to review the records. Johnson scathingly denounced Wallace's shenanigans at the contempt hearing, dismissing the charges because Wallace had, in fact, complied. But Wallace denied it all afterward, explaining to a bank of television cameras how he "was willing to risk my freedom" to fight the "evil Civil Rights Commission."

It was the unofficial launch of his 1962 campaign, and a harbinger of the demaguery to come. Political observers noticed how much livelier and hard-hitting Wallace's speeches were compared to his performances four years earlier. Aides attributed the change in tone to Wallace's new speechwriter, Asa Carter, the Citizens' Councilor-turned-Klansman whose racist extremism Nelle Harper had tried to capture in the character of Grady O'Hanlon in *Watchman*. One of Wallace's best applause lines was his pledge to "stand in the schoolhouse door" in order to preserve segregation in Alabama schools.

Wallace's chief opponent was his former mentor, Jim Folsom, who was vying for a third term. Back in 1946, one of Folsom's campaign stops at the University of Alabama had contributed to the liberal atmosphere on campus that young Nelle had found so invigorating. His first term was taken up with progressive efforts on behalf of small farmers and working people. Reelected in 1954, he planned to do battle once again with the Black Belt–Big Mule coalition. Yet his racially moderate administration foundered on the shoals of massive resistance, charges of cronyism and corruption, and his own monumental drinking problem. At parties at the mansion, Folsom would quietly slip out only to have aides find him later under the trees on the front lawn, his massive frame spread-eagled on the grass, an empty bottle beside him. "That second term, he literally bombed himself to pieces with the bottle," a political ally recalled.

Despite his troubles, Folsom remained a formidable figure. His down-home rallies still drew large crowds throughout north Alabama, the campaign band serenading the crowd with the Bill Monroe tune that served as Folsom's unofficial theme song, "Y'all Come." The race turned on an incident that would go down in Alabama lore. The Folsom campaign had bought statewide television time to broadcast a tribute film the night before the primary election. Folsom himself only needed to make a brief live appearance introducing the program. But when the Folsom team showed up at the studio, they realized that the studio technicians did not have the actual film. Folsom, who had been drinking heavily all day, decided to go on live with his family and ad-lib. It was a disaster. Introducing his children, he seemed to forget their names. "Now, which one are you?" he asked one. A technician quickly put on a different film, which appeared upside down. The fallout was clear the next day. Folsom dropped to third place, narrowly missing the runoff election to the other racial moderate in the race, state representative Ryan DeGraffenried. Wallace defeated DeGraffenried to become the Democratic nominee, and, in the fall, easily won the general election.

It's doubtful that these dramatics were followed closely in the Lee home that spring. In April, just a few months after meeting Peck on his visit to Monroeville, A. C. Lee suffered a second heart attack. His first one had drawn Nelle home from New York, and initiated a pattern of her coming home more often, and for longer stretches. But this one he would not survive. He died early on the morning of Palm Sunday, April 15, 1962. He was laid to rest the next day in the Pineville cemetery, next to the Methodist church that he had helped build, and that he had served faithfully for so many years. The inspiration for Atticus Finch had passed, just as a new vision was being born.

THE FILMING COMPLETED, Robert Mulligan worked up a series of rough cuts of the film. Gregory Peck watched them and sent comments to his agent, and later, a studio executive. Peck wasn't happy, and neither were the studio executives, at what he called Mulligan's "anti-heroic concept." Atticus came off as "wishy-washy" and a "supporting character," Peck wrote. He felt that Mulligan was "bending over backwards to avoid having Atticus do anything heroic." Mulligan continued to recut the film in ways that reflected the preferences of Peck.

Another artistic difference pitted Horton Foote on one side and Peck, Pakula, and Mulligan on the other, and it, too, shaped the image of Atticus that appeared onscreen. It involved a revision of Atticus's summation to the jury that the three had asked Foote to write late in the filmmaking. In the original version that Foote had written, the summation followed closely the language in the book while also incorporating several of Atticus's comments to his children in other parts of the novel. What Pakula, Mulligan, and Peck objected to in Foote's version is unclear. Yet the revised language that Foote wrote dispensed with Atticus's contemptuous comments about a generalized "low-grade white man," and focused instead on two very specific low-grade white people, Bob and Mayella Ewell, and their "cynical confidence" that the jury would conspire in their "evil assumption" about Negroes. Foote wrote to Pakula and Mulligan that he had "worried considerably" over the revisions. He explained why in a letter that attempted to contextualize Atticus's summation historically.

> In studying the material I think it should perhaps be kept in mind that particularly at this period a Southerner like Atticus is not an unprejudiced man speaking to a group of prejudiced ones. He is surely a man that has had to fight the prejudice in himself, so in a measure one might say he is addressing the speech to a part of himself as well as to the jurors. In other words, he is not a "noble man" explaining the obvious facts to a group of ignorant, unenlightened dirt farmers, but a man who has shared their prejudices, struggled with them, and who is determined to be free of them at all costs. And, too, he knows the depth of the complexity of the prejudice that he is trying to get them to renounce in themselves.

Perhaps Foote was thinking of his own experience as a child growing up in the southeast Texas town of Wharton. His grandfather had held the young Foote in his arms, his grandmother, parents, aunts, and uncles standing beside them on the wide front gallery of their home on Richmond Road, watching the Klan march by, torches in hand, on the way to the Courthouse Square. Maybe he recalled the story of Henry Schulze, who lived with his senile mother in Wharton and was rumored to be sleeping

with the black woman he had hired to look after her. The Klan kidnapped
Schulze, whipped him, cut off his hair, tarred and feathered him, and then
dumped him naked on a corner in front of the courthouse. Schulze lived
as the town outcast the rest of his life, the Boo Radley of Wharton, and his
sad tale was told over and over, long after the Klan died off. In imagining
a man like Atticus fighting "the prejudice in himself," surely Foote had
in mind one particular event, which he related in his memoir. As a five-
year-old boy poking around in a kitchen cabinet while his mother fixed
supper, he stumbled upon a white robe, and, asking his mother what it
was, watched her, suddenly flustered, explain that it was his Daddy's Ku
Klux Klan robe, that lots of folks had gone to the meetings, they'd been
pressured to do so. But his Daddy and his Papa had been disgusted by

Screenwriter Horton Foote, Harper Lee, and director Robert Mulligan at a preview of *To
Kill a Mockingbird*. (1962 Pakula-Mulligan Productions, Inc., and Brentwood Productions, Inc./DeGolyer Library, Southern Methodist University, Horton Foote Papers)

what they had heard there and weren't going to them anymore, or at least his Mama hoped they weren't.

In the end, Foote's concerns fell by the wayside. We watch Atticus's entire speech from the perspective of the jurors, as though we are sitting in the jury box ourselves. In the background are the Ewells and their supporters, as well as the prosecutor, his leg slung over the arm of his chair, chewing on a pencil, evoking a casual confidence that the jury would agree with him. In his script notes on the summation scene, Peck wrote of the jury, "Fighting not to convince them of evidence but to break down their prejudice." Peck's Atticus never struggles with prejudice. He has none. The script called for reaction shots of the jurors at the beginning of Atticus's speech and near the end, before he begins the soaring conclusion about the courts being the country's great levelers. But the final version had no close-up shots of the poor white men on the jury. The only two cutaways were to the African Americans in the courtroom, one to Tom Robinson, to remind the audience of the object of Atticus's heroism, and the other to the colored balcony, where, when Atticus speaks of all men being created equal, a few members look around in astonishment, not believing what they had just heard that white man say.

For Peck, as well as for Mulligan and Pakula, the noble Atticus served the needs of the film. It was necessary to sharpen the conflict during the summation, the dramatic climax of the court scene. Good and evil were embodied and set against one another, Atticus versus the Ewells.

Yet so many of the criticisms that would be lobbed at the movie's Atticus over the years were already expressed in Foote's letter. Atticus was too much the "noble man," a historical anachronism, an untethered ideal. His goodness was set too starkly against the bigotry of poor whites, the "ignorant, unenlightened dirt farmers." Foote had foreseen it all before the scene was ever filmed. Harper Lee would have seen it, too, how the character that she had first conceived back in 1957 in the midst of her own ambivalence—her outrage over militant resistance but also her resentment of northern liberal condescension—and that she had painstakingly revised into a calculated portrait of a principled "Black-Belt Bourbon," as she would describe Atticus of *Mockingbird* decades later to a friend, had become something else altogether. Only the trappings remained: the tortoiseshell glasses, the three-piece suit, the watch fob, the southern accent, although even that was pretty erratic in Peck's performance. What emerged was the handsome, dignified, blandly white face of mid-twentieth-century American liberalism.

MAYBE THAT WAS why Harper Lee was so nervous. She hated the publicity events for the film. She was shy by nature, uncomfortable with her appearance, always feeling that she needed to lose a few pounds, a sentiment never discouraged by her birdlike older sister Alice. Harper Lee adored the movie, and heaped lavish, sincere praise on Foote, the filmmakers, and the cast at every opportunity. But the film quickly took on a life of its own. What could she say about it, and about herself, her family, and her hometown, that had provided the inspiration for all of it? "It is and it isn't autobiographical," she told a reporter in April 1962, which was precisely true.

Her friends didn't understand her trepidation. Though she dreaded the interviews, with the press she was wry, charming, and smart. She more than held her own at the dinner parties, which sometimes included fourteen people around the table—editors, press agents, producers, authors, actors, and actresses. They all loved her. "Nelle really does a splendid job, but she doesn't know it!" Annie Laurie Williams wrote to Alice. So many people had told Williams how wonderful Nelle had been before audiences, large and small. "[B]ut when she gets through, she always thinks she didn't do so well and gets real surprised when you tell her how good she is."

A photograph from these days captures both the thrill and the dread. It was taken in Washington in November 1962, at a pre-release screening of *Mockingbird* for members of Congress and the White House staff. Pakula would remember it as one of the worst nights of his life. The studio had sent him the wrong print of the film; images that should have appeared in sharp black and white came out in dull shades of gray. In the photo, Lee, dressed in a black satin smock and a modest gold necklace, no earrings, clutches her purse. She is on the far left, the only woman standing next to four men: the Harvard historian Arthur Schlesinger Jr.,

President Kennedy's in-house intellectual and the administration's singular, unabashed liberal; Philip Gerard, publicity director for Universal
Pictures; Pakula; and George Stevens Jr., head of the film and television
division of the US Information Agency. Schlesinger, wearing his signature
bow tie, is in mid-witticism, a cigar and near-empty highball glass in his
left hand. Gerard, standing slightly behind Schlesinger, cranes his neck
forward, trying to gauge Lee's reaction. Pakula, fresh-faced, boyish, looks
straight into the camera. Stevens, who could easily have passed as a Kennedy and who, along with Gregory Peck, would help establish and become

Harper Lee at a preview of *To Kill a Mockingbird* in Washington, DC, November 1962.
From left to right: Arthur Schlesinger Jr., special assistant to President John F. Kennedy; Philip Gerard, publicity director for Universal Pictures; producer Alan Pakula;
and George Stevens Jr., head of the film and television division of the United States
Information Agency. (Rare Book & Manuscript Library, Columbia University in the City
of New York)

the founding director of the American Film Institute, looks straight at Lee. She's smiling, eyebrows raised, eyes cut to the camera, turning her face only enough to acknowledge that she's being photographed, documented, scrutinized. One imagines her turning back to the men in front of her, dutifully holding up her end of the conversation, keeping things light and clever, or trying to, having no idea how she was actually coming across, enduring it all gamely, if warily, still not quite sure how it had all come to pass so quickly.

The success of the film had surpassed what anyone could have imagined back when the relatively unknown Pakula had bought the film rights in January 1961. Back then, he had yet to find financing. Lee had yet to win the Pulitzer. Gregory Peck had yet to sign on to play Atticus. In pre-production, Mulligan talked to reporters about the importance of the film not jumping on the "segregation-integration soap box," about it not making speeches. But now that they had the thing in the can, and had Gregory Peck on film in the performance of his career, one that seemed to speak so directly to vital issues in the nation and the world, speeches seemed entirely appropriate. "There existed in the 1930's, and before that, and certainly today," Mulligan lectured a reporter in January 1963 on one of the central lessons of the film, "men of real conscience who are real southerners who are working and are committed to continue working, in their own quiet ways, to establish the kind of justice toward the Negro that must exist if this nation is to fully realize its position as a free and democratic country."

TO KILL A MOCKINGBIRD premiered in Los Angeles on Christmas Day 1962, a mere six years to the day after Joy and Michael Brown's life-changing gift to Harper Lee. The idea was to have it out in time for award season in 1963. It opened nationally on Valentine's Day at New York's Radio City Music Hall. In between those dates, on January 14, newly elected governor George Wallace took office in Montgomery with a fervid inaugural speech that drew national news coverage. Thus did George Wallace and Atticus Finch, the id and the superego of the descendants of the Confederacy, enter together the mainstream of American political and cultural life.

Shortly before his inauguration, Wallace met with a group of state senators one evening. "I'm gonna make race the basis of politics in this state," he told them, "and I'm gonna make it the basis of politics in this country." The Klansman Asa Carter would help him do it. He wrote Wallace's inaugural speech, just as he had his campaign speeches, despite efforts of more temperate members of the staff to keep Carter at arm's length now that Wallace was in the governor's mansion. The speech is most often remembered today for its infamous pledge: "I draw the line in the dust and toss the gauntlet before the feet of tyranny, and I say . . . segregation today . . . segregation tomorrow . . . segregation forever." It's tempting to think of it as one of the last gasps of the militant segregationists. After all, Congress would outlaw legalized segregation the very next year—so much for Wallace's forever. But the civil rights bill, far from spelling Wallace's doom, became evidence to Wallace and his supporters of how black civil rights leaders were calling the shots in Washington, of how weak-willed liberals had given things over to the radicals and the revolutionaries. Over the course of the 1960s, the size, zeal, and venom of Wallace's rallies would only grow.

In Asa Carter, Wallace had found not just any old silver-tongued race-baiter. He was Wallace's grand strategist of white nationalism, the man who would help him take his political message far beyond the Tennessee Valley. At his inaugural, Wallace, his traditional morning attire covered by his overcoat, which he kept on due to the frosty weather, called on "the Great Anglo-Saxon Southland" to "rise to the call of freedom-loving blood that is in us." Yet he also summoned the southerners who had left the region, but whose hearts had "never left Dixieland," as well as the "sons and daughters" of New England, the Midwest, and West. "[F]or you are of the Southern spirit . . . and the Southern philosophy . . . you are Southerners too," he said, by which he meant that they were white, and that they resented the changes that blacks were demanding.

Asa Carter even had a foreign policy, a vision of the colonial racial order retooled for the Cold War space age. The liberal internationalists had substituted "human rights" for individual rights, he had Wallace say in the speech. They had ceded too much ground to the "false doctrine of communistic amalgamation." They spoke of new necessities in a changing world, but at its core it was "degenerate and decadent" (this last word Wallace mispronounced "de-kay-dent"). The "international white minority" was persecuted at "the whim of the international colored majority." The two superpowers fell over each other competing for the hearts and minds of the "Afro-Asian bloc." Yet no war crimes commission would hear the appeals of the Belgian survivors of the Congo, the Portuguese in Angola, the dissidents in Castro's Cuba, or, in reference to the desegregation of the University of Mississippi a few months earlier, "the citizens of Oxford, Mississippi."

Years later Wallace would defend his inaugural as an expression of constitutional principles. "We were against big government," he said. "What we were really talking about was states' rights or state responsibilities, and so forth, and we never were against black people." The last point was absurd on its face. The speech was explicitly "against black people." And yet still Wallace wasn't entirely wrong. There *was* a lot in the speech about "big government," which is to say that it was full of the overheated, conspiracy-minded rhetoric of the American far right. Much of Wallace's speech would have been standard fare for a John Birch Society audience or any of the like-minded groups of the era, whose fervent, grassroots membership was upending conservative politics. Few of the people attending such rallies would have turned up their noses at Wallace's talk of race and identity. They believed it all, too, that America was a white man's country.

IN HIS INAUGURAL address, George Wallace made his bid to define what he called "the southern spirit . . . the southern philosophy." Harper Lee had done something very similar in *Mockingbird*. Atticus was the embodiment of the spirit and philosophy of *her* South. And an amped-up, spit-shined, cinematized version of it was playing in movie houses throughout the nation, and soon would be playing throughout the world.

Mockingbird would eventually be celebrated as a Hollywood classic, but some of the early reviews in national weeklies were not so kind. The *New Republic* described the film as a "soft-caramel" version of *Intruder in the Dust.* The *New Yorker* noted the story's conflict between Atticus's high-minded appeals to the rule of law and his complicity in Heck Tate's ruse that saved Boo Radley from being tried for the murder of Bob Ewell: "The moral of this can only be that while ignorant rednecks musn't take the law into their own hands, it's all right for *nice* people to do so." *Time's* criticisms were sharper still, dismissing the movie's "side-porch sociology" as "fatuous" and Peck's performance as a weak attempt at being "the Abe Lincoln of Alabama." *Newsweek* described Peck playing Atticus in a "dreamy, almost ectoplasmic way. He is careful never to exist too much." The review captured well the challenge of the filmmakers in reconciling the novel's sentimental portrait of small town life with the injustice of Tom Robinson's conviction: "The narrator's voice returns at the end, full of warmth and love—for Atticus, Maycomb, and the South—but we do not pay her the same kind of attention any more. We have seen that outrageous trial, and we can no longer share the warmth of her love."

There were positive reviews, too. The *Baltimore Sun* called Peck "superb," his performance was, "without question, the greatest thing he has ever done." The *Boston Globe* believed that if Peck didn't win the best actor award, "then Hollywood is doing him an injustice." *Variety* thought Peck's role was "especially challenging . . . requiring him to conceal his natural physical attractiveness yet project through a veneer of civilized restraint and resigned, rational compromise the fires of social indignation and humanitarian concern that burn within the character."

Reviewers in southern newspapers greeted the movie with an almost palpable sigh of relief. "[H]ere at last is the real South," Mildred Williams wrote in the *Richmond News Leader.* She hoped that the film would "help our neighbors to the North to understand us and our problems." In the *Atlanta Constitution,* Marjory Rutherford praised the film as "an understated, honest and compassionate story," one "not likely to offend any but the most bigoted viewers." The *Birmingham News* reviewer admitted having approached the film warily, mindful of "the 'slant' Hollywood gives pictures dealing with race." Yet she was delighted to see the film's treatment of controversial issues. Writing in the *Alabama Journal,* published in Montgomery, Arch McKay Jr. praised the filmmakers for the "dignity and integrity" with which they handled the courtroom scene. "There is no attempt to press any issue to the front other than the issue of justice for which the trial is being held," he wrote. "True, some glaring errors of the social system are shown in the film, but is it the fault of the film for showing them or the system for having them?"

In her history and memoir of the Birmingham civil rights movement, Diane McWhorter, a Birmingham native, recalled the powerful emotions the film stirred for her and her fellow fifth graders. McWhorter was actually a classmate of Mary Badham's at a private girls' school in Mountain Brook, the wealthy white suburb. She and her classmates joined Badham for a sneak preview of the movie the night before the official debut. She recalled how the film brought her and her friends "face to face with the central racial preoccupation of the southern white psyche, the dynamics that justified and ennobled Our Way of Life: the rape of a white woman by a black man." She remembered how she and the other girls couldn't understand how the jury could fail to acquit Tom Robinson, "especially since his lawyer was Gregory Peck." They were not yet schooled in the "meaning of southern justice," McWhorter observed. Her experience is a reminder of how many Americans who saw the film before reading the book first encountered Atticus—not as Harper Lee imagined him, as a rough proxy for her conservative, south Alabama father, but as Hollywood's handsome, familiar leading man.

McWhorter tried hard to hold back her tears that night but couldn't. She and her fellow students shared a secret bond, she recalled—the "racial guilt . . . in rooting for a Negro man"—one they acknowledged to each other by reciting the lines from Scout's innocent address to Mr. Cunningham outside the Maycomb Jail. McWhorter returned to the Saturday matinee showing with friends to "weep clandestinely." They kept up the ritual for several weeks, until their mothers forbade them from going downtown. It was too dangerous given the civil rights marches that had become regular occurrences in the spring of 1963.

Nominated for eight Academy Awards, *Mockingbird* took home three: Henry Bumstead, Alexander Golitzen, and Oliver Emert won for Best Art Direction; Horton Foote won for Best Adapted Screenplay; and Gregory

Peck prevailed in a crowded Best Actor field that included Jack Lemmon in *Days of Wine and Roses,* Burt Lancaster in *Birdman of Alcatraz,* and Peter O'Toole in *Lawrence of Arabia.* As Sophia Loren read out his name, Peck clutched A. C. Lee's pocket watch, a memento Harper Lee had given him after her father's death.

In a fitting twist of fate, the award for Best Supporting Actor went to Ed Begley for his portrayal of Boss Finley, a crass, corrupt political king-pin in Tennessee Williams's *Sweet Bird of Youth.* It was the Boss Finleys of southern politics to whom A. C. Lee had taken such exception on his editorial page. Among the first and the most profound lessons that the young Nelle Harper had learned from her father was the importance of standing up to the demagogue, of speaking out for honesty and decency in public life. If A. C. hadn't done it at all times on all issues, he had done it enough to inspire his daughter to create a character that would outlive them both as a model of the civic ideal.

The juxtaposition of the virtuous and the corrupt in southern politics, of Atticus and Boss Finley, had long fascinated Harper Lee. And if the Academy Awards were a reliable cultural barometer, it also fascinated a great number of her fellow Americans in 1963, that most fateful of all years in the southern civil rights movement. But while movie stars handed out their awards in Hollywood, back in Alabama, in Birmingham, the civil rights protests that had so alarmed the mothers of Mountain Brook had raised a critical question about white Americans' role in the unfinished struggle for freedom and justice in the South: Would decency be enough?

Chapter 6

Letter from Maycomb Jail

Hundreds of people jammed the sidewalks of downtown Birmingham, spilling out into the street, blocking traffic. A massive klieg light lit up the night sky. Reporters and photographers jockeyed to get close to the action. April 1963 in Birmingham, Alabama, would come to be remembered as a turning point in American history. The sight of police dogs and high-powered fire hoses turned on nonviolent civil rights protestors shocked the nation, setting off a chain of events that led to the passage of the 1964 Civil Rights Act, the most far-reaching civil rights legislation since Reconstruction. Yet before there were protests, there was a party.

It was the north Alabama premiere of *To Kill a Mockingbird*. The throngs were waiting to catch a glimpse of Mary Badham and Phillip Alford, the hometown heroes who had made good in Hollywood. On a flatbed truck outside the Melba Theater, the child actors fielded questions from the press. Behind them, the theater marquee spelled out their names in two-foot-high letters. Badham wore a pale yellow party dress with white gloves and a black headband; the next day's papers described Alford as handsome, poised, and gallant. An official awarded them keys to the city. The president of the Birmingham Junior Chamber of Commerce presented them with a plaque.

The Junior Chamber had led the campaign to bring *Mockingbird* to Birmingham after local theater owners had refused to show it, scared off by the film's depiction of southern injustice. Yet getting Atticus in front of local audiences was only one of the triumphs in recent months for Birmingham's young, white professional leaders. The most significant had taken place the night before *Mockingbird*'s premiere.

Albert Boutwell, the former Alabama lieutenant governor and, by Birmingham standards, a racial moderate, won a decisive victory in a bitterly fought campaign for mayor against Eugene "Bull" Connor, Birmingham's arch-segregationist public safety commissioner. This is what put many people in Birmingham in the mood for a party. City papers hailed it as a watershed moment in Birmingham's history. Connor had ruled Birmingham with an iron fist for nearly three decades. Though his reign had been briefly interrupted by a scandal in the early 1950s when a reporter discovered him in a hotel room with his secretary, the rise of the militant segregationist movement a few years later gave Connor a political lifeline. He capitalized on it with an ugly race-baiting campaign in 1956. With contacts that reached deep into the fetid corners of white racist extremism, Connor was more responsible than anyone for making Birmingham the South's most recalcitrant big city.

Connor's defeat was a coup for Birmingham's moderate business leaders, although the fact that Boutwell would be tapped as the reform candidate says much about how bad things had gotten in the city. As a state senator, he had been the brains behind the Freedom of Choice legislation that had given segregationists an end run around the *Brown* decision. A good friend of the Citizens' Council, he had delivered the Council-sponsored radio address that denounced the 1957 Civil Rights Act as "monstrous legislation." He was the kind of politician that Dick Gregory, the comedian and civil rights activist, had in mind when he joked: "You know the definition of a Southern moderate? That's a cat that'll lynch you from a low tree." But reformers in the city knew him as a segregationist who could still be swayed by a smart argument, and in the early 1960s that distinguished him among Alabama's political class. The smart argument by that time was that segregation was doomed, and the best thing to do was get out in front in managing its demise.

The mayor's race had come about only after a narrowly won referendum that had changed city government in Birmingham from a commissioner to a mayor-council system, which had been another, earlier victory for the city's young white progressives. Prominent among them were the lawyers David Vann, a future mayor of Birmingham, and Charles Morgan, Birmingham's real-life Atticus Finch—that is, if Atticus's law practice had been ruined and he'd been forced to leave Alabama. That's what happened to Morgan after he gave a speech and a follow-up editorial in the *New York Times* publicly acknowledging white Birmingham's collective guilt in the September 1963 church bombing that killed four African American girls. Vann, Morgan, and the other young Turks believed that with Connor's ouster, Birmingham had turned a corner.

Not everyone was convinced. A vanguard within Birmingham's black community, led by the intrepid and tempestuous civil rights leader Fred Shuttlesworth, had been planning a direct-action campaign for months. Bull Connor had closed down city parks, and promises by downtown merchants to desegregate stores and open jobs for blacks had led to no real action. Shuttlesworth, along with Martin Luther King Jr. and several others, had been a founding member of the Atlanta-based Southern Christian Leadership Conference (SCLC), and he had been urging King to come to Birmingham. The SCLC needed a successful protest, Shuttlesworth knew. The previous year, their campaign in Albany, Georgia, had been widely condemned as a failure. The Albany police chief, Laurie Pritchett, had met peaceful protest with peaceful policing, filling the jails in Albany and surrounding areas, and depriving King of the dramatic confrontations needed to draw sympathy and support for the cause. King signed off on plans for a Birmingham campaign to start in early 1963, yet the runoff in the mayoral election prompted him to put things on hold. Protests in the midst of a political campaign would only fuel white reaction and help Bull Connor in the race.

The night after Boutwell's victory—the same night as *Mockingbird*'s premiere—King addressed the first mass meeting of the Birmingham campaign. Earlier that day, twenty protestors had been arrested during sit-ins at lunch counters downtown. King coached the crowd in nonviolent tactics, and vowed to stay in Birmingham until the movement's demands were met.

It is easy to forget how few people, white or black, welcomed King's presence in Birmingham. Shuttlesworth, King's main contact, was hardly the spokesman for a united black Birmingham. He didn't live in the city any longer, having left for a pastorate in Cincinnati two years earlier. Many of Birmingham's black leaders believed that negotiations with whites still held promise, and that direct action would only poison the well of good feeling after Boutwell's election. The young white business and professional leaders who had engineered Bull Connor's ouster were flabbergasted that King would begin a campaign the very day after their labors had finally born fruit. In Washington, Burke Marshall, head of the civil rights division at the Justice Department, personally called the SCLC command post in Birmingham to convey his opinion, one shared by his boss Robert Kennedy, that King should forgo protests and give Boutwell's new administration a chance. In the early weeks of the campaign, national publications—*Time, Newsweek,* the *Washington Post*—weighed in with their skepticism, both about the timing of the protests and the motivations of the protestors.

Schoolchildren today are shown the famous photo of one of Bull Connor's police dogs attacking a young black protestor—which reportedly made President Kennedy sick to his stomach when he saw it—and taught how this and other horrible images finally turned American public opinion against Jim Crow. They did, but not immediately. In April, in both local and national papers, incidents of dogs attacking marchers were described in ways that would have led readers to sympathize with the Birmingham police. The *Birmingham News* reported that a police dog had attacked a protestor only after the man had flashed a pipe at the dog. An article in the *New York Times* claimed that a police dog had pinned one protestor to the ground after the man had slashed at the dog with a large knife.

What turned the tide in King's favor was civil rights leaders' decision in late April to use children as marchers. Before that, about 350 demonstrators had been arrested and the ranks of volunteers from the black community were depleted. It looked like Birmingham would be another Albany. But the addition of hundreds of young protestors filled the jails. And when that happened, Bull Connor finally showed himself to be the hothead that everyone had known he was. He set loose his officers with firehoses and police dogs and thoroughly disgraced his city for all the world to see. King, Shuttlesworth, and the other movement leaders finally got what they had come for.

Before that point, on April 12, 1963, Good Friday, eight of Alabama's most prominent white religious leaders published an open letter critical of the protests. Among them were bishops of the Methodist and Episcopal churches, the moderator of the Synod of the Alabama Presbyterian Church in the United States, an auxiliary bishop of the Catholic Church, the pastor of the First Baptist Church in Birmingham, and the rabbi of Birmingham's Temple Emanu-El. Albert Boutwell's election had brought "days of new hope," the men wrote, and "extreme measures" like direct-action protest were "unwise and untimely." They argued that the protests were "directed and led in part by outsiders," evoking not only King but Shuttlesworth, too, and called for direct negotiations with city leaders, which, they pointed out, a number of local black leaders had called for. Hatred and violence could not be tolerated, the men wrote, but neither should protests that incite others to hatred and violence, "however technically peaceful those actions may be."

The ministers' letter was a follow-up to one they had published three months earlier, only two days after Governor Wallace's inflammatory inaugural speech. That initial letter would have been remarkable if for no other reason than the diversity of its authors. The fact that Methodists and Baptists—the two largest but in most ways parochial of southern denominations—would join in a statement with a Catholic, much less a rabbi, was unheard of in Alabama.

Their January letter explicitly denounced the militant segregationists, the same forces that had prompted Harper Lee to recalibrate the moral and political aims of her fiction. Recent court decisions would soon force the desegregation of some schools and colleges in Alabama. "[D]efiance is neither the right answer nor the solution," they wrote. With Wallace's bellicose and intransigent rhetoric still ringing in Alabamans' ears, they warned that "rebellious statements can lead only to violence, discord, confusion and disgrace for our beloved state." They reminded their followers that the "American way of life" depended on "obedience to the decisions of courts of competent jurisdiction," and they reaffirmed the importance of protecting freedom of speech. Sounding a universalist theme of which Martin Luther King himself was fond, they advised that "no person's freedom is safe unless every person's freedom is equally protected."

The January statement was titled "An Appeal for Law and Order and Common Sense." That phrase, "law and order," had often been used as a bludgeon against progressive advocates of reform. And later in the decade, George Wallace would trumpet it nationally, paving the way for its utilization by right-wing politicians up to the present day. Yet it should not be dismissed as merely the dog whistle of reactionaries. In earlier decades in southern history, decent white people had used it as a defense against the reactionaries themselves. That was how these ministers used it here, as an admonition to the demagogues sowing hatred and division. The appeal to law and order was part of a long and often tragic struggle to turn the legal, political, and judicial system in the South into something more than a formalized proxy for mob rule. This is what A. C. Lee had tried to do in Monroe County in the 1920s and 1930s. It was of a piece with what the young businessmen and lawyers in Birmingham—white leaders who by 1963 had accepted the necessity of desegregation—tried to do in ousting Bull Connor. It was part of a southern tradition that had arisen in opposition to the detestable and appalling ones—the lynchings and political buffoonery—a tradition of civic-minded, conscientious, conservative men defending the rule of law. Harper Lee knew it, and cherished it, and had worked so hard to try to capture it in the figure of Atticus Finch.

But it would never be a simple or straightforward thing to explain or defend, as Lee herself knew all too well. White southerners lived in a moral thicket of their own making, and it was easy to lose one's way. That's

Policemen arresting Martin Luther King Jr. and Ralph Abernathy in Birmingham, Alabama, April 12, 1963. (Associated Press)

what happened to the ministers in their follow-up letter in April. They used that same phrase, "law and order," to urge an end to black protests, thereby equating George Wallace's defiance of federal courts with the civil disobedience of King and his followers. Yet Wallace was protesting the right to segregate, and subjugate, blacks, while King was protesting the laws that subjugated him and his people.

This misjudged second letter—not the first one that gave hell to George Wallace—was the one for which the men would be remembered. In fact, they came to face a peculiar kind of infamy. For the same day that their second missive was published, Martin Luther King was arrested and sent to the Birmingham Jail. It was there, several days later, that he read the men's statement, and decided that he would write a letter of his own.

IF THERE IS any document from the civil rights–era South more widely read than *To Kill a Mockingbird,* it is Martin Luther King's "Letter from Birmingham Jail." King began writing it in the margins of the newspaper in which the eight ministers' statement had appeared. A friendly prison trusty supplied him with scraps of paper on which he expanded his thoughts. King's lawyers carried the fragments back to SCLC headquarters for staff to assemble. In its explication of just and unjust law, its condemnation of racism and the moral callousness of white America, and its analysis of the political and moral costs of continued indifference, King's letter would take its place in history alongside Paine's *Common Sense,* or Lincoln's *Gettysburg Address,* as an essential document of American democracy. In the years to come it would inspire millions of freedom-seeking people around the world, from Johannesburg to Gdansk to Tiananmen Square.

It began, however, as a polite, professional response to the objections of King's fellow clergymen. King patiently explained why he had come to Birmingham. He was the president of the Southern Christian Leadership Conference, he wrote, which had an affiliate in Birmingham that had asked him and his organization for help. He had come because it was his professional duty, but even more, he had come for the same reason that Paul had come to the aid of the Macedonians. Injustice in Birmingham was a threat to justice everywhere, according to King, echoing the universalist principle that the religious leaders themselves had offered in their January statement. His fellow ministers may deplore the demonstrations, King wrote, yet they said nothing about the conditions that precipitated them: the police brutality, the rigged judicial system, the unsolved and unpunished bombings of homes and churches. Earlier negotiations had resulted in promises by Birmingham merchants that had gone unmet. What else were King and his colleagues to do? Negotiation may be preferable to protest, but in every instance in his people's long struggle, protests had been the only means for blacks to win genuine negotiations.

King's defense of the protests included a gallery of indelible images: children witnessing the lynching of mothers and fathers; the "hate-filled" policemen kicking and cursing; the "airtight cage of poverty"; the "degenerating sense of 'nobodiness.'" He also described a scene that Harper Lee had evoked in *Mockingbird,* that of a father confronted by young children asking the most innocent and impossible of questions. Only, unlike Atticus, King had no answer for why colored children couldn't go to the amusement park, no soothing words to clear the "ominous clouds of inferiority" slowly forming in his daughter's "mental sky," no tender wisdom for his son about why white people were so mean to colored people.

One of the most famous passages was King's condemnation of white moderates, those decent, well-meaning defenders of law and order.

> I have almost reached the regrettable conclusion that the Negro's great stumbling block in his stride toward freedom is not the White Citizen's Counciler or the Ku Klux Klanner, but the white moderate, who is more devoted to "order" than to justice; who prefers a negative peace which is the absence of tension to a positive peace which is the presence of justice; who constantly says: "I agree with you in the goal you seek, but I cannot agree with your methods of direct action"; who paternalistically believes he can set the timetable for another man's freedom; who lives by a mythical concept of time and who constantly advises the Negro to wait for a "more convenient season." Shallow understanding from people of good will is more frustrating than absolute misunderstanding from people of ill will. Lukewarm acceptance is much more bewildering than outright rejection.

King explained that he had "almost" reached this regrettable conclusion—that the moderates were worse than the reactionaries. He wasn't all the way there yet. And he still wouldn't be a year later when he revised the "Letter" and included it in his 1964 book *Why We Can't Wait.* He made numerous small emendations in language and emphasis from the version of the letter first published in May 1963 to the one published in his book, but he kept that important qualifier, "almost." It's important to understand why. That "almost" is evidence of King's own ambivalence about the decent white southerners that Harper Lee represented, both in her person and in her fiction.

On the level of practical politics, it's clear that King didn't truly believe that moderates were bigger stumbling blocks to him and his movement than Councilors and Klansmen. If he had, he never would have delayed the start of the protests in hopes of helping Albert Boutwell defeat Bull Connor. King had no illusions that Boutwell would "bring the millennium to Birmingham," as he wrote in his letter. Boutwell was a segregationist, just like Connor. Yet King knew that not all segregationists were the same.

In 1957, for example, King cultivated a relationship with the Tuscaloosa newspaper editor Buford Boone, the Pulitzer Prize winner for his editorials denouncing the Citizens' Council's role in the riots at the University of Alabama. Boone was a southern conservative and a segregationist. Unlike some of his fellow southern editors of the era, whose battles with militant reactionaries pushed them to the left politically, Boone remained a solid man of the right. In 1964, when President Lyndon Johnson invited him to serve on an advisory committee to the Community Relations Service, which had been established as part of the 1964 Civil Rights Act, Boone declined. He pledged to use his newspaper to "promote respect for law and order and a proper regard for human rights as well as individual freedoms," yet he "conscientiously believe[d] certain portions of the Civil Rights Bill violate the letter and spirit of our Constitution." He hoped that "they will be declared unconstitutional at an early date."

After the announcement of Boone's Pulitzer in May 1957, King wrote him a letter of glowing praise. King had had "unspeakable admiration" for Boone ever since he had read Boone's editorial denouncing the Councils earlier that year. He praised him for his "moral courage," "profound dignity," and willingness to "sacrifice and even face abuse for the cause of freedom and truth." He hoped other white southerners would "rise up and courageously give to the type of leadership that you have given." King was convinced that "this is no day for the rabble rouser, whether he be Negro or white." His conclusion had the rousing tone of his sermons: "[T]hose of us who stand amid the bleak and desolate midnight of man's inhumanity to man are given new hope for the emerging daybreak of freedom and justice when we know that such persons as you live in our great nation and in our great southland."

If King's praise seems excessive, especially when contrasted with his harsh words about the defenders of law and order in his "Letter," this owed in part to what had changed in the intervening years. In May 1957, Alabama was still in the midst of militant segregationists' hostile takeover. Boone's willingness to speak out at that early point required more moral courage than such stands would later. King's criticism of the moderate ministers of Birmingham in 1963 came at a moment when he was being criticized from nearly all sides for raining on Albert Boutwell's parade. He had to remind these moderate whites what had and had not actually taken place in Birmingham.

King did offer a bit of flattery in "Letter from Birmingham Jail" when he praised another group of white southerners, one that had "grasped the meaning of this social revolution and committed themselves to it." Or, at least, one of those listed, Lillian Smith, would have seen this as flattery. Smith's name appeared second behind that of Ralph McGill, the distinguished editor and publisher of the *Atlanta Constitution*. Smith had locked horns with McGill for years, criticizing him in the exact terms that King used to denounce white moderates. In fact, King's critique of moderates was anticipated by Smith by more than a decade in her book *Killers of the Dream*. "It is hard to decide which is more harmful to men's morals," she wrote, "the 'moderate' or reactionary, in this confused South." Moderates, Smith said, were "those who spoke for law and order but would not speak against the segregation that threatened law and order; they would protest the lynching of men's bodies but not the lynching of their spirits; they opposed the mob on the street but not the mob in men's minds; they wanted laws obeyed but would not defend the moral values on which law is grounded."

King's solicitation of figures like Boone and McGill was shrewd. It sampled from the hard-earned experience of southern blacks in the Jim Crow era, when, as King wrote, "Negroes defended themselves and protected their jobs—and, in many cases, their lives—by perfecting an air of ignorance and agreement." But it was rooted also in King's experience as a Christian, and in the charge that Jesus gave to his disciples in Matthew, a passage that King invoked at staff retreats to inspire his fellow soldiers in the cause of justice: "I am sending you out like sheep among wolves. Therefore be as shrewd as snakes and as innocent as doves."

It was with the innocence of doves that King addressed his fellow clergymen in "Letter from Birmingham Jail." It is vital to hear in that document the voice of the *Reverend* Martin Luther King. To whatever degree it was a philosophical or political tract intended to persuade, King's "Letter" was also a sermon written to redeem. His fellow Christian ministers would have recognized the idiom immediately, because they would have relied on it themselves in their own ministries to challenge the procrastinators and the prevaricators among their flock. King's "Letter" recalled the prophetic warning to the church in Laodicea received as part of the Revelation to John of Patmos: "I know your deeds, that you are neither cold nor hot. I wish you were either one or the other! So, because you are lukewarm— neither hot nor cold—I am about to spit you out of my mouth."

Indeed, King wrote his letter precisely because he believed that these fellow men of the cloth could be converted. He accepted that their criticisms were "sincerely set forth," however wrongheaded they might be, and he answered their objections with equal sincerity. He condemned not just the white moderate, but also the white church. He described how on his travels throughout the South he often drove by the beautiful churches with their lofty spires and massive education buildings nearby, and wondered to himself, "What kind of people worship here? Who is their God?" Yet King wrote not just to persuade, or even to sway these men morally. He wrote that they might be *convicted*—that the Holy Spirit might work within them to soften their hearts and open their eyes, so that seeing the error of their ways, they might repent.

Most of the men never did. A few bore a sense of grievance for the rest of their lives. They felt like they were among the tiny handful of white

Alabamans willing to speak out in a terrible, tumultuous moment, yet King had mischaracterized them, and had used them for his own purposes. Particularly galling to several would have been King's rhetorical question near the end of the letter asking where religious leaders had been "when Governor Wallace gave a clarion call for defiance and hatred?" These eight clergymen, of course, had been at the front of the line denouncing Wallace.

But a few of them did hear King's message, and they did repent. Earl Stallings, the pastor of Birmingham's First Baptist Church, and the one clergyman King mentioned by name for having welcomed black worshipers at his church, held firm against hardline segregationists among his flock who tried to reverse his open-door policy, and, failing that, to run him out of the church. In May 1963, Stallings preached a blistering sermon, "Pilate's Wash Bowl," reminding his congregation of how the Roman governor of Judea had absolved himself of personal responsibility for the injustices of his day. "Ah, Pilate, we condemn you because your position, your security, meant more to you than truth," Stallings said. "But, are we any better? We hear the call of truth, of righteousness, of justice, but we are not men enough to heed its challenge. Selfishness, caution, expediency, opportunism, all together slam shut the doors and we never cross the threshold of truth, of freedom, of justice."

The Catholic priest Joseph Durick was another. As part of a religious minority in the South, Durick had long had a heart for those at society's margins. But King's letter was instrumental in convincing him that segregation was not merely a political problem, but a moral one, with grave implications for the church. In 1966 he was appointed the bishop of the diocese of Tennessee, which covered the entire state, and took prophetic stands on issues of racial and economic inequality. In 1968, during the strike of black sanitation workers in Memphis, Bishop Durick donated $1,000 to feed the families of striking workers, which provoked a sharp rebuke from the city's mayor. Two days after King was assassinated in Memphis on the balcony of the Lorraine Motel, Durick led a local interfaith service honoring King as a prophet of "dignity and freedom" for all people. Reading aloud the passage from King's letter condemning white moderates, Durick asked God to "examine our individual conscience—to assess my part of the blame in the death of Dr. King." He dedicated himself to "work to make our morality meaningful—as with greater vigor we translate it into the social power structure and into living laws and social institutions."

BUT MOST OF that was still to come. King expanded on the themes in "Letter" in *Why We Can't Wait*, published in June 1964. The text was written largely by a ghostwriter, Al Duckett, and later approved by King with input from Stanley Levison, the former communist whose closeness to the minister the FBI had used to obtain a warrant to wiretap Levison, and eventually King himself. The book told the story of the Birmingham campaign. One chapter was a slightly revised version of "Letter." Another, titled "The Sword That Heals," represented King's most urgent defense to date of nonviolence. It was a response to the increasing pressure King felt from the rising black nationalist movement. Rather than a replacement for the legal attack on Jim Crow, nonviolence was only a supplement, he explained. It showed the "sophistication" of the freedom movement because it broke with Americans' "old, ingrained concepts," rooted in the frontier tradition, the eye-for-an-eye philosophy valorized as "the highest measure of American manhood," and the heroes "who champion justice through violent retaliation against injustice."

Running counter to this outdated philosophy, King argued, was "something in the American ethos that responds to the strength of moral force." And who for King was an example of an American responding to moral force? None other than Atticus Finch himself. King wrote,

> I am reminded of the popular and widely respected novel and film *To Kill a Mockingbird*. Atticus Finch, a white southern lawyer, confronts a group of his neighbors who have become a lynch-crazed mob, seeking the life of his Negro client. Finch, armed with nothing more lethal than a lawbook, disperses the mob with the force of his moral courage, aided by his small daughter, who, innocently calling the would-be lynchers by name, reminds them that they are individual men, not a pack of beasts.

What Abraham Lincoln had done for Harriet Beecher Stowe when, as legend has it, he referred to her as "the little woman who wrote the book that started this great war," Martin Luther King did for Harper Lee in invoking her most famous character as the example for those Americans who might yet do what's right.

Whether it was actually Scout helping Atticus or the other way around wasn't important. What was important was King's enduring faith in the strength of moral force. This, it must be remembered, was always the counterbalance to his cynicism about white moderates. In his nod to Atticus Finch, as in his appeals to Buford Boone and other white moderates in earlier years, King signaled his belief that within the oppressor race were people with the modicum of decency and empathy without which democratic change is impossible. King didn't know for certain when he wrote his book—before civil rights forces in Congress broke a southern filibuster for the first time in American history, and Lyndon Johnson signed the 1964 Civil Rights Act—whether there were enough moral white people in America to defeat the legalized subjugation of black southerners through peaceful, nonviolent, legislative means. But he believed it to be true, and through his belief, and the belief of millions of others inspired by him, it became true.

Even before the historic legislation of 1964, King had seen enough to confirm his faith in the power of moral witness. "The striking thing about the nonviolent crusade of 1963 was that so few felt the sting of bullets or the clubbing of billies and nightsticks," he wrote in *Why We Can't Wait*. "[T]he Revolution was a comparatively bloodless one." He wrote this in spite of the evil, cowardly murder of the four girls at Sixteenth Street Baptist Church, in spite of the bombing in Birmingham of his own brother's home and of the motel room where it was assumed he would be staying, in spite of the death threats he had received for years and would continue to receive until he himself was killed by another racist murderer.

Yet we would do well today to remember King's faith in the power of moral example, and the essential role that it plays in democratic society. We should remember, too, the strange way that Atticus Finch emerged as a token of that faith. President Kennedy summoned it in one of the signature presidential addresses of the era, his nationally televised "Report to the American People" on June 11, 1963. A president best known for his strong, masculine rhetoric about bearing burdens and meeting hardships sounded like a Sunday School teacher when he spoke of how Americans were "confronted primarily with a moral issue" that was "as old as the scriptures and is as clear as the American Constitution." He raised his own version of the Golden Rule: Were Americans "going to treat our fellow Americans as we want to be treated?" Echoing Atticus's counsel to Scout about crawling into another person's skin and walking around in it, as well as King's condemnation of those urging members of his race to wait, the president asked, "[W]ho among us would be content to have the color of his skin changed and stand in [the Negro's] place? Who among us would then be content with the counsels of patience and delay?"

King was convinced that the oppressors in Birmingham had been restrained not merely because the world looked on. The moral example of the protestors themselves had moved them. As King put it, the "hundreds, sometimes thousands, of Negroes who for the first time dared to look back at a white man, eye to eye," revealed that "the Negro did not merely give lip service to nonviolence." Despite the violence that had occurred, far greater violence that had been threatened never came to pass, King wrote, as "one side would not resort to it and the other was so often immobilized by confusion, uncertainty and disunity."

THE DISUNITED WHITE South. That was the side that Harper Lee and her people were on. It was to them that she had written a novel that would eventually be read and celebrated around the world as a timeless expression of universal values of moral courage, tolerance, and understanding. But she began the project confused and uncertain. In her first attempt at writing a novel, she had wanted to reconcile her abiding love and respect for her father with the hypocrisy and injustice that he and his generation of southerners had too easily abided, all while defending him from the condescension of the northern liberals. Yet through that process, and shaped, too, by the shifting politics of the day, she stumbled upon a simpler narrative: a father, inspired by his love and hope for his children, doing the right thing in a time of crisis. In that story, Atticus rose to the occasion. At the moment when it really mattered, he was his best self. Of course, *Mockingbird* doesn't tell us that. We know it because in *Watchman* we see this other side of Atticus. In *Mockingbird*, we know of him only as the children do, because that is the internal logic of the novel.

With the publication of *Watchman*, however, we know now not only that the Atticus of *Mockingbird* was always too good to be true, but that Harper Lee knew it as well. She knew all the things that Jean Louise discovers in *Watchman*: that Atticus's kindly paternalism covered ugly beliefs about racial difference; that his willingness to represent black clients was in service to the racial status quo; that Calpurnia and all of Maycomb's black population lived behind a veil; that what as a child she had assumed was genuine, reciprocal love and devotion across the color line was more like an elaborate act intended to ease, for whites, the guilt and, for blacks, the burden of racial injustice.

She knew all of these things and yet never told us. Why?

Epilogue

The truth is that she intended to. Or at least she planned on it for a time. In the letter that she wrote to her friends Joy and Michael Brown in July of 1957 she described how Maurice Crain had convinced her to divide the novels that she had been trying to combine into one. He told her to finish the childhood novel, write a bridge, and it would flow into "Watchman." But she never wrote the bridge—by which Crain and she presumably meant a third novel, to appear between the two existing ones—and she never came back to her other manuscript, "Watchman," the one that she had actually written first.

Perhaps she never took the idea of a trilogy terribly seriously, or she didn't hold to it for very long. As far as we know, it is only mentioned in this one letter to the Browns written in 1957. Maybe she continued to work secretly on this plan after *Mockingbird* was published. Or perhaps the idea had always been a fleeting one, devised at a time when she was desperately trying to figure out which of the manuscripts that she had written could be worked into decent enough shape to land a book contract. And once one of them sold, and the contract was signed, and the manuscript was revised, and the book was published, and made into a movie, and hailed as a great American classic, and the movie was hailed as a great American classic, and the characters in it became as familiar to readers as members of their own family, that old idea about writing a bridge and following Atticus into old age and Scout into adulthood seemed utterly ridiculous.

Yet some evidence suggests that in the years after Mockingbird's publication, Lee was still trying to work through unresolved themes from *Watchman*. In 1961, after *Mockingbird* had taken flight and Lee had emerged as the freshest face on the southern literary scene, Harold Hayes, an editor at *Esquire*, commissioned her to write a short feature concerning the current state of affairs in the South. No record has yet been found of what Lee wrote. To a friend she described what she had produced as a "pastiche" that "had some white people who were segregationists & at the same time loathed & hated the K.K.K." In late October, Hayes wrote an awkward letter rejecting the piece. "What seemed to have gone wrong—from our point of view," Hayes wrote, "is that the piece is working too hard to carry a lot of weight—humor, characterization, the barbarity of the Klan, the goodness of a brave man and so on. A novel's worth, in fact, with the result that it never quite makes it on either of these levels as a short feature." Interestingly, Hayes said that he was "sympathetic to your decision to change it to a fictional form."

In a letter to a friend, Lee shrugged it off as another example of a New York editor ignorant of southern complexities. Her piece didn't "conform to their Image (or the one they wish to project) of the South," she wrote. She marveled that Hayes couldn't believe that there were segregationists who also despised the Ku Klux Klan: "This is an axiomatic impossibility, according to Esquire! I wanted to say that according to those lights, nine-tenths of the South is an axiomatic impossibility."

But Hayes was no obtuse outsider. He was a southerner himself, a native North Carolinian. It may have been that what was wrong with the piece was akin to what was wrong with Lee's math. In 1961, when right-wing racists still had a veritable hotline to the Alabama governor's office, nine-tenths of "the South"—by which Harper Lee would have meant the white South—did not despise the Ku Klux Klan. Nine-tenths of the Monroeville Kiwanis Club maybe, but probably not even that.

Interviews that Lee gave in these years suggest that *Watchman* was still fresh in her mind. In March 1963 she described to an interviewer how

Mockingbird had "tried to give a sense of proportion to life in the South, that there isn't a lynching before every breakfast." That line was also Jean Louise's characterization of the *New York Post*'s coverage of the South in *Watchman*. More telling, however, was an interview Lee gave in March 1964 to Roy Newquist, host of the radio program *Counterpoint,* on WQXR in New York. When asked why the South produced so many writers, she spoke of how southerners "run high to Celtic blood and influence," how they were "mostly Irish, Scottish, English, Welsh," how they "grew up in a society that was primarily agricultural," which had made the region one of "natural storytellers, just from tribal instinct." All of these themes Lee had written about in *Watchman*. She put them in the mouth of Uncle Jack, who attempts to school Jean Louise on how Maycomb County was composed of "the living counterparts of every butt-headed Celt, Angle [sic], and Saxon who ever drew breath," how this fact prompted "tribal feelin'," how the South was populated by "small landowners and tenants by the thousands," how it was "a little England in its heritage and social structure."

These were all fragments of the conservative worldview that Uncle Jack sketches for Jean Louise in *Watchman*. Presumably Lee would have included them in any second book about Atticus Finch, one not written from a child's perspective. She would have had to explain the roots of Atticus's traditionalism, the loss of which Uncle Jack mourns in *Watchman*. "Men like me and my brother are obsolete and we've got to go," he tells Jean Louise, "but it's a pity we'll carry with us the meaningful things of this society."

Even if these themes were on her mind, however, Lee faced a problem in any attempt to make *Watchman* a viable novel. What exactly were the "meaningful things" that were worth preserving from the "tribal instinct" of a racially and ethnically homogenous white South? In both *Mockingbird* and the interview with Newquist, it was clear that it was not the passing of Uncle Jack's ethno-racial order that Harper Lee herself lamented, but rather the loss of small town southern life, with its simple pleasures, traditional values, and dense network of relationships. "There is a very definite social pattern in these towns that fascinates me," she told Newquist. "I think it is a rich social pattern. I would simply like to put down all I know about this because I believe that there is something universal in this little world, something decent to be said for it, and something to lament in its passing." But the "social pattern" in the Jim Crow small towns that so fascinated Harper Lee was predicated on the "tribal instinct" of the white South. One did not exist without the other. And the one thing that was clear both in the overt moral outrage of Jean Louise in *Watchman* and in the quieter, more profound moral outrage of *Mockingbird* was that Harper Lee could no longer abide the tribalism of white southerners. She was unable to reconcile her love of small town southern life—and of the values and principles of her father that grew out of it—with the commitment to racial hierarchy that defined both her hometown and her father. This, more than any single factor, was the thing that would have prohibited her from trying to rewrite *Watchman,* and that, ultimately, frustrated her ambition to become "the Jane Austen of south Alabama."

Thanks to men like George Wallace and Asa Carter, the southern tradition that Atticus and Uncle Jack embodied in *Watchman* had become the rallying cry of the reprehensible. By June 1963, Wallace had begun to follow through on his pledge to make race "the basis of politics in this country." His inaugural had launched him into the national political conversation, but it was Wallace's stand in the schoolhouse door on June 11, 1963, that secured his place there. Wallace's theatrics did nothing to stop the enrollment of Vivian Malone and James Hood at the University of Alabama, the first African American students to enroll since Autherine Lucy's brief stay in 1956, but he had known they wouldn't. What he wanted was to set up a scenario in which he could stand up and denounce the tyrannical forces of federal authority for a national television audience. And in this he succeeded marvelously. He caught a break when Assistant Attorney General Nicholas de Katzenbach decided to approach Wallace himself, without Malone and Hood. It was prudent not to subject the two black students to potential violence, but the result was that Wallace wasn't turning away polite, qualified black students. He was standing up to the government's hatchet man, defending constitutional principles against federal overreach, or so he said. And many people around the country, a surprising number of them outside of the South, loved him for it, as signaled by the avalanche of letters and telegrams that poured into Wallace's offices in the days and weeks following.

Buoyed by the response, Wallace entered the 1964 Democratic presidential primaries with a vow to "shake the eyeteeth of the liberals in Washington." He won roughly a third of the vote in primaries in Wisconsin and Indiana and very nearly won the Maryland primary outright. His rally at Serb Memorial Hall on Milwaukee's South Side on April 1 was a preview of the seething, raucous gatherings that would come to characterize his future presidential campaigns. Seven hundred people jammed into the low-ceilinged community center adjacent to the St. Sava Serbian Orthodox church, with another three hundred outside. Tensions escalated when three black civil rights activists, who had staked out a place up front to confront Wallace directly, refused to stand during the national anthem. When one of them, Reverend Leo Champion, yelled at Wallace, "Get your dogs out!," the rally organizer, Bronko Gruber, an ex-Marine tavern owner, grabbed the mike. "I'll tell you something about your dogs, padre!" he shouted. "[T]hree weeks ago tonight a friend of mine was assaulted by three of your countrymen or whatever you want to call them . . ." Roars from the crowd drowned out the rest of the sentence. "They beat up old ladies 83-years old, rape our womenfolk. They mug people. They won't work. They are on relief. How long can we tolerate this? Did I go to Guadalcanal and come back to something like this?" Wallace himself took the mike and the crowd calmed enough so that Reverend Champion and his associates could make their way out, showered by jeers. In his speech, Wallace implored the audience to send a message to Washington to let them know that "we want them to leave our homes, schools, jobs, business and farms alone." When he finished, the throngs roared for five minutes. It took him an hour to shake all the hands and sign all the autographs.

In those years when George Wallace was forging the politics of rage for the national scene, it would have been a strange project indeed for Harper Lee to rework *Watchman* to provide a more complex, historically grounded understanding of Atticus and his ilk. The Atticus of *Mockingbird* was already the symbolic antithesis of Wallace, sprung from the same south Alabama soil. In 1964 he still had a lot of important work to do. He had to make sure that George Wallace didn't get to define the southern spirit.

And not just the southern spirit, but the American one, too. In February 1963, the Hollywood Guilds Festival Committee had chosen *Mockingbird* to represent the United States at the Cannes Film Festival the following May. This was when participating countries still nominated only one film. It was screened on May 18, while conflict in Birmingham smoldered. One week before, bombs had destroyed the home of Martin Luther King's brother, A. D. King, and parts of the A. G. Gaston Motel. The reaction to the film among the audience at the festival was mixed. Some people clapped during Peck's more heroic moments, yet at the film's conclusion

Gregory Peck as Atticus Finch giving his summation to the jury. (Getty Images)

boos and catcalls were interspersed with the applause and shouts of "bravo."

Afterward, an international group of reporters grilled Peck in a nearly hour-long news conference. "Wasn't the picture an example of southern racism?" a French reporter asked. "The word racist has become a label that doesn't mean much," Peck answered. "The film represents a middle class moderate Southerner who is concerned about a Negro's rights. I think this is how the Southern white moderate feels today." Peck's comments about white moderates came roughly a week before the publication of Martin Luther King's condemnation of that group in "Letter from Birmingham Jail." Another reporter asked Peck, "[D]o you like Negroes as you did in the film?" Peck said that he had never felt intolerance: "I'm thankful that I was born in an area where this type of prejudice doesn't exist." Peck was referring to southern California, where the very next year voters overturned an open housing law, where the year after that the Watts riot broke out, and where a few years after that, George Wallace's 1968 campaign would tap deep and abiding strains of prejudice. An Israeli reporter asked Peck whether the character of Atticus was not too good to be true. "This is an ordinary type of American," Peck replied. "My father was like this, and the father of Harper Lee . . . is like this also."

Quibble as one might, Peck was playing a bit role in a much larger drama. Allen Rivkin, the screenwriter who headed the American delegation at Cannes, noted that Peck's press conference was the first time an American performer had answered questions from international reporters since Birmingham. "It is still a great problem," Rivkin said, referring to racial tension, "but we are solving it and we are not afraid to talk about it or bring a picture on the race question to an international film festival." The Kennedy administration was deeply concerned about how the violence in Birmingham was being covered internationally. A report sent to Secretary of State Dean Rusk on June 14, 1963, estimated that Soviet coverage of Birmingham was seven times that of the crisis in Oxford, Mississippi, where in 1962 James Meredith had become the first African American student to enroll at the University of Mississippi. Soviet foreign service news programs that were broadcast globally were reporting that racism was inevitable under the capitalist system, that the violence in Birmingham mocked US claims of leadership of the free world, and that racism in Alabama was "indicative of [US] policies toward colored peoples throughout the world." The US Information Agency saw to it that editions of *To Kill a Mockingbird* were published in various Indian and Middle Eastern languages. Here in the middle of the ongoing Cold War, in the titanic struggle between democratic capitalism and communist authoritarianism, the heartwarming tale of an Alabama Brahmin defending an Untouchable seemed like a story all the world should hear.

CLOSER TO HOME, other, more personal reasons inhibited Lee's progress on another novel. She had worked out her first book in cheerful anonymity, but after *Mockingbird* there were new expectations, and new pressures. On the first anniversary of her book's publication, Maurice Crain had gently inquired about a follow-up in a jokey telegram from "The Mockingbird." "Tomorrow is my first birthday," it read. "My agents think there should be another book written to keep me company. Do you think you can start one before I am another year old[?]" The pressure to match or exceed her first book wore on Lee. With *Mockingbird* she had been hoping "for a quick and merciful death at the hands of the reviewers," she told an interviewer in 1964, "but at the same time I sort of hoped that maybe someone would like it enough to give me encouragement. Public encouragement." She had hoped for a little, but had gotten a lot, which she said "in some ways . . . was just about as frightening as the quick, merciful death I'd expected."

In fact, the public encouragement, both critical and commercial, would have been daunting to the most seasoned and confident of novelists. There was the Pulitzer Prize, for one, as well as the fact that the sales figures for every edition of the book could not be measured in fewer than seven figures. By 1964 an estimated five million had sold through the Popular Library; two million had been distributed by Reader's Digest; another one million copies of a volume in which *Mockingbird* had been included with other books in an "all-time best" collection had sold. The Book of the

Month and Literary Guild Book clubs had run out of books. *Mockingbird* was selling actively all over the world: Britain, Australia, New Zealand, South Africa. Six hardbound editions had been published in German. An Italian edition was selling handsomely, and the book was published as well in Hungary, Romania, and Greece.

Yet the money that came with this success, rather than freeing Lee to pursue her creative instincts, turned out to be another source of anxiety. Incredible sums dropped into her life like rain through a leaky roof. Her sister Alice was responsible for funneling it all where it needed to go. The two sisters fretted over the tax implications of Nelle's constant stream of income, reflecting their father's old irritability over taxes and the prospect of profligate government. "The Procurator of Judea is breathing heavily down my neck," Nelle wrote to Hal Caufield in December 1960. "[A]ll the lovely, lovely money is going straight to the Bureau of Internal Revenue tomorrow, why during the Christmas season I shall never know. It has left me totally devoid of anything resembling good thoughts toward my brethren, especially when my brethren drive around Washington in Cadillacs I've paid for." In October 1963, Williams passed on to Alice a royalty check from Universal Pictures for over fifty-eight thousand dollars (this was minus the agent's commission; the full check was for over a half million dollars in today's money), and warned that there might be another one before the end of the year. Alice and Nelle tried not to worry. They were just hoping to take things in stride, Alice wrote. "Nelle Harper nearly flipped when I did a running total of her income for 1963, and she worried terribly for a short while, then she took off to the golf course and had a good time." The following August, Williams sheepishly sent along yet another check from Universal. "We know that Nelle Harper wishes these checks would not come in every few months," she wrote, "but I'm sure we all understand that there's no way of stopping them."

Nelle's complaints about the tax man recalled the contrarian, cantankerous young woman of her college days. Her crankiness was on display in the interview she gave to Roy Newquist in March 1964. Summarizing her educational background, she spoke of having resisted "all efforts of the government to educate me." How had she adjusted to living in New York?

Newquist asked. She didn't live in New York, she said; she was there only two months a year. Thus began the hopeless tradition of reporters trying to pin down where she was and when—New York or Monroeville—and what clues her location held about her loyalties, sensibilities, and work habits. What advice would she give to young writers? Newquist wondered. "Young people today, especially the college kids, scare me to death," she said, sounding about a quarter-century older than her actual age, which was thirty-eight. To writers foolish enough to think they could learn how to write in school, she offered: "Well, my dear young people, writing is something that is within you, and if it isn't there, nothing can put it there." Indulging her Anglophilia, she recommended to struggling writers the advice given by the Reverend John Keble, the priest and poet whose book *The Christian Year* (1827) was the most popular volume of verse in nineteenth-century England. To a friend who had asked Keble how to get his faith back, the reverend responded, "By holy living." Perhaps Nelle felt a kinship with Keble as a fellow best-selling author of a book of moral instruction. She spoke of the writer's life being akin to the "medieval priesthood." Writing was "the one form of art and endeavor that you cannot do for an audience," she said. Whatever else one can say about Harper Lee over her remaining fifty-two years, she followed her own advice. She never sat for another interview, or finished another book, for the rest of her life.

Acknowledgments

M any people have helped me in the researching and writing of this book. Edwin Conner, Molly Lee, and Hank Conner shared their memories of their grandfather and their aunt, and have answered questions, large and small, along the way. Ed very generously read the entire manuscript and offered suggestions and corrections. Jonathan Burnham at HarperCollins was extraordinarily generous in sharing documents that made clear important details about what Harper Lee was writing and when in the late 1950s. He also went to great lengths to ensure that I would be able to quote from the bulk of those documents. Paul Kennerson went out of his way to allow me to read and quote from his private collection of Harper Lee letters. Steve Stewart, a former editor of the *Monroe Journal* and the son of the man who bought the paper from A. C. Lee, answered many questions about Monroeville and the newspaper business in Alabama. In Monroeville, Wanda Green and the entire staff at the Monroe County Museum helped with a variety of research questions. Charles Shields generously shared research materials with me, and answered questions about sources.

Several colleagues read the entire manuscript on a very quick turnaround, and offered suggestions that improved the book enormously. Thank you Samuel Freedman, Patrick Allitt, Benjamin Reiss, Danny LaChance, and David Payne. Hank Klibanoff helped me with important questions about both Alabama and journalism, and opened his expansive Rolodex for me on a number of occasions. Sameer Pandya, Farrell Evans, Bruce Schulman, and Jim Campbell have been great sounding boards about this project as it evolved over many years.

Erica Bruchko at the Woodruff Library at Emory helped me locate sources and used money from her budget to buy microfilm copies of the *Monroe Journal*, which expedited my research greatly. It would have been impossible to write this book without the help of the entire staff at the Interlibrary Loan Office at Emory. They do fantastic work.

I wrote the bulk of this book during a year I spent as a senior fellow at the Fox Center for Humanistic Inquiry at Emory. Martine Brownley, Keith Anthony, Amy Erbil, and Colette Barlow all helped make my year there productive and fun. Thanks as well to the other senior fellows: Robin Fivush, Noelle McAfee, and especially Sarah McPhee, with whom I had a number of important conversations about history and biography.

Thanks to Sue Williams for inviting me to participate in a panel discussion at Emory with Natasha Trethewey and Kevin Young on the intersections of history and poetry. Natasha's and Kevin's writings have been an inspiration to me for many years, and our discussion that day sharpened my ideas and approach to this book.

Julian Zelizer and Kevin Kruse invited me to present a chapter of this book at their Political History seminar at Princeton. Sean Wilentz's commentary on the paper was brilliant and challenging, and the entire conversation with students and faculty there was inspiring.

I was fortunate to have two very smart and able Emory undergraduates who served as research assistants for the book, Mary Hollis McGreevy, who helped with some of the early research, and Hannah Fuller, who did yeoman's work checking the notes. I also benefitted from comments on the manuscript from the Emory undergraduates in my seminar on Atticus Finch and American History in the fall of 2017. Colleagues at Emory such as Tom Rogers, Yanna Yannakakis, Jeff Lesser, Jamie Melton, and Jonathan Prude provided insight and encouragement. The entire staff in the History Department—Kelly Yates, Becky Herring, Katie Wilson, and Alison Rollins—are a joy to work with. Their efficiency and professionalism make it easier to do things like researching and writing this book. Also making it easier are friends who lend their intelligent, balanced perspective—so thank you Randy, Charles, James, Walter, Berkeley, Bruce, Terry, and the entire Horseshoe gang.

My agent, Geri Thoma, is a sage and experienced guide and advocate. I appreciate her expertise and her friendship. Thank you Lara Heimert, publisher at Basic Books, for taking on this unorthodox project. Thanks can't begin to cover all that my editor, Dan Gerstle, did to help with the book. That guy doesn't miss a lick, and I'm grateful for his support and enthusiasm from the earliest stages on through to the last edit.

My daughter, Carrie, my son, Sam, and my wife, Caroline Herring, have lived this project with me over the last couple of years. Caroline also gave the book one of its best reads, and saved me from some foolish mistakes. Editorial assistance, however, has been among the least of her contributions. I'm a lucky man.

Notes

Prologue

xiii **"Whatever you please. Merry Christmas.":** Harper Lee, "Christmas to Me," *McCall's*, December 1961; *Chicago Tribune*, May 14, 1961; Charles Shields, *Mockingbird: A Portrait of Harper Lee, From Scout to Go Set a Watchman* (New York: Henry Holt, 2016), 73–78.

xiv **Friends had shown her:** Lee, "Christmas to Me."

xiv **With the title "Go Set a Watchman.":** "Lee, Nelle Harper," Author Cardfile, Box 210, Annie Laurie Williams Papers, Rare Book & Manuscript Library, Columbia University. Hereinafter cited as Lee, Author Cardfile, ALWP.

xiv **Later explain to a reporter:** *Birmingham Post-Herald*, January 3, 1962.

xiv **Author of *Gone with the Wind*:** Ellen F. Brown and John Wiley Jr., *Margaret Mitchell's* Gone with the Wind: *A Bestseller's Odyssey from Atlanta to Hollywood* (Lanham, MD: Taylor Trade Publishers, 2011), 12–25.

xiv **Help with her next book:** Maurice Crain to Lois Cole, February 28, 1957; Lois Dwight Cole to Maurice Crain, April 5, 1957; Maurice Crain to Nelle Harper Lee, April 5, 1957, HarperCollins Collection. This collection consists of letters and other documents taken primarily from the files of HarperCollins. It was assembled on behalf of Jonathan Burnham, senior vice-president and publisher of HarperCollins, in preparation for the publication of *Go Set a Watchman*. I was allowed to read all of the material, and given permission to quote from all but one letter. The documents remain in the possession of HarperCollins. I learned of their existence after watching the video recording of "Re-Discovering Harper Lee: Jonathan Burnham in Conversation with Joan Acocella and Tuzyline Allan," which took place October 7, 2015, at the Center for the Humanities at the Graduate Center, CUNY. In his presentation, Burnham quotes from a number of the documents from the collection. See https://www.centerforthehumanities.org/programming/re-discovering-harper-lee-jonathan-burnham-in-conversation-with-joan-acocella-and-tuzyline-allan.

xiv   **"In the segregation battle.":** Maurice Crain to Evan Thomas, April 10, 1957, HarperCollins Collection.

xv   **If this one didn't sell:** Interoffice Memorandum, Annie Laurie Williams to Maurice Crain, May 13, 1957, HarperCollins Collection.

xv   **At J. B. Lippincott on May 13:** Maurice Crain to Lynn Carrick, May 13, 1957, HarperCollins Collection.

xv   **First fifty pages of "Watchman.":** Lee, Author Cardfile, ALWP.

xv   **Titled "The Long Goodbye.":** Lee, Author Cardfile, ALWP.

xv   **"Sister to a lonely childhood.":** Maurice Crain to Lynn Carrick, June 13, 1957, HarperCollins Collection.

xvi   **Flow into "Watchman.":** Nelle Harper Lee to Joy and Michael Brown, July 9, 1957, HarperCollins Collection.

xvi   **"Charm to the telling.":** Portions of Crain's letter to McMillion are reproduced in Ari N. Schulman, "The Man Who Helped Make Harper Lee," *Atlantic*, July 14, 2015. McMillion's book, *So Long at the Fair*, would not be published until 1964. Writing to McMillion in February 1961, when *Mockingbird* had already emerged as a commercial hit, Crain recalled proudly how he "handled it from the time it was a short story and a gleam in the author's eye."

xvi   **Lippincott's records as "Atticus.":** J. B. Lippincott Company, *The Author and His Audience* (Philadelphia, PA, 1967), 27–28.

xvi   **Pages throughout the summer:** Lee, Author Cardfile, ALWP.

xvi   **Typed "To Kill A Mocking Bird.":** Lee, Author Cardfile, ALWP. Since the publication of *Go Set a Watchman* in 2015, the working assumption has been that *Mockingbird* emerged out of wholesale revisions that Lee made to *Watchman* under the guidance of Tay Hohoff. This is the theory put forth in Charles Shields's biography of Lee, *Mockingbird: A Portrait of Harper Lee, from Scout to* Go Set a Watchman. Yet documents in the HarperCollins Collection, make clear that the two manuscripts emerged in succession in the first half of 1957, and that Lee imagined them as part of one continual story.

xvii   **"Pure and simple.":** Quoted in Shields, *Mockingbird*, 150.

xix   **"And walk around in it.":** *New York Times*, January 10, 2017.

Chapter 1

4   **Was the highest he completed:** Year: *1940;* Census Place: *Monroeville, Monroe, Alabama;* Roll: *T627_66;* Page: *10A;* Enumeration District: *50-4.*

4   **Army of northern Virginia:** Ed Conner, email to author, March 6, 2017, Joseph Crespino papers, Rose Library, Emory University (hereinafter cited as Crespino papers); Wayne Flynt, *Mockingbird Songs: My Friendship with Harper Lee* (New York: HarperCollins, 2017), 124.

5   **"Defenceless people imaginable.":** Albert James Pickett, *History of Alabama and Incidentally of Georgia and Mississippi from the Earliest Period* (Charleston, SC: Walker and James, 1851), 521.

5   **Markers in and around Monroe:** Hank Conner, interview by author, March 3, 2017, Crespino papers.

5   **Junior of her closest sibling:** *Monroe Journal*, June 10, 1954.

6   **Bought on Alabama Avenue:** *Monroe Journal*, October 5, 1922; Shields, *Mockingbird*, 20.

7   **Fully to the service:** Monroe County Heritage Museum, *Monroeville: The Search for Harper Lee's Maycomb* (Charleston, SC: Arcadia Publishing, 1999), 76.

8   **Size of the tax:** *Anniston Star*, August 17, 1932.

8   **Solely on a cash basis:** *Monroe Journal*, September 12, 1935.

8   **That year's legislative session:** *Anniston Star*, February 22, 1935.

8   **Never came to pass:** Flynt, *Mockingbird Songs*, 43.

8   **"Lucrative position recently.":** *Monroe Journal*, April 20, 1933. Also see *Monroe Journal*, January 12, 1933, and February 9, 1933.

8   **"Calling us names.":** *Monroe Journal*, June 21, 1934.

9   **Anything in her book:** Harper Lee, *To Kill a Mockingbird* (New York: Warner Books, 1982), 116. All page numbers cited refer to this edition of the book; hereinafter cited as *TKM*.

11   **"Pride the name Alabamians.":** *Monroe Journal*, August 28, 1930.

11   **Against a white woman:** For more on the history of prosecutions of black-on-white rape trials in the Jim Crow South, see Lisa Lindquist Dorr, *White Women, Rape, and the Power of Race in Virginia, 1900–1960* (Chapel Hill: University of North Carolina Press, 2004).

11   **A. C. Lee ever took:** Shields, *Mockingbird*, 94–96.

12   **"Practice of criminal law.":** Lee, *TKM*, 5.

12   **"A Truly Great Man Passes.":** See for example *Monroe Journal*, April 14, 1932; December 21, 1933; May 17, 1934; and October 2, 1941.

12   **"Passions of the mobs.":** Mark K. Bauman, *Warren Akin Candler: The Conservative as Idealist* (Metuchen, NJ: Scarecrow Press, 1981), 156–159.

12   **Stood up to the lynch mob:** Whether A. C. Lee himself ever personally stood up to the Klan is doubtful. In her book reporting the childhood memories of Jennings Faulk Carter, a first cousin of Truman Capote's, Marianne M. Moates recounts a story in which in the early 1930s A. C. Lee, described as "a big strong man" (which he wasn't), dressed in an undershirt (it's hard to imagine the formal Lee walking out in public in an undershirt), confronted a group of Klansmen who had come to harass Truman's Halloween costume party. There's no indication from the *Monroe Journal* that the Klan was active in Monroe County in these years. Charles Shields records a similar story in his biography of Harper Lee, citing a letter written to him about the incident from local Monroeville historian George Thomas Jones. When I asked Jones about the incident, he said that Shields had been mistaken, and that the story was likely made up. Marianne M. Moates, *Truman Capote's Southern Years: Stories from a Monroeville Cousin* (Tuscaloosa: University of Alabama Press, 2014), 61–63; Shields, *Mockingbird*, 38, 273n82; George Thomas Jones, interview by author, May 2, 2017, Crespino papers.

12   **Actions "utterly reprehensible,":** *Monroe Journal*, June 26, 1930.

13   **Attacking a white woman:** *Monroe Journal*, July 3, 1930.

13   **Earlier in the day:** Crowd estimates vary. A reporter who was present put the number at between one thousand and two thousand. Another reporter in Marianna estimated between three thousand and five thousand. In his report for the NAACP, Howard Kester estimated between three thousand and seven thousand. James R. McGovern, *Anatomy of a Lynching: The Killing of Claude Neal* (Baton Rouge: Louisiana State University Press, 1992), 77; Howard Kester, "The Lynching of Claude Neal" (Montgomery, AL: Southern Rural Welfare Association, 1971), originally published by the National Association for the Advancement of Colored People, November 20, 1934. The spelling of Lola Cannidy's last name varies across secondary accounts. All original newspaper sources from the 1930s that I have consulted spell her name as I do here.

14   **Courthouse square in Marianna:** McGovern, *Anatomy of a Lynching*, 68–84; Kester, "Lynching of Claude Neal."

14   **Details of the lynching:** *Monroe Journal,* November 22, 1934.

14   **Neal and the other prisoners:** Kester, "Lynching of Claude Neal."

15   **Arrived from Apalachicola:** Kester, "Lynching of Claude Neal."

16   **"Not yet even alarmed.":** William Faulkner, *Intruder in the Dust* (New York: Random House, 1948), 138.

16   **Out at Old Sarum:** Lee, *TKM,* 144–146.

16   **Wrote in an editorial:** *Monroe Journal,* January 20, 1938, and February 24, 1938.

16   **Complied in both cases:** *Monroe Journal,* November 9, 1933; February 1, 1934; and July 12, 1934. In one of the cases, Leo Fountain had been convicted of killing another black man, Robert Martin, as part of a life insurance scam. The other case was notable because the convicted black man, Walter Lett, had been charged with criminally assaulting a white woman. Letters from Monroe citizens to the governor and the state parole board expressed doubts that Lett was guilty.

17   **"In the orderly way.":** *Monroe Journal,* October 5, 1933.

17   **Get a fair hearing:** *Monroe Journal,* January 28, 1932.

17   **"Disposition of justice.":** *Monroe Journal,* February 13, 1936.

18   **Took much note of it:** For more on Judge Horton's decision, see Dan T. Carter, *Scottsboro: A Tragedy of the American South* (Baton Rouge: Louisiana State University Press, 1969), 265–273.

18   **"Conception of the proprieties.":** *Monroe Journal,* April 13, 1933. In his history of the Scottsboro trial, James Goodman explains how many white Alabamans came to view the second Scottsboro trial as a fair and legitimate exercise of legal authority, as A. C. Lee clearly did in this editorial. See Goodman, *Stories of Scottsboro* (New York: Vintage Books, 1994), 136–146. Also see *Monroe Journal,* July 29, 1937.

19   **Interest in the trial that followed:** See, for example, the trial of Tom Perkins, a black man, for the murder of Clifton McNeil. Perkins was convicted and sentenced to death. The *Journal* reported, "The trial evoked a great deal of interest throughout the county . . . Despite the bad weather, a capacity crowd filled the court room and the judge ordered those who were unable to find seats to retire from the room." *Monroe Journal,* April 9, 1936.

19   **Dancing and a "Negro quartette.":** See, for example, *Monroe Journal,* February 4, 1932; December 13, 1934; and February 28, 1935.

19   **Banner "White Supremacy.":** *Monroe Journal,* October 30, 1930.

19   **"Her white people.":** *Monroe Journal,* July 31, 1930.

19   **"Fealty and integrity.":** *Monroe Journal,* March 2, 1933.

19   **Between corporations and government:** *Monroe Journal*, March 23, 1933, and June 29, 1933.

20   **Bottom was dictatorship:** A long run of editorials through the mid- and late 1930s reflect this general theme. See the following issues of the *Monroe Journal* by year for examples. 1935: February 21; May 9; June 13; July 25; August 8; October 31. 1936: April 2. 1937: September 2. 1938: May 19; May 26; June 23. 1939: July 13; September 14; September 21. 1940: January 4; August 1.

20   **Session to discuss it:** *Monroe Journal*, March 26, August 27, and September 3, 1931.

20   **Legislators, and judges alike:** See *Monroe Journal*, May 19, 1932; August 10, 1933; September 7, 1933; January 18, 1934; August 9, 1934; September 6, 1934; December 20, 1934; and January 24, 1935.

21   **Power in Europe:** For Roosevelt's views on Long see T. Harry Williams, *Huey Long* (New York: Knopf, 1969) 640, 794–795; and Alan Brinkley, *Voices of Protest: Huey Long, Father Coughlin, and the Great Depression* (New York: Knopf, 1982), 62–64, 79–81.

22   **Died two days later:** Williams, *Huey Long*, 859–871; Brinkley, *Voices of Protest*, 249–251.

22   **Dangers of "iron handed rule.":** *Monroe Journal*, September 19, 1935.

22   **Example of the Louisiana Kingfish:** See, for example, *Monroe Journal* editorials on July 13 and August 3, 10, and 24, 1939; and February 22 and March 14, 1940.

22   **Eventually probate judge:** *Monroe Journal Centennial Edition, 1866–1966*, 27C.

22   **Fought to defeat Millsap:** *Monroe Journal Centennial Edition, 1866–1966*, 7B; Monroe County Heritage Museums, *Monroeville: The Search for Harper Lee's Maycomb*, 64–65.

23   **"Factotum in local affairs.":** V. O. Key Jr., *Southern Politics in State and Nation* (New York: Vintage Books, 1949), 53–54.

23   **Casually over the arm:** Monroe County Heritage Museums, *Monroeville: The Search for Harper Lee's Maycomb*, 64–65.

23   **Paid for such service:** *Monroe Journal*, April 25, 1940.

23   **Cashed at election time:** *Monroe Journal*, May 2, 1940; Rayburn Williams, interview by author, May 2, 2017, Crespino papers.

24   **Promised them the world:** *Monroe Journal*, February 15, 1940; February 22, 1940; and March 14, 1940.

24   **"Make Us Free.":** *Monroe Journal*, April 4, 1940.

24   **"Built in the county.":** *Monroe Journal,* April 11, 1940.

24   **Subscription be discontinued:** *Monroe Journal,* April 18, 1940. Nelle Dailey census record at Year: *1940;* Census Place: *Perdue Hill, Monroe, Alabama;* Roll: *T627_66;* Page: *1A;* Enumeration District: *50-3.* Homer Dees census record at Year: *1930;* Census Place: *Ridge, Monroe, Alabama;* Roll: *42;* Page: *3A;* Enumeration District: 0008; Image: *901.0;* FHL microfilm: *2339777.*

24   **Boxes with loyal henchmen:** *Monroe Journal,* April 25, 1940; *Monroe Journal,* May 2, 1940.

24   **3,900 votes cast:** *Monroe Journal,* May 9, 1940.

25   **"Upon the proper basis.":** *Monroe Journal,* May 16, 1940.

25   **"Properly appraise values.":** *Monroe Journal,* May 23, 1940.

25   **"Vote was Willoughby's.":** Harper Lee, *Go Set a Watchman* (New York: HarperCollins, 2015), 106. Hereinafter cited as *GSAW.*

25   **Southerners read the news:** Thomas D. Clark, *The Southern Country Editor* (Columbia: University of South Carolina Press, 1991), 332–338.

26   **"Liberty's Darkest Hour.":** *Monroe Journal,* June 20, 1940.

26   **"These things to be.":** *Monroe Journal,* June 27, 1940.

26   **Lee's heartiest endorsement:** *Monroe Journal,* June 13, 1940.

26   **"Our program of preparedness.":** *Monroe Journal,* June 27, 1940.

26   **"Him to come over here.":** Quoted in John Temple Graves, *The Fighting South* (New York: G. P. Putnam's Sons, 1943), 8. Also see John T. Kneebone, *Southern Liberal Journalists and the Issue of Race, 1920–1944* (Chapel Hill: University of North Carolina Press, 1985), 175–176.

27   **Nationalist forces in China:** *Monroe Journal,* June 11, 1931, and May 11, 1933 (Gandhi); *Monroe Journal,* February 8, 1934 (China).

27   **Frequently, the rise of Hitler:** *Monroe Journal,* March 23, 1933; September 2, 1937; and February 24, 1938 (Japan). *Monroe Journal,* September 19, October 3, and October 31, 1935; May 7, 1936; and May 6, 1937 (Italy). *Monroe Journal,* August 2, 1934; May 9, 1935; August 27, 1936; July 22, 1937; February 10, March 24, July 28, September 1, September 15, September 22, September 29, October 6, October 13, November 24, and December 22, 1938; and March 23, May 4, August 24, and September 7, 1939 (Germany).

27   **July putsch in Austria:** *Monroe Journal,* August 2, 1934.

27   **Protestant and Catholic organizations:** *Monroe Journal,* March 28 and August 22, 1935.

27   **"With their present-day Hitler.":** *Monroe Journal,* March 24, 1938.

27   **Fictionalize in *Mockingbird*:** Monroe County Heritage Museums, *Monroeville*, 60–61.

27   **Towns across the South:** Lee Shai Weissbach records an apocryphal story of small town Jewish life that involved a Jewish merchant who watched a parade of Klansmen with bemusement, identifying each hooded member by name based on the shoes the particular Klansman had bought at his store. See Lee Shai Weissbach, *Jewish Life in Small-Town America: A History* (New Haven, CT: Yale University Press, 2005), 273.

27   **"Progressive community," it read:** *Monroe Journal*, September 29, 1938.

28   **Mid-1930s, disgusted Lee:** *Monroe Journal*, January 23, 1936.

28   **Join the League of Nations:** *Monroe Journal*, February 18, 1932; May 25, 1933; March 24, 1938; November 17, 1938; April 6, 1939; November 9, 1939; and March 13, 1941.

28   **"Destruction of England and France.":** *Monroe Journal*, October 19, 1939.

28   **"World," Lee contended:** *Monroe Journal*, July 11, 1940.

28   **"Purposes of [the] government.":** *Monroe Journal*, May 8, 1941.

29   **"Beginning of another world war.":** *Monroe Journal*, September 2, 1937.

29   **"That is bound to come.":** *Monroe Journal*, March 24, 1938.

29   **"In this country of ours.":** *Monroe Journal*, February 9, April 20, and September 7, 1939.

29   **"Messages of his whole administration.":** *Monroe Journal*, September 28, 1939.

29   **In favor of revision:** David M. Kennedy, *Freedom from Fear: The American People in Depression and War, 1929–1945* (New York: Oxford University Press, 1999), 433.

29   **Established by George Washington:** *Monroe Journal*, August 26, 1937; June 13, 1940; August 22, 1940.

Chapter 2

31   **"I am Dill.":** Gerald Clarke, ed., *Too Brief a Treat: The Letters of Truman Capote* (New York: Random House, 2004), 290.

31   **Writing their first stories:** George Plimpton, *Truman Capote: In Which Various Friends, Enemies, Acquaintances, and Detractors Recall His Turbulent Career* (New York: Doubleday, 1997), 11–13; Shields, *Mockingbird*, 32.

32   **"she is a freak, too?":** Truman Capote, *Other Voices, Other Rooms* (New York: Vintage Books, 1948), 106, 155.

32   **US Army Air Corps:** Shields, *Mockingbird*, 42–43.

33   **"School of Ideals.":** *Monroe Journal*, August 31, 1922; Shields, *Mockingbird*, 17–18; and Marja Mills, *The Mockingbird Next Door: Life with Harper Lee* (New York: Penguin Books, 2014), 104.

33   **Nelle Harper, for him:** Mills, *Mockingbird Next Door*, 179–183.

33   **Presence in the house:** Mills, *Mockingbird Next Door*, 179–183; Shields, *Mockingbird*, 21–24.

33   **Lawyer in Monroe County:** *Monroe Journal*, October 7, 1943, and June 10, 1954.

34   **"Satisfied," the narrator nods:** Nelle Harper Lee, "A Wink at Justice," *The Prelude*, Spring 1945, 14–15.

34   **Comments on their work:** Nelle Harper Lee, "Nightmare," *The Prelude*, Spring 1945, 11.

34   **"Lee and Daughters, Lawyers.":** *Crimson-White*, November 26, 1946.

35   **Despite Lee's fervent opposition:** *Monroe Journal*, March 23, April 6, and April 27, 1944.

35   **Effort in regional development:** *Monroe Journal*, January 26, 1933.

35   **"Conception of public duty.":** *Monroe Journal*, April 6, 1933.

35   **Balance to the financial sector:** *Monroe Journal*, June 8, 1933.

35   **County's southern edge:** *Monroe Journal*, June 8, 1933.

35   **Controversial National Recovery Act:** *Monroe Journal*, June 22, 1933; April 19 and October 4, 1934; and June 6, 1935.

35   **People shouldn't panic:** *Monroe Journal*, November 17, 1932.

35   **"Leaders of all times.":** *Monroe Journal*, August 3, 1933.

36   **Lifeblood of south Alabama:** *Monroe Journal*, June 29, 1933.

36   **"Present occupant," Lee wrote:** *Monroe Journal*, January 16, 1936.

36   **"Bloodletting at the pigpens.":** Clark, *Southern Country Editor*, 333.

36   **Height of irresponsible demagoguery:** For Lee's editorials on Talmadge, see *Monroe Journal*, August 8, November 7, and December 19, 1935; April 23, May 14, May 21, June 11, and September 17, 1936; October 23, 1941; and August 20, 1942. For more on Talmadge's fight with Roosevelt, see William Anderson, *The Wild Man from Sugar Creek: The Political Career of Eugene Talmadge* (Baton Rouge: Louisiana State University Press, 1975), 105–123.

36 **Restructure the Supreme Court:** *Monroe Journal*, February 18, 1937. For more editorials on court-packing, see *Monroe Journal*, February 11, March 25, May 20, July 15, and July 29, 1937.

36 **"One of its policies.":** *Monroe Journal*, June 24, 1937.

37 **Compete under the new rules:** *Monroe Journal*, December 16, 1937.

37 **Industrialists of a nonunionized workforce:** *Monroe Journal*, June 16 and June 30, 1938.

37 **"Disguised as a humanitarian reform.":** Quoted in Kennedy, *Freedom from Fear*, 345.

37 **Short end of the stick:** *Monroe Journal*, May 19, June 2, and June 9, 1938. A. C. Lee would continue to write about the law and what he perceived as its harmful impact on the southern economy. See *Monroe Journal*, July 21, October 27, and November 3, 1938; and June 29 and October 26, 1939.

37 **Sparked the Vanity Fair deal:** Kathryn Tucker Windham, *Alabama, One Big Front Porch* (Huntsville, AL: Strode Publishers, 1975), 120.

38 **Climate of south Alabama:** Edward Boykin, *Everything's Made for Love in This Man's World: Vignettes from the Life of Frank W. Boykin* (Mobile, AL: Privately printed, 1973), 82.

38 **Operate a union shop:** Michelle Haberland, "It Takes a Special Kind of Woman to Work up There," in *Work, Family, and Faith: Southern Women in the Twentieth Century*, ed. Rebecca Sharpless and Melissa Walker (Columbia: University of Missouri Press, 2006), 258. For more on the history of Vanity Fair's relocation to Alabama, see Michelle Haberland, *Striking Beauties: Women Apparel Workers in the U.S. South, 1930–2000* (Athens: University of Georgia Press, 2015).

38 **Day, and for good reason:** *Monroe Journal*, June 16, 1938.

39 **Would have enjoyed immensely:** Haberland, "It Takes a Special Kind of Woman to Work up There"; and George T. Jones, interview by author, May 2, 2017, Crespino papers.

39 **Return home from New York:** Lee, *GSAW*, 80.

39 **Countless reactionary attacks:** For a firsthand account of these developments by a native, white, southern liberal, see Virginia Foster Durr, *Outside the Magic Circle: The Autobiography of Virginia Foster Durr* (Tuscaloosa: University of Alabama Press, 1985); also see Patricia Sullivan, *Days of Hope: Race and Democracy in the New Deal Era* (Chapel Hill: University of North Carolina Press, 1996).

40 **"Existence before the New Deal.":** Kennedy, *Freedom from Fear*, 340. Also see James Patterson, *Congressional Conservatism and the New*

Deal: The Growth of the Conservative Coalition in Congress, 1933–1939 (Lexington: University Press of Kentucky, 1967).

40 **Community along class lines:** Key, *Southern Politics*, 41–46. For more on A. C. Lee's sympathy with the Black Belt, see *Monroe Journal*, October 12, 1933. Lee advocated a measure to reduce membership in the House to one member per county. North Alabamans opposed it because it would give more power to the Black Belt, which had a smaller population. Lee said the measure was about cost-saving and efficiency, not exploiting the factional divide, though it's easy to see how north Alabamans would have viewed it otherwise.

41 **Votes with extravagant promises:** *Monroe Journal*, June 26, 1930.

41 **"Appeal of the demagogue.":** *Monroe Journal*, August 28, 1930.

41 **Did seem heaven-sent:** For a fuller examination of rural southerners' encounter with the Great Depression, see Alison Collis Greene, *No Depression in Heaven: The Great Depression, the New Deal, and the Transformation of Religion in the Delta* (New York: Oxford University Press, 2015).

41 **He wrote in 1938:** *Monroe Journal*, June 23, 1938.

41 **"Owes them a living.":** *Monroe Journal*, July 27, 1939.

41 **Out of control, he feared:** *Monroe Journal*, March 16 and December 28, 1939.

41 **"Our Income" once again:** *Monroe Journal*, March 25, 1939.

42 **Coherent liberal program:** Brinkley, *End of Reform*, 3–4.

42 **Lobbying on Heflin's behalf:** *Monroe Journal*, March 20, 1930. For more on race and labor and the 1920s Klan, see Glenn Feldman, *Politics, Society, and the Klan in Alabama, 1915–1949* (Tuscaloosa: University of Alabama Press, 1999).

42 **Influence on the Democratic Party:** *Monroe Journal*, October 16, 1930.

42 **Publicized on the *Journal's* editorial page:** *Monroe Journal*, September 18, 1930.

42 **"wages and hours legislation.":** *Monroe Journal*, December 16, 1937. Also see *Monroe Journal*, December 30, 1937; January 6 and January 20, 1938.

43 **"Language," Roosevelt explained:** Kennedy, *Freedom from Fear*, 346–347; *Monroe Journal*, June 30, 1938.

43 **"Chore to his enemies.":** *Monroe Journal*, August 18, 1938.

43 **"Sink the ship.":** *Monroe Journal*, September 15, 1938. For other of Lee's editorials on Roosevelt's attempted "southern purge," see *Monroe*

Journal, July 14, September 1, and September 22, 1938. For more on the politics of the purge, see Susan Dunn, *Roosevelt's Purge: How FDR Fought to Change the Democratic Party* (Cambridge, MA: Harvard University Press, 2012).

43 **Anti–New Deal sentiment:** For Alabama conservatives' challenge to Roosevelt's third term, see Robert J. Norrell, "Labor at the Ballot Box: Alabama Politics from the New Deal to the Dixiecrat Movement," *Journal of Southern History*, vol. 57, no. 2 (May 1991): 219–220. Lee wrote editorials opposed to the principle of a third term for Roosevelt, but when push came to shove in the summer of 1940, he was firmly in Roosevelt's camp. See *Monroe Journal*, August 26, 1937, and June 13, 1940.

43 **Denounced in a 1934 editorial:** *Monroe Journal*, August 30, 1934.

43 **Lee lapped them up:** For more on the anti–New Deal business lobby, see Kimberly Phillips-Fein, *Invisible Hands: The Businessmen's Crusade against the New Deal* (New York: W. W. Norton, 2010).

44 **His with the credit line:** For more on the Industrial News Review, see *Congressional Record*, Senate, April 6, 1965, 6951–6957.

44 **"State Leads to Despotism.":** *Monroe Journal*, December 5, 1940; February 6, 1941; and April 10, 1947. I did not record every Industrial News Review editorial published in the *Monroe Journal*, but a good sampling can be seen in issues on October 20, 1938; October 26, 1939; February 15 and 22, 1940; and January 27, 1944, as well as numerous editorials in 1945 and 1946.

44 **Early years of the war:** *Monroe Journal*, April 3, May 15, June 12, October 30, and November 20, 1941; and July 30, September 24, October 1, and December 17, 1942. There were also numerous other editorials on this subject in 1943.

44 **Take its place:** *Monroe Journal*, May 25, 1944; June 8, 1944; and May 16, 1946.

44 **"Headed for Statism?":** *Monroe Journal*, September 23, 1943; November 30, 1944; September 27, 1945; October 11, 1945; and May 2, 1946.

44 **"That way everywhere else?":** Quoted in Norrell, "Labor at the Ballot Box," 219.

45 **Age of eligibility:** George C. Stoney, "Suffrage in the South—Part I: The Poll Tax," *Survey Graphic* 29, no. 1 (January 1, 1940): 5–9.

46 **Candidates in the preceding years:** Sheldon Hackney, *Populism to Progressivism in Alabama* (Princeton: Princeton University Press, 1969), 147–208.

46   **Pepper, an Alabama native:** *Monroe Journal,* November 19 and 26, 1942; December 3, 1942; July 27, 1944; February 22, 1945; and March 8, 1945.

46   **Community in fundraising efforts:** *Monroe Journal,* May 8, 1941, and February 4, 1954.

47   **"Relationships between the races.":** *Monroe Journal,* October 1, 1942.

47   **"Hearts of the people of America.":** *Monroe Journal,* January 14, 1943.

47   **"Fair country of ours.":** *Monroe Journal,* July 26, 1945. For other anti-FEPC editorials, see January 31 and June 20, 1946. Also see two guest editorials Lee published on June 28, 1945, and January 10, 1946.

47   **"Bloc of the people.":** *Monroe Journal,* June 1, 1944.

47   **"Road to ultimate destruction.":** *Monroe Journal,* November 29, 1945.

48   **"À la Confederate era.":** *Crimson-White,* October 5 and 12, 1945.

48   **"regular on the staff.":** *Rammer-Jammer,* December 1945.

48   **Burglary at a sorority house:** *Crimson-White,* June 13, June 21, and August 2, 1946.

48   **"Something about it," she wrote:** *Crimson-White,* June 28, 1946.

49   **Whom were freshmen:** *Crimson-White,* May 27, 1947.

49   **Country club of the South:** For the impact of World War II veterans on the politics of the South, see Jennifer E. Brooks, *Defining the Peace: World War II Veterans, Race, and the Remaking of Southern Political Tradition* (Chapel Hill: University of North Carolina Press, 2011).

50   **"Since it was built.":** Folsom quoted in Carl Grafton and Anne Permaloff, *Big Mules & Branchheads: James E. Folsom and Political Power in Alabama* (Athens: University of Georgia Press, 1985), 60; *Crimson-White,* April 12, 1946.

50   **"Than its weakest element.":** *Crimson-White,* May 3, 1946.

51   **"South could be broken.":** *Crimson-White,* April 19, 1946.

51   **"Doctrine of the states' rights.":** *Crimson-White,* March 22 and May 24, 1946.

51   **Students at the summer convocation:** *Crimson-White,* June 13, 1946.

51   **"From somewhere in Mississippi.":** *Crimson-White,* August 16, 1946.

51   **"Activities of the Klan discontinued.":** *Crimson-White,* July 26, 1946.

51   **Cowardly to sign his name:** *Crimson-White*, August 2, 1946.

52   **"Our government was founded.":** *Monroe Journal*, August 22, 1946.

52   **African American veterans' hospital:** Robert J. Norrell, *Reaping the Whirlwind: The Civil Rights Movement in Tuskegee* (New York: Knopf, 1985), 59–63.

53   **Fall of 1946:** McCorvey quoted in Stephen F. Lawson, *Black Ballots: Voting Rights in the South, 1944–1969* (New York: Columbia University Press, 1976), 90. Also see Norrell, *Reaping the Whirlwind*, 56.

53   **"Proven themselves worthy.":** *Monroe Journal*, October 3, 10, 17, and 24, 1946.

55   **Protest their disfranchisement:** *Rammer Jammer*, October 1946, 7, 17–18.

55   **Before the Supreme Court:** Richard T. Rives, "Argument Against the Adoption of the Boswell Amendment," *Alabama Lawyer* 7, no. 3 (July 1946): 291–297.

55   **"Civilization known to man.":** Horace Wilkinson, "Argument for Adoption of the Boswell Amendment," *Alabama Lawyer* 7, no. 4 (October 1946): 375–382.

56   **Negroes demanding registration:** Norrell, *Reaping the Whirlwind*, 65–66.

57   **Back in January 1941:** *Monroe Journal*, January 23, 1941.

57   **"The Jackassonian Democrat.":** *Rammer Jammer*, February 1947.

57   **Editorship of the *Monroe Journal*:** Shields, *Mockingbird*, 65.

58   **"Wish to change.":** *Monroe Journal*, June 26, 1947.

58   **"Line of easiest resistance.":** *Washington Post*, November 17, 1960.

58   **With her head down:** Shields, *Mockingbird*, 62–64.

58   **Co-ed participation and leadership:** For example, the summer that Nelle had a column in the *Crimson-White*, the editorial and business staff of the paper included an equal number of men and women. By her senior year, however, only two of the nine leadership staff positions were held by women.

59   **"By actual belief.":** *Crimson-White*, February 9, 1948.

59   **"Government of Russia.":** *Crimson-White*, October 8, 1946.

59   **"Faults of the Communistic system.":** *Crimson-White*, February 9, 1948.

59   **"Idiotic generalities," she wrote:** *Crimson-White*, February 17, 1948.

59   **"Harsh in my interpretation.":** *Crimson-White*, March 2, 1948.

59   **"'God Save the King'":** *Crimson-White*, March 9, 1948.

60   **"Small towns forever.":** Nelle Lee, "Some Writers of Our Times," *Rammer Jammer,* November 1945.

60   **"Dark eddies of 'niggertown.'":** *Crimson-White,* October 1, 1946.

60   **Died later that evening:** Shields, *Mockingbird,* 70–72; Mills, *Mockingbird Next Door,* 143–144.

61   **Nine-month-old son, Edwin Jr.:** Shields, *Mockingbird,* 70–72; Mills, *Mockingbird Next Door,* 145–148.

62   **Also true to life:** Lee, *GSAW,* 32.

63   **Loved all things English:** Ed Conner, interview by author, March 7, 2017, Crespino papers.

63   **"A fuse onto dynamite.":** Ray Whatley, interview by author, May 16, 2017, Crespino papers.

64   **"Suspected of liberal tendencies.":** Lee, *GSAW,* 94–95.

65   **Reaction to victory:** Anderson, *Wild Man from Sugar Creek,* 231–233.

65   **Did not improve from there:** Ray Whatley, interview by author, May 16, 2017, Crespino papers.

65   **Lures of communism:** Ray E. Whatley, "The Laborer," September 2, 1951, Ray Whatley Papers, Methodist Archives Center, Huntingdon College Library, Montgomery, Alabama.

66   **"Me from Beulah Land.":** Hank Conner, interview by author, March 3, 2017, Crespino papers.

66   **Led toward communism:** A. C. Lee, "This Is My Father's World," c. 1952, Special Collections, Bounds Law Library, University of Alabama School of Law.

66   **"Rule in America.":** Ray Whatley, "My Brother's Keeper," February 8, 1953, Ray Whatley Papers, Methodist Archives Center, Huntingdon College Library, Montgomery, Alabama.

67   **"Stay off social issues.":** Ray E. Whatley, "Some Reflections on Race Relations in the South," April 19, 1965, Ray Whatley Papers, Methodist Archives Center, Huntingdon College Library, Montgomery, Alabama.

67   **Gesture of reconciliation:** Ray Whatley, interview by author, May 16, 2017, Crespino papers.

67   **Than Montgomery and Monroeville:** Ray Whatley, "A Review of Personal Experiences in Racial Issues," January 11, 1994, Ray Whatley Papers, Methodist Archives Center, Huntingdon College Library, Montgomery, Alabama.

68   **Church in the North:** L. Harold DeWolf to Rev. Ray E. Whatley, November 2, 1956, Ray Whatley Papers, Methodist Archives Center, Huntingdon College Library, Montgomery, Alabama.

68 **Service on the pension board:** Ray Whatley, interview by author, May 16, 2017, Crespino papers.

68 **Church in Monroeville:** Ray Whatley, interview by author, May 16, 2017, Crespino papers; Charles J. Shields, interview by author, June 21, 2017, Crespino papers.

69 **"Doing a great job.":** Flynt, *Mockingbird Songs,* 72–73.

Chapter 3

73 **And Annie Laurie Williams:** *Chicago Tribune,* May 4, 1961.

73 **"Yes, Mam and No Mam.":** P. Barnes to M. Crain, Subject Nelle Harper Lee, November 28, 1956, HarperCollins Collection.

73 **Connecticut to write:** *Los Angeles Times,* February 9, 1962.

73 **Cruise on the Mississippi River:** Alice Lee to Maurice Crain and Annie Laurie Williams, July 3, 1965, box 149, folder Lee, Nelle Harper—Motion Picture, Annie Laurie Williams Papers, Rare Book and Manuscript Library, Columbia University.

74 **Strength to hold a book:** Nelle Harper Lee to Harold Caufield, June 16, 1956, and n.d., Kennerson Collection. A number of letters that Harper Lee wrote from Monroeville to friends in New York in the late 1950s and early 1960s are in the private collection of Paul Kennerson, who allowed me to read, take notes on, and quote from the material. My notes on the letters are included in my research materials that are archived at the Rose Library at Emory University. For more on the Kennerson collection, see Rebecca Mead, "Yours Truly," *New Yorker,* June 8 and 15, 2015.

75 **She would fictionalize in *Watchman*.:** Nelle Harper Lee to "Dears," n.d., Kennerson Collection.

75 **"If such is possible.":** Nelle Harper Lee to Harold Caufield and friends, n.d., Kennerson Collection.

77 **"Gets into the newspapers.":** Lee, *GSAW,* 24.

77 ***Post* and the *New York Times*:** Gene Roberts and Hank Klibanoff, *The Race Beat: The Press, the Civil Rights Struggle, and the Awakening of a Nation* (New York: Knopf, 2006), 212–214.

78 **"Bloodshed" would ensue:** David Halberstam, "The White Citizens Councils: Respectable Means for Unrespectable Ends," *Commentary* 22 (October 1, 1956): 293–302 (quotation on 294); Joseph Crespino, *In Search of Another Country: Mississippi and the Conservative Counterrevolution* (Princeton, NJ: Princeton University Press, 2007), 23.

78   **"Renew a mortgage.":** Quoted in J. Mills Thornton, *Dividing Lines: Municipal Politics and the Struggle for Civil Rights in Montgomery, Birmingham, and Selma* (Tuscaloosa: University of Alabama Press, 2009), 393.

78   **Membership was twelve thousand:** Thornton, *Dividing Lines*, 73.

78   **Membership of forty thousand:** Neil R. McMillen, *The Citizens' Council: Organized Resistance to the Second Reconstruction* (Urbana: University of Illinois Press, 1971), 43–44.

78   **Political power for years:** McMillen, *Citizens' Council*, 47; Norrell, *Reaping the Whirlwind*, 79.

79   **"Negroes in every county office.":** Lee, *GSAW*, 243.

79   **Out of three members:** *New York Times* (*NYT* hereinafter) March 13, 1956.

79   **Case to the nation:** *NYT*, February 11, 1956.

79   **Leading to a conviction:** *Washington Post*, February 1, 1956.

80   **In and around Birmingham:** David M. Chalmers, *Hooded Americanism: The First Century of the Ku Klux Klan, 1865–1965* (New York: Doubleday, 1965), 344–347; Diane McWhorter, *Carry Me Home: Birmingham, Alabama: The Climactic Battle of the Civil Rights Revolution* (New York: Simon and Schuster, 2001), 100–101. In one of the more bizarre second acts in American history, in the 1970s Carter took the pen name Forest Carter and penned a string of successful novels set in the American West, including one that would be made into a major motion picture, *The Outlaw Josey Wales*, starring Clint Eastwood, and *The Education of Little Tree*, a fictional memoir of a Native American childhood that became a sleeper hit in the late 1980s, some ten years after Carter's death. *NYT*, October 4, 1991.

80   **Whites with integrationist ideas:** *NYT*, March 30, 1956.

80   **"Only in maintaining segregation.":** *NYT*, March 6, 1956.

80   **Performance in Birmingham:** *Atlanta Constitution*, April 12, 1956.

80   **Cars with black passengers:** *Atlanta Constitution*, September 1, 1956.

80   **Violence in Clinton:** *NYT*, September 25, 1956.

81   **Klan meeting in Birmingham:** *Atlanta Constitution*, January 24, 1957.

81   **Charges were eventually dropped:** McMillen, *Citizens' Council*, 55.

81   **Buses were unconstitutional:** *Washington Post*, November 14, 1956.

81   **Segregation on Birmingham buses:** *Christian Science Monitor*, December 28, 1956.

81   **"Dynamite with a short fuse.":** *Philadelphia Tribune,* January 1, 1957.

81   **Determined to maintain segregation:** *NYT,* December 16, 1956.

81   **Calming the troubled waters:** Taylor Branch, *Parting the Waters: America in the King Years, 1954–1963* (New York: Simon and Schuster, 1989), 164–167; *New Journal and Guide,* December 29, 1956.

82   **"Creature all his life.":** Nelle Harper Lee to Hal Caufield, n.d., Kennerson Collection.

82   **"Colored and white people.":** *Monroe Journal,* March 8, 1956.

82   **"Time in a Christian Democracy.":** *Monroe Journal,* February 16, 1956.

82   **"Feet on the ground.":** *Monroe Journal,* March 1, 1956.

82   **Whites in Monroe County:** *Monroe Journal,* March 15, 1956.

83   **Monroe in the twentieth century:** Steve Stewart, interview by author, January 13, 2017, Crespino papers.

83   **On them soon enough:** In Macon County, in addition to the white-controlled board of registrars refusing to meet, Engelhardt had introduced a bill in the state legislature to gerrymander the Tuskegee city boundaries to dilute black voting strength. For more on Engelhardt and white resistance in Macon County, see Norrell, *Reaping the Whirlwind,* 93–110.

83   **Representative from Harlem:** *Monroe Journal,* March 22, 1956.

83   **Over seven hundred members:** *Monroe Journal,* May 31, 1956.

83   **Mississippi judge Tom Brady:** *Monroe Journal,* June 14, 1956 (Harris); July 19, 1956 (Brady); September 13, 1956 (Grant).

83   **He had helped incite:** Lee, *GSAW,* 238.

84   **Kills a white man:** The Selma case involved William Earl Fikes, a twenty-seven-year-old service station attendant accused of entering the home of the daughter of Selma's mayor. See Thornton, *Dividing Lines,* 387–392.

84   **"Like this to happen.":** Lee, *GSAW,* 148–149.

84   **"Maycomb County council membership.":** Lee, *GSAW,* 250. In other places Lee disassociates Atticus from the extremists. Jean Louise is appalled to find among Atticus's reading material a copy of a scurrilous pamphlet titled *The Black Plague,* yet we never hear Atticus defend the publication; it is only the insipid Aunt Alexandra who blithely suggests that "[t]here are a lot of truths in that book" (Lee, *GSAW,* 102). Atticus's membership in the Klan in the 1920s, a revelation that Henry Clinton

makes to Jean Louise, is explained by a moderate, pragmatic sensibility. "He had to know who he'd be fighting if the time ever came to," Henry says of Atticus, "he had to find out who they were" (Lee, *GSAW*, 230).

84 **"Be in such a hurry.":** Lee, *GSAW*, 229.

84 **Mechanics, storekeepers, and small clerks:** David M. Chalmers, *Hooded Americanism: The First Century of the Ku Klux Klan, 1865–1965* (New York: Doubleday, 1965), 345.

85 **Would write him off:** Lee, *GSAW*, 232.

85 **Henry explains to Jean Louise:** Lee, *GSAW*, 230.

85 **"Supreme Court decision?":** Lee, *GSAW*, 238.

85 **"Bid for immortality.":** Lee, *GSAW*, 24.

86 **"Liberal by comparison":** All quotations in this paragraph are taken from Lee, *GSAW*, 238–240.

86 **"Contemporary social justice.":** *NYT*, May 18, 1954.

87 **Difficult but necessary transition:** Richard Kluger, *Simple Justice: The History of* Brown v. Board of Education *and Black America's Struggle for Equality* (New York: Knopf, 1975), 700–747.

88 **"Law of the land.":** *Congressional Record*—Senate, March 12, 1956, 4459–4460.

88 **"Supreme Court's order.":** *NYT*, February 26, 1956.

88 **"Land I love.":** Quoted in Joseph Crespino, *Strom Thurmond's America* (New York: Hill and Wang, 2012), 116.

89 **Opposition to the loudmouth Talmadge:** Keith M. Finley, *Delaying the Dream: Southern Senators and the Fight Against Civil Rights, 1938–1965* (Baton Rouge: Louisiana State University Press, 2008), 142–147; Crespino, *Strom Thurmond's America*, 105–107.

89 **Use them wisely:** Lee, *GSAW*, 244–245.

89 **"Good things in it.":** Lee, *GSAW*, 200.

90 **"If he wants to.":** All quotations in this paragraph are taken from Lee, *GSAW*, 197–198.

90 **"Members of society fearlessly.":** *Monroe Journal*, December 19, 1935; also see *Monroe Journal*, January 30, 1941.

90 **Jefferson, "the Great Democrat":** *Monroe Journal*, August 22, 1946.

91 ***South and the Agrarian Tradition:*** Twelve Southerners, *I'll Take My Stand: The South and the Agrarian Tradition* (New York: Harper, 1930).

91 **"Marshall were busily forwarding.":** Donald Davidson, *The Attack on Leviathan: Regionalism and Nationalism in the United States*

(Chapel Hill: University of North Carolina Press, 1938), 106–107, 265–267.

91   **Conservative intellectual movement:** Paul V. Murphy, *The Rebuke of History: The Southern Agrarians and American Conservative Thought* (Chapel Hill: University of North Carolina Press, 2001), 146–149.

92   **"Viewpoint of conservative white Southerners.":** George H. Nash, *The Conservative Intellectual Movement in America: Since 1945* (New York: Basic Books, 1976), 307.

92   **(Response of the Citizens' Council movement.):** Lee, *GSAW*, 193–195.

92   **"Minority are to be satisfied.":** Donald Davidson, "The New South and the Conservative Tradition," *National Review* 9 (September 10, 1960): 141–146 (quotation on 146).

92   **"It is the advanced race.":** "Why the South Must Prevail," *National Review* 4 (August 24, 1957): 148–149.

93   **"Tyrant over society.":** Davidson, "New South and the Conservative Tradition," 146.

94   **"Himself with the Communists.":** Joel Williamson, *William Faulkner and Southern History* (New York: Oxford University Press, 1995), 302.

94   **"Survive, and probably won't.":** Williamson, *William Faulkner and Southern History*, 303.

94   **"'Tell us this in time?'":** Quoted in John Egerton, *Speak Now Against the Day: The Generation Before the Civil Rights Movement in the South* (New York: Knopf, 1994), 619.

94   **"Several French writers.":** Williamson, *William Faulkner and Southern History*, 308.

95   **"Citizens' Council nor NAACP.":** Lee, *GSAW*, 188.

95   **"Law or economic threat.":** William Faulkner, "A Letter to the 95," *Life*, March 5, 1956, 51–52. Faulkner implied that the Supreme Court was responsible for creating the conditions that led to Emmett Till's lynching. His regional defensiveness compelled him to balance southern violence with racial riots in the North and West, and his ultimate concern was not with the ongoing injustices suffered by black southerners but with the white southerner finding some "peace," so that he was "not to be faced with another legal process or maneuver every year, year after year, for the rest of his life."

95   **Comments attributed to him:** *Time*, April 23, 1956.

95   **Covered southern racial matters:** Lee, *GSAW*, 24.

96   **"So drop the act.":** All quotations in this paragraph are from Lee, *GSAW*, 177–178.

96   **"Do right," she says:** Lee, *GSAW*, 241.

96   **Aspects of his views:** Lee, *GSAW*, 242, 245–246.

97   **"Far from it yet.":** Lee, *GSAW*, 245–246.

97   **"Big overgrown Negroes.":** Quoted in Stephen E. Ambrose, *Eisenhower: Soldier and President* (New York: Simon and Schuster, 1990), 367.

98   **Cal shakes her head:** Lee, *GSAW*, 160.

98   **Good white southerner:** Micki McElya, *Clinging to Mammy: The Faithful Slave in Twentieth Century America* (Cambridge, MA: Harvard University Press, 2007).

99   **"Hostile to black demands.":** Eugene D. Genovese, *The Southern Tradition: The Achievement and Limitations of an American Conservatism* (Cambridge, MA: Harvard University Press, 1994), 86–87.

Chapter 4

101   **Work was untitled:** Lee, Author Cardfile, ALWP; Maurice Crain to Lynn Carrick, June 13, 1957, HarperCollins Collection. There is some discrepancy in the historical record about these events. Annie Laurie Williams lists the revisions that Lee handed over in July and August 1957 on a cardfile labeled "Go Set a Watchman," which suggests that these revisions were to "Watchman." But both the June 13, 1957, letter from Maurice Crain to Lynn Carrick and the July 9, 1957, letter from Harper Lee to Joy and Michael Brown make clear that by this time Lee had accepted Crain's advice to put aside "Watchman" to work full-time on the childhood novel that she had titled "The Long Goodbye."

101   **Taken their husband's name:** Clarissa Atkinson, "Once Upon a Time," The Oldest Vocation, August 8, 2014, https://oldestvocation .wordpress.com/2014/08/08/once-upon-a-time/.

102   **"Sound plot structure.":** *The Author and His Audience*, 27–28.

102   **Far too long:** Shields, *Mockingbird*, 90.

102   **Might in fact do so:** *The Author and His Audience*, 28–29; Maurice Crain to Lynn Carrick, June 13, 1957, HarperCollins Collection.

102   **Expected to take six months:** Shields, *Mockingbird*, 91; Lee, Author Cardfile, ALWP; *The Author and His Audience*, 28.

103   **"Tom Heflin," he chuckles:** Lee, *TKM*, 205, 250.

104 **About an idealistic man:** Shields, *Mockingbird*, 89.

104 **"Work of his whole life.":** Tay Hohoff, *A Ministry to Man: The Life of John Lovejoy Elliott* (New York: Harper and Brothers, 1959), 226.

104 **"Obey his inner light.":** *Los Angeles Times*, September 9, 1960.

105 **That she herself had:** Lee, *GSAW*, 118.

105 **"Always be his answers.":** Lee, *GSAW*, 265. One of Lee's nephews, Ed Conner, who owns the family's lone doctorate in literature and who taught for years at Kentucky State University, a historically black institution, holds to this interpretation. He believes that the act of writing *Watchman* served as a kind of emotional catharsis for his aunt. It was written as she saw her father in dramatic physical decline, and it allowed her to forgive him and to expunge, as it were, the years of frustration she felt toward him. Ed Conner, email to author, March 6, 2017, Crespino papers.

106 **Hypothetical black student:** *NYT*, May 7, 1959; Roberts and Klibanoff, *The Race Beat*, 132–138. For attempts in Tuscaloosa to start a rival newspaper, see "Notes of The People Speak Broadcast," March 12, 1957 and "Notes from Janette," March 13, 1957 in folder 7, box 255, Buford Boone Papers, Hoole Special Collections Library, University of Alabama.

107 **Patience became dirty words:** Thornton, *Dividing Lines*, 93, 96, 168–173, 195, 405.

108 **The Statesmen Quartet:** *Monroe Journal*, June 10, 1954; and April 10 and May 1, 1958.

108 **To attract new industries:** Thornton, *Dividing Lines*, 108–109, 474–475.

108 **"Alabama sun for demagoguery.":** *Monroe Journal*, September 26, 1957.

109 **"Life," the man said:** Quoted in Carter, *Politics of Rage*, 95.

109 **"Out-nigger me again.":** Thornton, *Dividing Lines*, 108–109. Also see Dan Carter, *The Politics of Rage: George Wallace, the Origins of the New Conservatism, and the Transformation of American Politics* (New York: Simon and Schuster, 1995), 90–96.

110 **"Efforts were stopped cold.":** Quoted in Thornton, *Dividing Lines*, 97.

110 **"People to preserve segregation.":** *Monroe Journal*, December 5, 1957.

110 **Klan in Monroe County:** *Monroe Journal*, August 7, 1958.

110 **Meetings at rural churches:** *Monroe Journal*, August 28, 1958.

110 **"Attention All White People.":** *Monroe Journal*, March 19, 1959.

111   **"Monroe County Klaverns 46-202.":** *Monroe Journal,* July 2 and December 31, 1959.

111   **"That way down here.":** Monroe County Heritage Museums, *Monroeville: The Search for Harper Lee's Maycomb* (Charleston, SC: Arcadia Publishing, 1999), 19.

111   **"Bayonets in public schools.":** *Monroe Journal,* August 7, 1958.

112   **"Directly on the U.S. Supreme Court.":** *Monroe Journal,* May 7, 1959.

112   **"Carving up on each other.":** *Monroe Journal,* January 15, 1959; for the connection between the *Home News* and the Klan, see Thornton, *Dividing Lines,* 97.

112   **"NAACP, which God forbid.":** Nelle Harper Lee to Hal Caufield, June 16, 1956, Kennerson Collection.

114   **Becomes a heroic choice:** Cultural assumptions about single fathers are backed up by psychological research. See Amanda R. Haire and Christi R. McGeorge, "Negative Perceptions of Never-Married Custodial Single Mothers and Fathers: Applications of a Gender Analysis for Family Therapists," *Journal of Feminist Family Therapy* 24, no. 1 (January 1, 2012): 24–51; and Sarah L. DeJean, Christi R. McGeorge, and Thomas S. Carlson, "Attitudes Toward Never-Married Single Mothers and Fathers: Does Gender Matter?" *Journal of Feminist Family Therapy* 24, no. 2 (April 1, 2012): 121–138.

115   **"Boy! It's great.":** *Chicago Tribune,* April 29, 1962. For more on the politics and culture of the baby boom, see Steve M. Gillon, *Boomer Nation: The Largest and Richest Generation Ever, and How It Changed America* (New York: Free Press, 2004).

115   **"Bitterness toward white people.":** *Brown v. Board of Education of Topeka,* 347 U.S. 483 (1954); Martin Luther King, "Letter from Birmingham Jail." The essential study of how theories of the black damaged psyche shaped American racial liberalism is Daryl Michael Scott, *Contempt and Pity: Social Policy and the Image of the Damaged Black Psyche* (Chapel Hill: University of North Carolina Press, 1997). Also see Eric Sundquist, *Strangers in the Land: Blacks, Jews, Post-Holocaust America* (Cambridge, MA: Belknap Press, 2005), 220–227. For more on children and civil rights politics, see Rebecca de Schweinitz, *If We Could Change the World: Young People and America's Long Struggle for Racial Equality* (Chapel Hill: University of North Carolina Press, 2009). For a study of how the preservation of childhood innocence shaped debates over race in nineteenth- and early twentieth-century America, see Robin Bernstein,

Racial Innocence: Performing American Childhood from Slavery to Civil Rights (New York: New York University Press, 2011).

116   **"Embarrassed" the South:** *Crimson-White,* October 1, 1946.

116   **"After the household sleeps.":** Lillian Smith, *Killers of the Dream* (New York: W. W. Norton, 1949, 1961, 1994), 25.

116   **"Thing in all my life.":** Smith, *Killers of the Dream,* 53.

116   **"He is a gentleman,"** Lee, *GSAW,* 113.

116   **"Unless we run away.":** Smith, *Killers of the Dream,* 51, 54. For more on the socialization of white children, see Kristina DuRocher, *Raising Racists: The Socialization of White Children in the Jim Crow South* (Lexington: University Press of Kentucky, 2011). For a comparative study of white and black socialization, see Jennifer Ritterhouse, *Growing Up Jim Crow: How Black and White Southern Children Learned Race* (Chapel Hill: University of North Carolina Press, 2006).

117   **"At home anywhere else.":** Lee, *GSAW,* 248.

117   **Fate of Tom Robinson:** Lee, *TKM,* 200–201; 213.

117   **"They had to do it.":** Lee, *GSAW,* 241.

118   **Began with the rising generation:** Eric Sundquist observes that *Brown* and *Mockingbird* both "started from the simple premise that today's children are tomorrow's adults." Sundquist, *Strangers in the Land,* 221.

118   **"That was enough.":** Lee, *TKM,* 157. Eric Sundquist has written, "The novel's beguiling proposition that juries, police forces, and whole communities of sympathetic children would make for a more just world, and, most famously, Scout's naïve routing of the lynch mob that has come to drag Tom Robinson from jail—all are calculated to substantiate the ethical authority driving *Brown v. Board of Education.*" Sundquist, *Strangers in the Land,* 228–229.

118   **Corpse with sharpened sticks:** Kester, "Lynching of Claude Neal."

118   **As "a child's book.":** Flannery O'Connor, *The Habit of Being: Letters of Flannery O'Connor* (New York: Farrar, Straus and Giroux, 1988), 411.

118   **Audience that it enjoyed:** Mills, *Mockingbird Next Door,* 225.

119   **From riotous white protestors:** *NYT,* August 28 and 31, 1956; September 2 and 3, 1956; December 8, 1956.

119   **"That had turned violent.":** Lee, *GSAW,* 238.

119   **Yelling God-knows-what:** David Margolick, *Elizabeth and Hazel: Two Women of Little Rock* (New Haven, CT: Yale University Press, 2012).

119   **"Negro comes up.":** Lee, *TKM,* 88.

120   **Train for Kansas:** Gerald Clarke, *Capote: A Biography* (New York: Simon and Schuster, 1988), 318–319.

120   **"Somebody your size.":** *Monroe Journal,* December 17, 1959.

121 **"All are one in Christ.":** *Monroe Journal,* December 24, 1959; Galatians 3:27–28.

121 **"Did right, son.":** Mills, *Mockingbird Next Door,* 21. The canceled Christmas parade would become a proud moment for Monroeville's civic leaders. See Steve Stewart, "'Watchman,' 'Mockingbird,' and the Real Monroeville," *Montgomery Advertiser,* July 26, 2015.

121 **"try and stop it?":** Lee, *GSAW,* 267–268.

122 **"Giants in the KKK.":** *Monroe Journal,* January 14, 1960.

122 **Suspected of being a Klansman:** *Monroe Journal,* December 31, 1959, and February 18, 1960.

122 **Decked in Confederate flags:** *Monroe Journal,* December 17, 24, and 31, 1959; January 14 and 21, February 18, and March 31, 1960.

123 **Books were leftover:** *New York Herald Tribune,* April 15, 1962.

Chapter 5

127 **Campaigns could surely ensue:** R. Barton Palmer, *Harper Lee's* To Kill a Mockingbird: *The Relationship Between Text and Film* (London: Methuen Drama, 2008), 113–115.

128 **Star to play Atticus:** James P. Yarbrough to Miss Sullivan, October 17, 1960, and Annie Laurie Williams to James P. Yarbrough, November 4, 1960, Box 149, folder Lee, Nelle Harper—Motion Picture, Annie Laurie Williams Papers, Rare Book and Manuscript Library, Columbia University.

128 **Would have to wait:** Annie Laurie Williams to George Wood, August 8, 1960, and George Wood to Annie Laurie Williams, October 6, 1960, box 149, folder Lee, Nelle Harper—Motion Picture, Annie Laurie Williams Papers, Rare Book and Manuscript Library, Columbia University.

128 **Cooper and John Huston:** Robert P. Richards to Annie Laurie Williams, November 8, 1960, Box 149, folder Lee, Nelle Harper—Motion Picture, Annie Laurie Williams Papers, Rare Book and Manuscript Library, Columbia University.

128 **Psychologically abusive father:** *Chicago Tribune,* Janurary 30, 1961; *NYT,* May 6, 1962; also see Jared Brown, *Alan J. Pakula: His Life and His Films* (New York: Back Stage, 2005).

128 **"Burble a single note.":** Maurice Crain to Alice Lee, March 22, 1961, box 149, folder Lee, Nelle Harper—Motion Picture, Annie Laurie Williams Papers, Rare Book and Manuscript Library, Columbia University.

129 **Hill behind the town:** *NYT,* April 19, 1961; *NYT,* May 6, 1962; and John Griggs, *The Films of Gregory Peck* (Secaucus, NJ: Citadel Press, 1984), 179–184.

129 **Lee, initially imagined:** Palmer, *Harper Lee's* To Kill a Mockingbird, 200.

130 **Straight over to tell him:** *Chicago Tribune*, May 14, 1961.

130 **Ask for identification:** *Boston Globe*, February 11, 1963.

130 **Outlawed the previous year:** *Washington Post*, May 5, 1961.

130 **"Make it through Alabama.":** Raymond Arsenault, *Freedom Riders: 1961 and the Struggle for Racial Justice* (New York: Oxford University Press, 2006), 132–133.

131 **Escaped with their lives:** Arsenault, *Freedom Riders*, 140–145.

131 **("Goddamned niggers except me").:** Arsenault, *Freedom Riders*, 204–205.

131 **Up the National Guard:** McWhorter, *Carry Me Home*, 233–235.

131 **Disapproved of the Freedom Rides:** Branch, *Parting the Waters*, 478.

131 **"But they respect it.":** Quoted in Mary McDonagh Murphy, *Scout, Atticus, & Boo: A Celebration of Fifty Years of* To Kill a Mockingbird (New York: Harper, 2010), 36.

132 **Birmingham's militant segregationists:** McWhorter, *Carry Me Home*, 218, 222–223.

132 **Other white leaders:** Thornton, *Dividing Lines*, 123.

132 **"Undivided white community.":** Thornton, *Dividing Lines*, 140.

133 **A half million copies:** *Los Angeles Times*, August 27, 1961.

133 **Week they were offered:** *NYT*, May 6, 1962.

133 **Secretary of the NAACP:** *Chicago Tribune*, September 18, 1960.

133 **Remembered, was *To Kill a Mockingbird*:** Sheldon Stern, Interview with James Farmer, April 25, 1979, John F. Kennedy Presidential Library. The other book that Wilkins brought Farmer was A. J. Liebling, *The Earl of Louisiana. Chicago Defender*, June 15, 1961.

134 **His presence as well:** Ari N. Schulman, "The Man Who Helped Make Harper Lee," *Atlantic*, July 14, 2015.

134 **"Who rarely speak out.":** Maurice Crain to Harper Lee, January 27, 1961, Box 149, folder Lee, Nelle Harper—Motion Picture, Annie Laurie Williams Papers, Rare Book and Manuscript Library, Columbia University.

134 **"Patterns of a small Southern town.":** *NYT*, May 19, 1961.

135 **Lee opted out:** Lucy Kroll to Horton Foote, February 6, 1961, Box 23, folder 12, Horton Foote Papers, DeGolyer Library, Southern Methodist University.

135 **Publication royalties with Foote:** *NYT*, March 4, 2009.

135 **"View of the children.":** Brown, *Alan J. Pakula*, 43–44.

135   **"Inheritance from him.":** "Discussion with Bob Mulligan on 'Mockingbird' at Luncheon Meeting," c. 1962, Box 142, folder 16, Horton Foote Papers, DeGolyer Library, Southern Methodist University.

135   **Quickly as he could:** Palmer, *Harper Lee's* To Kill a Mockingbird, 199.

136   **Image of Gregory Peck:** "Characters in a novel . . . are verbal constructs," observes film scholar Barton Palmer, "[b]ut characters in a film are embodied by particular human beings, whose presence in the story world . . . is a complex source of pleasure and psychological connection, potentially exceeding . . . their function as characters within the story." Palmer, *Harper Lee's* To Kill a Mockingbird, 194.

136   **"I could *be* him.":** Quoted in Griggs, *The Films of Gregory Peck*, 180.

136   **Those two topics alone:** Gary Fishgall, *Gregory Peck: A Biography* (New York: Scribner, 2002), 116.

136   **"People of good will.":** Palmer, *Harper Lee's* To Kill a Mockingbird, 197.

136   **"Hidden in a backwater.":** "To Kill A Mockingbird—Script," n.d., Box 67, folder 662, Gregory Peck Papers, Margaret Herrick Library.

136   **Assigned the case to Atticus:** Palmer, *Harper Lee's* To Kill a Mockingbird, 183.

137   **Take on Tom Robinson's defense:** Horton Foote, *The Screenplay of* To Kill a Mockingbird (New York: Harcourt, Brace and World, 1962), 22–23.

137   **"Atticus is aroused.":** "To Kill A Mockingbird—Script," n.d., Box 67, folder 662, Gregory Peck Papers, Margaret Herrick Library.

138   **"That much," Atticus observes:** Lee, *TKM*, 235.

138   **Misses his aim:** Palmer, *Harper Lee's* To Kill A Mockingbird, 229–230.

139   **"What real courage is.":** Notes of Robert Mulligan on *To Kill A Mockingbird*—Script, c. 1962, Box 3, folder 29, Robert Mulligan Papers, Margaret Herrick Library. The script that Mulligan and Peck made notes on included the scenes with Mrs. Dubose. Because the scenes were not included in the final version of the film, they do not appear in Horton Foote's published screenplay.

139   **Slow developing movie:** "Fearful Symmetry: The Making of *To Kill a Mockingbird*," a documentary included with bonus material in the fiftieth anniversary edition DVD of *To Kill a Mockingbird*. Pakula said that while he and Mulligan loved the performances, the scenes stopped the film's momentum.

140 **His every mannerism:** Ed Conner, email to author, May 21, 2017, Crespino papers.

140 **With his watch fob:** *"Fearful Symmetry"* film; Shields, *Mockingbird*, 172–173.

140 **"From that small Southern town.":** Quoted in Fishgall, *Gregory Peck*, 233.

140 **DC; New Orleans; and Atlanta:** *Monroe Journal*, April 27, 1944; April 15, 1920; June 12, 1924; February 10, 1921; and July 5, 1923.

140 *If a Man Answers:* *Los Angeles Times*, April 22, 1962.

140 **Way for the new Dodger Stadium:** *NYT*, January 19, 1962.

141 **Pond on the back lot:** *NYT*, May 6, 1962.

142 **"Stomped the floor.":** Quoted in Carter, *Politics of Rage*, 109.

143 **"Evil Civil Rights Commission.":** Carter, *Politics of Rage*, 96–104.

143 **Segregation in Alabama schools:** Carter, *Politics of Rage*, 105–109.

143 **Political ally recalled:** Marshall Frady, *Wallace* (New York: Meridian Books, 1968), 107.

144 **Won the general election:** Carl Grafton and Anne Permaloff, *Big Mules & Branchheads: James E. Folsom and Political Power in Alabama* (Athens: University of Georgia Press, 1985), 230–236.

144 **Preferences of Peck:** Gregory Peck, "Interoffice Correspondence with George Chasin," June 18, 1962, and Gregory Peck, "Confidential Memo to Mel Tucker," July 6, 1962, Box 70, folder 689, Gregory Peck Papers, Margaret Herrick Library.

145 **"To renounce in themselves.":** Horton Foote to Alan Pakula and Robert Mulligan, March 28, 1962, Box 115, folder 791, Alan J. Pakula Papers, Margaret Herrick Library.

147 **Mama hoped they weren't:** Horton Foote, *Farewell: A Memoir of a Texas Childhood* (New York: Scribner, 1999), 28–32.

147 **"Break down their prejudice.":** "To Kill A Mockingbird—Script," n.d., Box 67, folder 662, Gregory Peck Papers, Margaret Herrick Library.

147 **"Unenlightened dirt farmers":** Horton Foote to Alan Pakula and Robert Mulligan, March 28, 1962, Box 115, folder 791, Alan J. Pakula Papers, Margaret Herrick Library.

148 **Something else altogether:** Flynt, *Mockingbird Songs*, 60.

148 **Erratic in Peck's performance:** A note in the dailies urged Peck to "cut down Southern accent"; a screening note called for Peck to make a loop, or re-record, Atticus's line "Come in here, Scout, and have your breakfast" to "get rid of southern accent." "Dailies," March 16, 1962, and "Screening Notes," April 12, 1962, both in Box 114, folder 781, Alan J. Pakula Papers, Margaret Herrick Library.

148 **Mid-twentieth-century American liberalism:** Quoted in Flynt, *Mockingbird Songs*, 58.

148 **Birdlike older sister Alice:** Alice once wrote to Annie Laurie Williams, "Nelle Harper called on Thursday evening and said that she would be going to the farm with you on Friday and would probably spend the hours there in hard labor in the hope of taking off extra pounds which do have a way of accumulating when she is inactive." Alice Lee to Annie Laurie Williams, June 25, 1962, Box 149, folder Lee, Nelle Harper— Motion Picture, Annie Laurie Williams Papers, Rare Book and Manuscript Library, Columbia University.

148 **Cast at every opportunity:** *Boston Globe*, February 11, 1963.

148 **Which was precisely true:** *New York Herald Tribune*, April 15, 1962.

148 **"How good she is.":** Annie Laurie Williams to Alice Lee, February 16, 1963, Box 149, folder Lee, Nelle Harper—Motion Picture, Annie Laurie Williams Papers, Rare Book and Manuscript Library, Columbia University.

150 **All come to pass:** Gerard sent a copy of the photo to Annie Laurie Williams. See Philip Gerard to Annie Laurie Williams, December 1, 1962, Box 86, folder Nelle Harper Lee, To Kill a Mockingbird, Publicity and Fan Mail, Annie Laurie Williams Papers, Rare Book & Manuscript Library, Columbia University.

150 **Not making speeches:** *NYT,* May 19, 1961.

150 **"Free and democratic country.":** *Christian Science Monitor,* January 23, 1963.

151 **"Politics in this country.":** Frady, *Wallace,* 140.

151 **"Tomorrow . . . segregation forever.":** In his speech Wallace actually said, "Segregation Now," which ruined Carter's more poetic today, tomorrow, forever sequence.

151 **"You are Southerners too,":** "Inaugural Address of Governor George Wallace," January 14, 1963, Alabama Department of Archives and History, http://archives-alabama-primo.hosted.exlibrisgroup.com/01ALA BAMA:default_scope:01ALABAMA_ALMA215244160002743.

152 **"Citizens of Oxford, Mississippi.":** Ibid.; video of the speech can be found at https://www.youtube.com/watch?v=_RC0EjsUbDU.

152 **"Never were against black people.":** Quoted in Carter, *Politics of Rage,* 109.

153 **"Warmth of her love.":** *New Republic,* February 2, 1963; *New Yorker,* February 23, 1963; *Time,* February 22, 1963; *Newsweek,* February 18, 1963.

153   **"Burn within the character.":** *Baltimore Sun,* February 24, 1963; *Boston Globe,* February 16, 1963; *Film Facts,* February 28, 1963.

153   **"Us and our problems.":** *Richmond News Leader,* March 29, 1963.

153   **"Most bigoted viewers":** *Atlanta Constitution,* March 21, 1963.

153   **Treatment of controversial issues:** *Birmingham News,* February 10, 1963.

154   **"System for having them?":** *Alabama Journal,* April 5, 1963.

154   **Spring of 1963:** Diane McWhorter, *Carry Me Home: Birmingham, Alabama: The Climactic Battle of the Civil Rights Revolution* (New York: Simon and Schuster, 2001), 322.

155   **After her father's death:** *Christian Science Monitor,* April 10, 1963.

Chapter 6

158   **Depiction of southern injustice:** *Birmingham News,* April 4, 1963; McWhorter, *Carry Me Home,* 325.

158   **Most recalcitrant big city:** McWhorter, *Carry Me Home,* 37–39, 50–51, 63–64, 84–86, 120.

158   **As "monstrous legislation.":** McWhorter, *Carry Me Home,* 313.

158   **"Lynch you from a low tree.":** *NYT,* August 19, 2017.

159   **Four African American girls:** See Charles Morgan Jr., *A Time to Speak* (New York: Harper & Row, 1964).

160   **Movement's demands were met:** Glenn T. Eskew, *But for Birmingham: The Local and National Movements in the Civil Rights Struggle* (Chapel Hill: University of North Carolina Press, 1997), 217–223.

160   **After Boutwell's election:** Thornton, *Dividing Lines,* 297–300.

160   **New administration a chance:** McWhorter, *Carry Me Home,* 323–325.

160   **Motivations of the protestors:** *Birmingham News,* April 15, 1963; and McWhorter, *Carry Me Home,* 354.

160   **Opinion against Jim Crow:** McWhorter, *Carry Me Home,* 25.

160   **Pipe at the dog:** *Birmingham News,* April 8, 1963.

160   **Dog with a large knife:** *NYT,* April 8, 1963. The classic photograph that has survived in history of a police dog attacking a protestor was taken by the Associated Press photographer Bill Hudson and published in early May. Diane McWhorter reports that the person attacked, Walter Gadsden, a sophomore at Parker High School, was not in fact a demonstrator but had merely come out to see his classmates march (McWhorter, *Carry Me Home,* 372–375). Mills Thornton points out that only once before May 3 did Bull Connor use police dogs, on April 17, and this sparked the incident reported in the *New York Times* in which a black onlooker in

the crowd, Leroy Allen, had drawn a knife when a dog lunged at him (Thornton, *Dividing Lines*, 314).

161 **They had come for:** Thornton, *Dividing Lines*, 310–312.

161 **"Those actions may be.":** *Birmingham News*, April 13, 1963.

162 **"Freedom is equally protected.":** S. Jonathan Bass, *Blessed Are the Peacemakers: Martin Luther King Jr., Eight White Religious Leaders, and the "Letter from Birmingham Jail"* (Baton Rouge: Louisiana State University Press, 2001), 233–234.

163 **Him and his people:** Diane McWhorter describes the use of the term "law and order" in these years as "the old Bourbon warning cry against Populist insurrection now a euphemism for integration" (McWhorter, *Carry Me Home*, 315). Jonathan Rieder dismisses the ministers' call for law and order as "morally compromised," and criticizes them for failing to condemn segregation outright and for failing to call for white Alabamans to "love Negroes because they were their brothers." Rieder does not comment on the passage in their January letter where they wrote that "every human being is created in the image of God and is entitled to respect as a fellow human being with all basic rights, privileges, responsibilities which belong to humanity" (Rieder, *Gospel of Freedom*, 90). S. Jonathan Bass, who has written the most sympathetic account of the eight ministers, characterized their use of the term as "naïve, misguided, and obtuse" (Bass, *Blessed Are the Peacemakers*, 26).

165 **"Bewildering than outright rejection.":** All quotes from King's "Letter from Birmingham Jail" come from the documentary edition in Appendix 3 in Bass, *Blessed Are the Peacemakers*, 237–256 (white moderate quotation on 246).

166 **"Unconstitutional at an early date.":** Buford Boone to Lyndon Johnson, July 2, 1964, Box 254, folder 1, Buford Boone Papers, Hoole Special Collections Library, University of Alabama.

167 **"In our great southland.":** Martin Luther King Jr. to Buford Boone, May 9, 1957, Box 254, folder 9, Buford Boone Papers, Hoole Special Collections Library, University of Alabama.

167 **"Law is grounded.":** Smith, *Killers of the Dream*, 199, 231–232. For more on the rift between Smith and McGill, see Anne C. Loveland, *Lillian Smith: A Southerner Confronting the South* (Baton Rouge: Louisiana State University Press, 1986), 94, 103–104, 118, 127–128, 135, 142, 145–146, 152, 160.

168 **"Air of ignorance and agreement.":** Martin Luther King Jr., *Why We Can't Wait* (New York: New American Library, 1964), 28.

168 **"As innocent as doves.":** Rieder, *Gospel of Freedom*, 72; Matthew 10:16.

168 **Sermon written to redeem:** For more on how the African American oral culture affected King's writing, see Jonathan Rieder, *Gospel of Freedom*.

168 **"Spit you out of my mouth.":** Revelation 3:15–16.

169 **"Of freedom, of justice.":** Bass, *Blessed Are the Peacemakers*, 215–216.

170 **"Laws and social institutions.":** Bass, *Blessed Are the Peacemakers*, 187–193.

170 **Eventually King himself:** David J. Garrow, *Bearing the Cross: Martin Luther King, Jr., and the Southern Christian Leadership Conference* (New York: Vintage Books, 1988), 299–300; 679n9.

170 **"Retaliation against injustice.":** King, *Why We Can't Wait*, 37.

170 **"Not a pack of beasts.":** King, *Why We Can't Wait*, 37–38.

171 **"Comparatively bloodless one.":** King, *Why We Can't Wait*, 39–40.

172 **"Counsels of patience and delay?":** John F. Kennedy, "Report to the American People on Civil Rights," June 11, 1963, John F. Kennedy Library.

172 **"Confusion, uncertainty and disunity.":** King, *Why We Can't Wait*, 40.

Epilogue

175 **Flow into "Watchman.":** Nelle Harper Lee to Joy and Michael Brown, July 9, 1957, HarperCollins Collection.

175 **After *Mockingbird* was published:** On February 5, 2015, in answer to criticism that Harper Lee had been manipulated into publishing *Watchman*, Lee's agent, Andrew Nurnberg, cited as evidence "old letters between Lee and her agent" (which, presumably, is the HarperCollins Collection) to claim that Lee and Crain had agreed that Lee would write a trilogy. He went further, however, saying, "[I]t is clear that Lippincott was planning on publishing *Watchman*." But in fact there is no evidence that I have found in the HarperCollins Collection that indicates that Lippincott planned to publish *Watchman*. See "Harper Lee's 'Lost' Novel Was Intended to Complete a Trilogy, Says Agent," *Guardian*, February 5, 2015.

176 **"Hated the K.K.K.":** Nelle Harper Lee to Hal Caufield, November 21, 1961, Kennerson Collection.

176 **"Change it to a fictional form.":** Harold Hayes to Nelle Harper Lee, October 27, 1961, Box 149, folder Lee, Nelle Harper—Motion Picture, Annie Laurie Williams Papers, Rare Book and Manuscript Library, Columbia University.

176 **"South is an axiomatic impossibility.":** Nelle Harper Lee to Hal Caufield, November 21, 1961, Kennerson Collection.

177 **Coverage of the South in *Watchman*:** Lee, *GSAW*, 24. For the transcript of the March 1963 interview, see Shields, *Mockingbird*, 192.

177 **On WQXR in New York:** Shields, *Mockingbird*, 210.

177 **"Just from tribal instinct.":** Roy Newquist, "Harper Lee," in *Counterpoint*, ed. Roy Newquist (London: George Allen and Unwin, 1965), 407.

177 **"Heritage and social structure.":** Lee, *GSAW*, 190, 194.

177 **"Things of this society.":** Lee, *GSAW*, 200.

178 **"Jane Austen of south Alabama.":** Newquist, "Harper Lee," 412.

178 **"Politics in this country.":** Frady, *Wallace*, 140.

179 **Days and weeks following:** Carter, *Politics of Rage*, 133–155.

179 **"Liberals in Washington.":** Carter, *Politics of Rage*, 208.

179 **"Back to something like this.":** Carter, *Politics of Rage*, 206–207.

179 **Sign all the autographs:** Carter, *Politics of Rage*, 207.

181 **"White moderate feels today.":** *Atlanta Constitution*, May 20, 1963.

181 **"Like this also.":** *Jerusalem Post*, May 27, 1963.

181 **"International film festival.":** *Atlanta Constitution*, May 20, 1963, 4A.

182 **"Peoples throughout the world.":** Thomas L. Hughes to Secretary of State Dean Rusk, June 14, 1963, Papers of John F. Kennedy. Presidential Papers. National Security Files. Subjects. Civil rights: General, June 1963: 11–14.

182 **Middle Eastern languages:** Annie Laurie Williams to Alan J. Pakula, December 18, 1964, Box 149, folder Lee, Nelle Harper—Motion Picture, Annie Laurie Williams Papers, Rare Book and Manuscript Library, Columbia University. For more on the civil rights struggle seen through an international lens, see Mary Dudziak, *Cold War Civil Rights: Race and the Image of American Democracy* (Princeton, NJ: Princeton University Press, 2000).

182 **"Another year old[?]":** Maurice Crain to Nelle Harper Lee, July 12, 1961, box 149, folder Lee, Nelle Harper—Motion Picture, Annie Laurie Williams Papers, Rare Book and Manuscript Library, Columbia University.

182 **"Death I'd expected.":** Newquist, "Harper Lee," 405.

183 **Hungary, Romania, and Greece:** Annie Laurie Williams to Alan J. Pakula, December 18, 1964, Box 149, folder Lee, Nelle Harper—Motion

Picture, Annie Laurie Williams Papers, Rare Book and Manuscript Library, Columbia University.

183 **"Cadillacs I've paid for.":** Nelle Harper Lee to Hal Caufield, December 12, 1960, Kennerson Collection.

183 **Before the end of the year:** Annie Laurie Williams to Alice Lee, October 21, 1963, Box 149, folder Lee, Nelle Harper—Motion Picture, Annie Laurie Williams Papers, Rare Book and Manuscript Library, Columbia University.

183 **"Had a good time.":** Alice Lee to Annie Laurie Williams, November 14, 1963, Box 149, folder Lee, Nelle Harper—Motion Picture, Annie Laurie Williams Papers, Rare Book and Manuscript Library, Columbia University.

183 **"No way of stopping them.":** Annie Laurie Williams to Alice Lee, August 3, 1964, Box 149, folder Lee, Nelle Harper—Motion Picture, Annie Laurie Williams Papers, Rare Book and Manuscript Library, Columbia University.

184 **Rest of her life:** Newquist, "Harper Lee," 404–412.

Bibliography

Adamson, June N. "Few Black Votes Heard: The Black Community and the Desegregation Crisis in Clinton, Tennessee, 1956." *Tennessee Historical Quarterly* 53 (Spring 1994): 30–41.

Ambrose, Stephen E. *Eisenhower: Soldier and President.* New York: Simon and Schuster, 1990.

Anderson, William. *The Wild Man from Sugar Creek: The Political Career of Eugene Talmadge.* Baton Rouge: Louisiana State University Press, 1975.

Arsenault, Raymond. *Freedom Riders: 1961 and the Struggle for Racial Justice.* New York: Oxford University Press, 2006.

Bartley, Numan V. *The Rise of Massive Resistance: Race and Politics in the South During the 1950's.* Baton Rouge: Louisiana State University Press, 1969.

Bass, S. Jonathan. *Blessed Are the Peacemakers: Martin Luther King Jr., Eight White Religious Leaders, and the "Letter from Birmingham Jail."* Baton Rouge: Louisiana State University Press, 2001.

Bauman, Mark K. *Dixie Diaspora: An Anthology of Southern Jewish History.* Judaic Studies Series. Tuscaloosa: University of Alabama Press, 2006.

Bauman, Mark K. *Warren Akin Candler: The Conservative as Idealist.* Metuchen, NJ: Scarecrow Press, 1981.

Beck, Joseph Madison. *My Father and Atticus Finch: A Lawyer's Fight for Justice in 1930s Alabama.* New York: W. W. Norton and Company, 2016.

Bernstein, Robin. *Racial Innocence: Performing American Childhood from Slavery to Civil Rights.* New York: New York University Press, 2011.

Blackmur, R. P. "Scout Finch and the Wilderness Within." *Princeton Alumni Weekly,* December 2, 1960.

Boykin, Edward. *Everything's Made for Love in This Man's World: Vignettes from the Life of Frank W. Boykin.* Mobile, AL: Privately printed, 1973.

Branch, Taylor. *Parting the Waters: America in the King Years, 1954–1963.* New York: Simon and Schuster, 1989.

Branch, Taylor, and Claude Sitton. *Pillar of Fire: America in the King Years, 1963–1965*. New York: Simon and Schuster, 1998.

Brinkley, Alan. *The End of Reform: New Deal Liberalism in Recession and War.* New York: Alfred A. Knopf, 1995.

Brinkley, Alan. *Voices of Protest: Huey Long, Father Coughlin, and the Great Depression.* New York: Alfred A. Knopf, 1982.

Brooks, Jennifer E. *Defining the Peace: World War II Veterans, Race, and the Remaking of Southern Political Tradition.* Chapel Hill: University of North Carolina Press, 2011.

Brown, Ellen Firsching, and John Wiley. *Margaret Mitchell's* Gone with the Wind: *A Bestseller's Odyssey from Atlanta to Hollywood.* Lanham, MD: Taylor Trade, 2011.

Brown, Jared. *Alan J. Pakula: His Life and His Films.* New York: Back Stage Books, 2005.

Brown, Jerry Elijah. *Clearings in the Thicket: An Alabama Humanities Reader: Essays and Stories from the 1983 Alabama History and Heritage Festival.* Macon, GA: Mercer University Press, 1985.

Brundage, W. Fitzhugh. *Lynching in the New South: Georgia and Virginia, 1880–1930.* Urbana: University of Illinois Press, 1993.

Capote, Truman. *Other Voices, Other Rooms.* New York: Vintage Books, 1948.

Carmer, Carl. *Stars Fell on Alabama.* New York: Farrar and Rinehart, 1934.

Carter, Dan T. *The Politics of Rage: George Wallace, the Origins of the New Conservatism, and the Transformation of American Politics.* New York: Simon and Schuster, 1995.

Carter, Dan T. *Scottsboro: A Tragedy of the American South.* Baton Rouge: Louisiana State University Press, 1969.

Castleberry, Marion. *Blessed Assurance: The Life and Art of Horton Foote.* Macon, GA: Mercer University Press, 2014.

Chalmers, David Mark. *Hooded Americanism: The First Century of the Ku Klux Klan, 1865–1965.* New York: Doubleday, 1965.

Chappell, David L. *Inside Agitators: White Southerners in the Civil Rights Movement.* Baltimore, MD: Johns Hopkins University Press, 1994.

Chappell, David L. *A Stone of Hope: Prophetic Religion and the Death of Jim Crow.* Chapel Hill: University of North Carolina Press, 2004.

Clark, Thomas Dionysius. *The Southern Country Editor.* Southern Classics Series. Columbia: University of South Carolina Press, 1991.

Clarke, Gerald. *Capote: A Biography.* New York: Simon and Schuster, 1988.

Clarke, Gerald. *Too Brief a Treat: The Letters of Truman Capote.* New York: Random House, 2004.

Cole, Teju. "The White-Savior Industrial Complex." *The Atlantic*, March 2012.

Crespino, Joseph. *In Search of Another Country: Mississippi and the Conservative Counterrevolution.* Princeton, NJ: Princeton University Press, 2007.

Crespino, Joseph. *Strom Thurmond's America.* New York: Hill and Wang, 2012.

Cumming, Douglas O. *The Southern Press: Literary Legacies and the Challenge of Modernity.* Visions of the American Press. Evanston, IL: Medill School of Journalism, Northwestern University Press, 2009.

Davidson, Donald. *The Attack on Leviathan: Regionalism and Nationalism in the United States*. Chapel Hill: University of North Carolina Press, 1938.

Davidson, Donald. "The New South and the Conservative Tradition." *National Review*, September 10, 1960.

De Schweinitz, Rebecca. *If We Could Change the World: Young People and America's Long Struggle for Racial Equality*. Chapel Hill: University of North Carolina Press, 2009.

DeJean, Sarah L., Christi R. McGeorge, and Thomas Stone Carlson. "Attitudes Toward Never-Married Single Mothers and Father: Does Gender Matter?" *Journal of Feminist Family Therapy* 24, no. 2 (April 1, 2012): 121–138.

Dorr, Lisa Lindquist. *White Women, Rape, and the Power of Race in Virginia, 1900–1960*. Chapel Hill: University of North Carolina Press, 2004.

Dudziak, Mary L. *Cold War Civil Rights: Race and the Image of American Democracy*. Princeton, NJ: Princeton University Press, 2000.

Dunn, Susan. *Roosevelt's Purge: How FDR Fought to Change the Democratic Party*. Cambridge, MA: Harvard University Press, 2012.

DuRocher, Kristina. *Raising Racists: The Socialization of White Children in the Jim Crow South*. Lexington: University Press of Kentucky, 2011.

Durr, Virginia Foster. *Outside the Magic Circle: The Autobiography of Virginia Foster Durr*. Tuscaloosa: University of Alabama Press, 1985.

Dykeman, Wilma, and Jim Stokely. *Seeds of Southern Change*. Chicago, IL: University of Chicago Press, 1962.

Earley, Pete. *Circumstantial Evidence: Death, Life, and Justice in a Southern Town*. New York: Bantam Books, 1995.

Egerton, John. *Speak Now Against the Day: The Generation before the Civil Rights Movement in the South*. New York: Alfred A. Knopf, 1994.

Eskew, Glenn T. *But for Birmingham: The Local and National Movements in the Civil Rights Struggle*. Chapel Hill: University of North Carolina Press, 1997.

Faulkner, William. *Intruder in the Dust*. New York: Random House, 1948.

Faulkner, William. "A Letter to the North." *Life*, March 5, 1956, 51–52.

Feldman, Glenn. *From Demagogue to Dixiecrat: Horace Wilkinson and the Politics of Race*. Lanham, MD: University Press of America, 1995.

Feldman, Glenn. *Politics, Society, and the Klan in Alabama, 1915–1949*. Tuscaloosa: University of Alabama Press, 1999.

Finley, Keith M. *Delaying the Dream: Southern Senators and the Fight Against Civil Rights, 1938–1965*. Baton Rouge: Louisiana State University Press, 2008.

Fishgall, Gary. *Gregory Peck: A Biography*. New York: Scribner, 2002.

Flynt, Wayne. *Mockingbird Songs: My Friendship with Harper Lee*. New York: HarperCollins, 2017.

Flynt. Wayne. *Poor but Proud: Alabama's Poor Whites*. Tuscaloosa: University of Alabama Press, 1989.

Foote, Horton. *Beginnings: A Memoir*. New York: Scribner, 2001.

Foote, Horton. *Farewell: A Memoir of a Texas Childhood*. New York: Scribner, 1999.

Foote, Horton. *The Screenplay of* To Kill a Mockingbird. New York: Harcourt, Brace and World, 1962.

Frady, Marshall. *Wallace.* New York: Meridian Books, 1968.

Frederickson, Kari A. *The Dixiecrat Revolt and the End of the Solid South, 1932–1968.* Chapel Hill: University of North Carolina Press, 2001.

Garrow, David J. *Bearing the Cross: Martin Luther King, Jr., and the Southern Christian Leadership Conference.* Norwalk, CT: Easton Press, 1989.

Genovese, Eugene D. *The Southern Tradition: The Achievement and Limitations of an American Conservatism.* Cambridge, MA: Harvard University Press, 1994.

Gillon, Steven M. *Boomer Nation: The Largest and Richest Generation Ever, and How It Changed America.* New York: Free Press, 2004.

Gilmore, Glenda Elizabeth. *Defying Dixie: The Radical Roots of Civil Rights, 1919–1950.* New York: W. W. Norton and Company, 2008.

Goodman, James E. *Stories of Scottsboro.* New York: Vintage Books, 1994.

Goodwin, Stephen. "Resisting Atticus's Allure." *American Scholar,* July 13, 2015.

Grafton, Carl, and Anne Permaloff. *Big Mules & Branchheads: James E. Folsom and Political Power in Alabama.* Athens: University of Georgia Press, 1985.

Graham, Allison. *Framing the South: Hollywood, Television, and Race During the Civil Rights Struggle.* Baltimore, MD: Johns Hopkins University Press, 2001.

Gram, Margaret Hunt. "Matters of the State: American Literature in the Civil Rights Era." Harvard University, 2013.

Graves, John Temple. *The Fighting South.* New York: G. P. Putnam's Sons, 1943.

Greene, Alison Collis. *No Depression in Heaven: The Great Depression, the New Deal, and the Transformation of Religion in the Delta.* New York: Oxford University Press, 2015.

Griffin, Larry J., and Don Harrison Doyle. *The South as an American Problem.* Athens: University of Georgia Press, 1995.

Griffith, Sally Foreman. *Home Town News: William Allen White and the* Emporia Gazette. New York: Oxford University Press, 1989.

Griggs, John. *The Films of Gregory Peck.* Secaucus, NJ: Citadel Press, 1984.

Haberland, Michelle. *Striking Beauties: Women Apparel Workers in the U.S. South, 1930–2000.* Athens: University of Georgia Press, 2015.

Hackett, Alice Payne, and James Henry Burke. *80 Years of Best Sellers, 1895–1975.* New York: R. R. Bowker Company, 1977.

Hackney, Sheldon. *Populism to Progressivism in Alabama.* Princeton, NJ: Princeton University Press, 1969.

Haire, Amanda R., and Christi R. McGeorge. "Negative Perceptions of Never-Married Custodial Single Mothers and Fathers: Applications of a Gender Analysis for Family Therapists." *Journal of Feminist Family Therapy* 24, no. 1 (January 1, 2012): 24–51.

Halberstam, David. "The White Citizens Council: Respectable Means for Unrespectable Ends." *Commentary,* October 1, 1956.

Hohoff, Tay. *A Ministry to Man: The Life of John Lovejoy Elliott.* New York: Harper and Brothers, 1959.

Hollis, Daniel Webster. *An Alabama Newspaper Tradition: Grover C. Hall and the Hall Family.* Tuscaloosa: University of Alabama Press, 1983.

J. B. Lippincott Company. *The Author and His Audience: With a Chronology of Major Events in the Publishing History of J. B. Lippincott Company.* Philadelphia, PA: J. B. Lippincott Company, 1967.

Jackson, Harvey H. *Inside Alabama: A Personal History of My State.* Tuscaloosa: University of Alabama Press, 2008.

Jeffries, Hasan Kwame. *Bloody Lowndes: Civil Rights and Black Power in Alabama's Black Belt.* New York: New York University Press, 2010.

Johnson, Claudia Durst. To Kill a Mockingbird: *Threatening Boundaries.* New York: Twayne Publishers, 1994.

Katznelson, Ira. *Fear Itself: The New Deal and the Origins of Our Time.* New York: Liveright Publishing Corporation, 2013.

Kennedy, David M. *Freedom from Fear: The American People in Depression and War, 1929–1945.* New York: Oxford University Press, 1999.

Kester, Howard. "The Lynching of Claude Neal." Mongomery, AL: Southern Rural Welfare Association, 1971.

Key, V. O., Jr. *Southern Politics in State and Nation.* New York: Vintage Books, 1949.

King, Martin Luther. *Why We Can't Wait.* New York: New American Library, 1964.

Kirby, Jack Temple. *Rural Worlds Lost: The American South, 1920–1960.* Baton Rouge: Louisiana State University Press, 1987.

Kiselyak, Charles. "Fearful Symmetry." 1998.

Kluger, Richard. *Simple Justice: The History of* Brown v. Board of Education *and Black America's Struggle for Equality.* New York: Alfred A. Knopf, 1975.

Kneebone, John T. *Southern Liberal Journalists and the Issue of Race, 1920–1944.* Chapel Hill: University of North Carolina Press, 1985.

Lawson, Steven F. *Black Ballots: Voting Rights in the South, 1944–1969.* New York: Columbia University Press, 1976.

Lechner, Zachary J. "The South of the Mind: American Imaginings of Rural White Southernness." Temple University, 2012.

Leuchtenburg, William E. *The White House Looks South: Franklin D. Roosevelt, Harry S. Truman, Lyndon B. Johnson.* Baton Rouge: Louisiana State University Press, 2005.

Loveland, Anne C. *Lillian Smith, a Southern Confronting the South: A Biography.* Baton Rouge: Louisiana State University Press, 1986.

Margolick, David. *Elizabeth and Hazel: Two Women of Little Rock.* New Haven, CT: Yale University Press, 2012.

McElya, Micki. *Clinging to Mammy: The Faithful Slave in Twentieth-Century America.* Cambridge, MA: Harvard University Press, 2007.

McGill, Ralph. *The South and the Southerner.* Boston, MA: Little, Brown, 1964.

McGovern, James R. *Anatomy of a Lynching: The Killing of Claude Neal.* Baton Rouge: Louisiana State University Press, 1982.

McMillen, Neil R. *The Citizens' Council: Organized Resistance to the Second Reconstruction, 1954–64.* Urbana: University of Illinois Press, 1971.

McWhorter, Diane. *Carry Me Home: Birmingham, Alabama—The Climactic Battle of the Civil Rights Revolution.* New York: Simon and Schuster, 2001.

Mead, Rebecca. "Yours Truly." *New Yorker,* June 8 and 15, 2015.

Meyer, Michael J. *Harper Lee's* To Kill a Mockingbird: *New Essays.* Lanham, MD: Scarecrow Press, 2010.

Miller, James A. *Remembering Scottsboro: The Legacy of an Infamous Trial.* Princeton, NJ: Princeton University Press, 2009.

Mills, Marja. *The Mockingbird Next Door: Life with Harper Lee.* New York: Penguin Books, 2014.

Moates, Marianne M. *A Bridge of Childhood: Truman Capote's Southern Years.* New York: Henry Holt, 1989.

Moates, Marianne M. *Truman Capote's Southern Years: Stories from a Monroeville Cousin.* Tuscaloosa: University of Alabama Press, 2014.

Monroe County Heritage Museum. *Monroeville: The Search for Harper Lee's Maycomb.* Charleston, SC: Arcadia Publishing, 1999.

The Monroe Journal Centennial Edition, 1866–1966. Monroeville, AL: *Monroe Journal,* 1966.

Morgan, Charles. *A Time to Speak.* New York: Harper and Row, 1964.

Murphy, Mary McDonagh. *Scout, Atticus, and Boo: A Celebration of Fifty Years of* To Kill a Mockingbird. New York: Harper, 2010.

Murphy, Paul V. *The Rebuke of History: The Southern Agrarians and American Conservative Thought.* Chapel Hill: University of North Carolina Press, 2001.

Nash, George H. *The Conservative Intellectual Movement in America: Since 1945.* New York: Basic Books, 1976.

Nelson, Bruce. "Organized Labor and the Struggle for Black Equality in Mobile During World War II." *Journal of American History* 80 (December 1993): 952–988.

Newman, Roger K. *Hugo Black: A Biography.* New York: Fordham University Press, 1997.

Newquist, Roy, and Raymond Danowski. *Counterpoint.* London: George Allen and Unwin, 1964.

Norrell, Robert J. "Labor at the Ballot Box: Alabama Politics from the New Deal to the Dixiecrat Movement." *Journal of Southern History* 57, no. 2 (May 1991): 219–220.

Norrell, Robert J. *Reaping the Whirlwind: The Civil Rights Movement in Tuskegee.* New York: Alfred A. Knopf, 1985.

O'Connor, Flannery. *The Habit of Being: Letters of Flannery O'Connor.* New York: Farrar, Straus and Giroux, 1988.

Palmer, R. Barton. *Harper Lee's* To Kill a Mockingbird: *The Relationship Between Text and Film.* London: Methuen Drama, 2008.

Patterson, James T. *Congressional Conservatism and the New Deal: The Growth of the Conservative Coalition in Congress, 1933–1939.* Lexington: University Press of Kentucky, 1967.

Percy, William Alexander. *Lanterns on the Levee: Recollections of a Planter's Son.* New York: Alfred A. Knopf, 1945.

Phillips-Fein, Kim. *Invisible Hands: The Businessmen's Crusade Against the New Deal.* New York: W. W. Norton and Company, 2010.

Pickett, Albert James. *History of Alabama, and Incidentally of Georgia and Mississippi, from the Earliest Period.* Charleston, SC: Walker and James, 1851.

Plimpton, George. *Truman Capote: In Which Various Friends, Enemies, Acquaintances, and Detractors Recall His Turbulent Career.* New York: Doubleday, 1997.

Raines, Howell. *My Soul Is Rested: Movement Days in the Deep South Remembered.* New York: Penguin Books, 1983.

Rieder, Jonathan. *Gospel of Freedom: Martin Luther King, Jr.'s Letter from Birmingham Jail and the Struggle That Changed a Nation.* New York: Bloomsbury Publishing, 2013.

Ritterhouse, Jennifer Lynn. *Growing Up Jim Crow: How Black and White Southern Children Learned Race.* Chapel Hill: University of North Carolina, 2006.

Roberts, Gene, and Hank Klibanoff. *The Race Beat: The Press, the Civil Rights Struggle, and the Awakening of a Nation.* New York: Alfred A. Knopf, 2006.

Sarat, Austin, and Martha Umphrey. *Reimagining* To Kill a Mockingbird: *Family, Community, and the Possibility of Equal Justice Under Law.* Amherst: University of Massachusetts Press, 2013.

Schulman, Ari. "The Man Who Helped Make Harper Lee." *Atlantic*, July 14, 2015.

Schultz, Mark Roman. *Rural Face of White Supremacy: Beyond Jim Crow.* Champaign: University of Illinois Press, 2010.

Scott, Daryl Michael. *Contempt and Pity: Social Policy and the Image of the Damaged Black Psyche, 1880–1996.* Chapel Hill: University of North Carolina Press, 1997.

Sharpless, Rebecca, and Melissa Walker. *Work, Family, and Faith: Rural Southern Women in the Twentieth Century.* Columbia: University of Missouri Press, 2006.

Shields, Charles J. *Mockingbird: A Portrait of Harper Lee from Scout to* Go Set a Watchman. New York: Henry Holt, 2016.

Sims, George E. *The Little Man's Big Friend: James E. Folsom in Alabama Politics, 1946–1958.* Tuscaloosa: University of Alabama Press, 1985.

Smith, Lillian Eugenia. *Killers of the Dream.* New York: W. W. Norton and Company, 1949, 1961, 1994.

Smith, Lillian Eugenia, and Margaret Rose Gladney. *How Am I to Be Heard?: Letters of Lillian Smith.* Chapel Hill: University of North Carolina Press, 1993.

Sokol, Jason. *There Goes My Everything: White Southerners in the Age of Civil Rights, 1945–1975.* New York: Alfred A. Knopf, 2006.

Stevenson, Bryan. *Just Mercy: A Story of Justice and Redemption*. New York: Spiegel and Grau, 2014.

Sullivan, Patricia. *Days of Hope: Race and Democracy in the New Deal Era*. Chapel Hill: University of North Carolina Press, 1996.

Sundquist, Eric J. *Strangers in the Land: Blacks, Jews, Post-Holocaust America*. Cambridge, MA: Belknap Press of Harvard University Press, 2005.

Teel, Leonard Ray. *Ralph Emerson McGill: Voice of the Southern Conscience*. Knoxville: University of Tennessee Press, 2001.

Thornton, J. Mills. "Alabama Politics: J. Thomas Heflin and the Explusion Movement of 1929." *Alabama Review* 67 (January 2014): 10–39.

Thornton, J. Mills. *Dividing Lines: Municipal Politics and the Struggle for Civil Rights in Montgomery, Birmingham, and Selma*. Tuscaloosa: University of Alabama Press, 2009.

Twelve Southerners. *I'll Take My Stand: The Southern and the Agrarian Tradition*. New York: Harper, 1930.

Ward, Jason Morgan. *Defending White Democracy: The Making of a Segregationist Movement and the Remaking of Racial Politics, 1936–1965*. Chapel Hill: University of North Carolina Press, 2011.

Warren, Robert Penn. *Segregation: The Inner Conflict in the South*. Athens: University of Georgia Press, 1994.

Webb, Clive. *Massive Resistance: Southern Opposition to the Second Reconstruction*. New York: Oxford University Press, 2005.

Weissbach, Lee Shai. *Jewish Life in Small-Town America: A History*. New Haven, CT: Yale University Press, 2005.

Williams, T. Harry. *Huey Long*. New York: Alfred A. Knopf, 1969.

Williamson, Joel. *William Faulkner and Southern History*. New York: Oxford University Press, 1995.

Windham, Kathryn Tucker. *Alabama: One Big Front Porch*. Huntsville, AL: Strode Publishers, 1975.

Index

Kay Hinton

JOSEPH CRESPINO IS the Jimmy
Carter Professor of History at Emory
University. He is the author of *Strom
Thurmond's America* and *In Search of
Another Country*, winner of the 2008
Lillian Smith Book Award from the
Southern Regional Council. He lives
in Decatur, Georgia.